What People Are Saying About This Book
From the world of comedy, theology, and politics

"The humor and genuine pleasure of this story is all in the keenly observed details of small-town governance and the comedic cast of characters who alternately support and foil Nunes's plans as mayor."
> —ANNE LIBERA, Director of Comedy Studies,
> The Second City

"As a professional comedian from a small town (Dwight, IL), I thoroughly enjoyed Jeremy's book. It's full of colorful characters and funny stories. The book also gives you insight into how a small town operates. I knew Jeremy was a funny comedian, but now I know he is a gifted writer too. I highly recommend this book. It's a great read. That's a tip from your Uncle Lar.'"
> —"UNCLE" LARRY REEB, multi-time
> Chicago Comedian of the Year

"Jeremy Nunes's mayor story is one of hope, triumph, and the American Way. Enjoy. You will have to re-read this book because you're laughing so hard!"
> —MICHAEL PALASCAK, *Last Comic Standing* Finalist

"Jeremy Nunes has the unique distinction of getting to live THREE dreams at once! First he became a comedian, then a mayor, and now an author. Wow! Most of us don't even live one.

I have had the pleasure of living two myself (comedian and author) and I know how difficult each of those are. I have so much respect for Jeremy for becoming the mayor of his hometown, and I'm sure that's not easy either.

Comedy comes in threes, and Jeremy is well on his way to much success! He's a legitimate triple threat, and I hope he lets me drive his limousine as promised. I may need a gig soon."

—DOBIE MAXWELL, Chicago Comedy Icon,
Author of *Monkey in the Middle*

"In this book, Jeremy takes you on a journey full of laughs. If you've lived in a small town or just like to laugh at them, you need to read this."

—TIM GRABLE, President, The Grable
Group Entertainment Solutions

"With so many clowns in politics, why not elect a real comedian?! Well, one town did! Jeremy is a hilarious comedian and his book is a fun read."

—JASON DOUGLAS, President, Comedians
Nationwide & The Comedian Company

"Who knew small-town politics could be so intriguing? Jeremy Nunes has a knack for laying clear the absurd and oftentimes hilarious goings-on in his little corner of the world. Dawson, Illinois may not be on your map now, but after enjoying the mayor's story, it is a place you won't soon forget."

—MANDI MORRIS, President, Azalea Talent Agency

"It is so important for people to step up and serve in their local community. The mayor of a small town deals with many issues that directly impact the quality of life for people. The position can sometimes be thankless, and we all appreciate Jeremy's service and ability to do the job with a smile on his face. I think readers will enjoy hearing him reflect on his time in office!"

—CONGRESSMAN DARIN LAHOOD, IL-18

"Only someone who has personally experienced the palace intrigue of the Village Hall could write this book, and only a comedian would dare. From the employee who keeps right on serving the public from his deathbed, to the inane complaints from constituents who clearly don't understand how government works—and don't care to—Jeremy Nunes has captured the highs and lows of the dysfunctional family with the power to tax that is small-town American government."

—SILAS MCCORMICK, President, Lincoln Christian University, Associate Professor of Law and Government

"In this age of media noise, big-city protests, and larger-than-life headlines, there's the small town of Dawson. Comedian/Mayor Jeremy Nunes introduces us to the people, the problems, and the politics of small-town America and it feels a little like LIVING in Mayberry. As I began the book I felt like a stranger looking in, but by the end, I was part of the town, sad to leave the 'folks' I had gotten to know. This fun-to-read book will warm your heart, make you laugh, and remind you of what really matters. Merf would tell you, 'It's well worth the read.' And so would I."

—TODD WILSON, Founder of Familyman Ministries

"Living in a small town myself, I can vouch for the fact that Jeremy captures reality better than any Hollywood-produced reality show ever could. His comedic prowess captures the real but insane world of small-town government. There are some great and ironic parallels in small-town government and ministry to men! Well done, Jeremy!"

—Tom Cheshire, Founder of Relevant Practical Ministry to Men

YOU CAN'T
WRITE
CITY HALL

WHAT HAPPENED WHEN A STAND-UP
COMEDIAN GOT ELECTED MAYOR

JEREMY NUNES

Clovercroft Publishing

You Can't Write City Hall

©2021 by Front Porch Entertainment, Inc.

Published by Clovercroft Publishing, Franklin, Tennessee

Published in association with Larry Carpenter of
Christian Book Services, LLC
www.christianbookservices.com

Edited by Tiarra Tompkins and Ann Tatlock

Cover Design by Sandra Nunes

Interior Layout Design by Suzanne Lawing

Printed in the United States of America

978-1-950892-97-6

For my wife Sandra, who stood with me through it all.

FOREWORD

Hey you! Yes, the individual who is considering skipping the Foreword...STOP! The Foreword is placed at the beginning and not the end for a reason. It creates anticipation. Don't deny yourself the well-prepared anticipatory process, and thus enjoy this excellent book at only 95 percent of its possibly narrative ecstasy.

You hold in your hand a rare opportunity to get to know a great writer while he is still in the undiscovered stage. I've spent my life reading some of the great illustrators of the humorous life. People like Robert Fulgham, Dave Barry, and Lewis Grizzard topped many stacks on my IKEA-inspired desk. So, when a funny storyteller premieres a book, I take interest.

This is a triple-crown mashup of Amy Poehler's *Parks and Recreation*, Garrison Keillor's *Lake Wobegon Days*, and the wit and true-life experience of world-class comedian Jeremy Nunes. This could be a great sitcom. Prepare for a fun and engaging read that will become a treasured favorite for years to come.

—MIKE G. WILLIAMS, Author, Speaker,
CMA/GMA 2017 Comedian of the Year

INTRODUCTION

I have often told people that you have no idea how difficult it is to be a small-town mayor until you've lived it. Looking back at all I went through, it reminded me of the balance you have to maintain. A mayor has to keep his board happy so that they approve his ideas, keep the town employees happy so they get his projects done, keep the town happy so they reelect him, and keep his family happy so they don't kick him out! All the while, chaos is engulfing the town, and he has to control it. When I started in politics as a Village trustee, I had no idea how much being a mayor actually involved. It wasn't until later that I figured it out.

It seemed every month I had someone from the town complaining about something, and I share those complaints with you month by month. Similarly, it seemed like an employee had a complaint every month too, which I also share. At the time, those moments were frustrating, but looking back now they make me laugh.

Like my mayoral career and any good comedic story, this book first takes a little time to lay the foundation. As the story builds, so does the humor. In my biased opinion, once you understand the basic details of the story, you'll really settle into the laughter it brings as you continue through the pages.

As I wrote this book, I was reminded of the emotional pain I endured, but also of the joy of accomplishing goals and making new friends. I also remember all the laughs.

I'll end with something I used to write on my comedy CDs that I gave to girls I was trying to impress ... "I hope this makes you smile as much as you make me smile."

Jeremy Nunes
7/10/20

In my basement office under Illinois Coronavirus Lockdown

CHAPTER 1

IT STARTED WITH A BANK

The most common question people ask me when they find out I delayed my career as a comedian to work as a small-town mayor is, "Why would you do that to yourself?!" The answer is that I ran for office as a joke. I registered my name on the ballot as "Comedian Jeremy Nunes." Then, I distributed fliers with my campaign slogan: "Put a Real Joker in Office."

Of course, that is how I answer the question to be funny. The real answer is that I never intended to be a mayor. I never had any plans or aspirations to be in a political position. As I traveled across the United States doing comedy, I performed in some really gorgeous small towns. After seeing so many of these amazing towns, I started to think, "Why isn't my town like this?"

If you have ever started a business of any kind, you know the reputation-building can be tough. As I paid my dues as a full timer in the comedy business, money was tight. When I left Chicago to return to my hometown of Dawson, Illinois, I was the typical starving artist. Simultaneously, I regularly talked to people in my town about the amazing towns I saw across the country and the great ideas those towns had. The more people I talked to, the more they urged me to run for the Town Council. I wasn't quite sure, but when I was told that I'd get paid $75 a month, I was sold! It's not much, especially considering the headaches you endure, but it was a significant amount for me.

In Spring 2011, I launched my campaign. Of the three council members who were up for reelection, none ran for their seats. This, of course, should have been a warning! Three people had the chance to get away and took it! Instead of recognizing the warning, I viewed it as an opportunity to get my money! Longtime Councilman Barry Vance offered some assistance. He wasn't running for reelection, and said he'd be thrilled if I were to get it. My longtime friend Matt Butler made a living as a campaign strategist, so he took control of the campaign.

In all, there were five people running for three seats. Aside from me, there was the former fire chief and a guy I went to high school with, Mike Madison. There was former Mayor Greg Emerson and his daughter Sharon Yount. The fifth was Rita Robins, a longtime friend of current Mayor Carl Donaldson. I suspected that Mike Madison was quite popular and would be the top vote-getter. Greg Emerson had been the mayor and was a popular one at that. I suspected he was a lock for the second spot. That left the final spot up for grabs between Rita Robins, Sharon Yount, and me.

With my friend Matt at the helm, we launched a campaign that would be comparable to a congressional battle. Using my own money, I mailed an endorsement letter from the very popular Barry Vance, with his permission, to every registered voter in the town. I paid to have campaign brochures made, which were written by Matt. Then, one by one, I knocked on the door of every registered voter in the town and hand delivered those pamphlets. I was even brave enough to knock on the door of my opponents!! I waited until the weekend before the election to do this, because I didn't want to leave time for my opponents to react. It was my version of the October surprise.

On election night, the votes were in. I won! Not only did I win, but I was hands down the top vote-getter! Mike Madison came in second, and Rita Robins came in third, barely edging out Greg Emerson. Sharon Yount came in dead last, gathering something like eight total votes. I was as giddy as a pageant girl at the county fair. I later heard that Sharon was so unpopular that people in her own family didn't vote for her!

On the council, I quickly got a reputation for being fearless as well as intelligent. To me, I was just asking logical questions. Like, "How much will this cost?," "Did we budget for that?," and "Is there an alternative?" These may seem like basic questions to you, but word of mouth spread quickly that there was a highly intelligent new councilman shaking things up at City Hall! No one else had dared question then mayor Carl Donaldson. Carl was in his early 70s, thinning white hair, medium build, with thick, coke-bottle glasses. As he aged, it was sad to see his mobility decline and his shaking increase. He was an Army veteran, so he had my respect. However, I just couldn't let him get away with shady actions.

Before you ask what kind of "actions" I am talking about, let me tell you a story. Tina Elton was our young, 20-something treasurer, and Mayor Donaldson and long-time Town Clerk Rhonda Brown argued fiercely to give her a 100% raise.

During the meeting, we had two trustees missing, so there were only four of us to vote. Elderly Councilwoman Margie Baggio sat next to me and fiercely argued against it. I opposed it also, but knew we were outnumbered. Across the table from us sat Rita Robins, who was obviously going to do whatever Mayor Donaldson wanted. Mike Madison was rumored to be having an affair with Tina, so I was certain he'd be giving her a raise. If the vote tied 2-2, the mayor would break the tie in favor of his own proposal. With two trustees missing, I had a sneaky plan. I whispered to Margie, "Just vote yes, trust me."

"WHAT'D YOU SAY?!" she responded. I forgot she had trouble hearing in her old age. I had that feeling like when you're talking loud at a party and it gets quiet right when you say something like, "So now I have to use an ointment!" Embarrassed that my motives might be revealed, I just looked at her and spoke in a normal tone. "I think we should all vote for the raise." Then, I winked at her with my right eye, which no one could see but her, and mouthed, "Trust me." Luckily, Margie trusted me, and the raise passed 4-0.

Tina was thrilled. She had only worked for the town for a couple years, and only worked 20 hours a week at that. With the raise, she'd now be making more money than either of our two full-time employees, both of which had been with the town for decades. My biggest concern was whether or not the raise was so costly that it would lead to financial turmoil. I talked with our local bank, who told me it seemed there was no way our Village could afford such a raise. Rumblings of the raise spread through the town fast, and people were furious. Who could blame them? We have all felt the pain of someone being promoted when we felt it unjust. Additionally, many who had dealt with Tina felt she was rude, and to be blunt, not so bright. Likewise, our two full-time employees, Bill Murphy and Ron Butcher, were possibly the two most popular men in town. The employees and the people of the town felt that Bill and Ron both got hosed. I felt that way too, but if I revealed my strategy, those in favor of the raise would've had time to plan a defense. As you read this, you may think, "This is a lot of strategizing for a town of 500 people." To that I respond, "Yes."

The day before our next board meeting, I called our other two council members, Agnes Cobb and Ed Quentin, to inform them of my plan. Agnes was very uncomfortable with the raise, and she was on board to fight it. I was unable to reach Ed, only leaving a basic voicemail of the general situation. I was really taking a gamble without knowing where Ed stood. Sometimes you just have to roll the dice. Knowing that Agnes, Margie, and I were in favor of blocking the raise, and with Mike and Rita wanting to give the raise, we had three votes versus two. If the votes tied 3-3, Mayor Donaldson would break the tie in favor of the raise. Ed had to vote with us.

As the meeting started, Mayor Donaldson made his usual statement, "The first item is old business. Seeing none we will move on to – "

"Excuse me!" I said. "We made a significant decision last meeting, so I think it's very important that Ed Quentin and Agnes Cobb be allowed to review our decision. That being said, I make a motion to reconsider the vote regarding the raise to Tina Elton."

I looked left to the head of the table. Carl Donaldson and Rhonda Brown were stunned. But, in order for the vote to be reconsidered, I needed a second from someone who voted for the raise last meeting. That's why I previously told Margie to vote for the raise. I knew the loophole. I saw the smirk on Agnes Cobb's face when I made the bold move. Agnes was one of the older ladies in the town who had actually been friends with my Grandma before her passing. Agnes had glasses that made her big brown eyes even bigger. She had short gray hair and had been a trustee on the Town Board for what seemed like 40 years. Ed was tougher to read until he dropped one of his trademark jokes. He was around 50, with no hair left on top, but plenty of gray hair on the sides. He was a husky, avid hunter, who often forgot to shave, but really cared about the town, having also served numerous terms on the Town Board.

Now, earlier in the week, Margie had secretly agreed with me to make the second motion, knowing that Rita and Mike surely wouldn't. I looked to my right at Margie, waiting for the motion. Nothing. I had been tricked. I felt dumb. I did it all for nothing. I silently called her things I've never called anyone! Mayor Donaldson said, "Well, since we don't have a second, we–"

"Oh, you need someone to second the motion. I'll second it," said Margie. She looked at me and said, "I'm sorry, I don't hear so well. I didn't know you made the motion!" I was so relieved, and a little repentant for my inner monologue of name calling. Now, we just needed the votes. Madison – no, Cobb – yes, Baggio – yes, Nunes – yes, Robins – no. The votes were exactly as I thought, and it would come down to Ed Quentin. He looked around and said, "Seems to me this raise has the town as uncomfortable as a tick on your naughty parts! I vote yes!"

Tina angrily left the room. The argument to change the vote didn't take much, because they knew they were outnumbered. Just a few minutes later, the same people voted the same way and undid the raise. Since it was December, we had gathered up food for a Christmas potluck to follow the meeting. Tina angrily grabbed her Crock-Pot of meatballs and stormed out, hurling expletives my way. "Such a sweet woman," said Ed.

The next day, employees Ron Butcher and Bill Murphy separately knocked on my door and thanked me for what I had done. They both asked me the same question, "Have you thought about running for mayor?" Before this mention, the thought hadn't crossed my mind. Many in the town then began reaching out to me with the same suggestion. They felt Carl Donaldson had been in office too long, and it was time for a little less corruption and some more fresh ideas.

As I debated a run, Tina abruptly resigned. Mayor Donaldson quickly replaced her while the Town Council had been preoccupied trying to figure out what to do about the aging water superintendent, Ron Butcher. Someone was going to have to replace him in the near future, and we had no idea who. Agnes Cobb always pushed me to retire from comedy and apprentice as water superintendent. My grandfather had been the water superintendent for the nearby town of Riverton for decades. By the rules of small-town employment, this made me highly qualified for the job!

However, if I were to work for the Village, I couldn't be on the Town Council, nor could I run for mayor. I really had to consider both options.

I talked it over with my wife Sandra, who was then my fiancée. She wisely urged that I should run for mayor, not pursue the water job, and stay in comedy. With my longtime friend Matt Butler once again at the controls, we launched the campaign. A mayoral election was somewhat rare in our little town, because no one typically ever wanted the job other than Carl Donaldson. I had two years of experience on the City Council, and here I was taking on the person who'd been mayor for 24 years. We had our work cut out for us, but took the same approach as my Town Council race.

I once again sent letters to the town's registered voters, this time drafted and signed by three current council members: Agnes Cobb, Margie Baggio, and Ed Quentin. I spent my own money to mail them out, and purchased campaign signs and printed brochures. There are only about 70 homes in our town. Of them, 30 sported a "Jeremy Nunes for Mayor" sign. Three sported a sign for Carl Donaldson. I was starting to think I might have some momentum. At Matt's suggestion, my fiancé joined me as I knocked on the door of every registered voter and gave them a pamphlet. Side by side, it projected that this nice looking young couple wanted to settle down in this town for the long term. The older residents, who were most of the voters, seemed to love us and planned to vote for us. On the other hand, Carl Donaldson was one of them, so would they vote against him?

Election night in April 2013 was just a few days prior to my wedding. We knew that I'd either be really happy or really bummed as I headed to the church that Saturday.

My fiancée Sandra said, "You better not let this make you mad at our wedding."

I joked, "I'll be mad at our wedding anyways!"

I anxiously watched the election results refresh on my computer screen as I talked on the phone with Matt, who was doing the same. The results for the three council seats, again pursued by five people, came up first. Agnes Cobb and Ed Quentin were reelected, but Margie Baggio was edged out by Johnny Lynch, someone I'd never even met. Sharon Yount had run again, and again finished last. About 9:00 p.m., Matt started screaming, "WE WON!!! WE WON!!! Wow and we gave him a beat-down too!" My margin of victory was what you'd expect from the final score of a college basketball game between Duke and Southwest North Dakota State Community College Tech (79-21). My soon-to-be wife ran into the room and gave me a big hug and kiss. We were now the power couple in a town of 500.

CHAPTER 2

SWEARING AT CEREMONY

Accustomed to arriving around 6:45 as a trustee to scan through the monthly reports, I figured being the mayor was relevant and prestigious enough to commit an extra 15 minutes of my time to actually reading those reports. So, I arrived 30 minutes early to prepare for four years of work.

The Village Hall was a building trapped in the past. Let me give you the dime tour. After entering through the main door, you walk through a narrow hallway, which had a basic white tile floor and fluorescent lights in the drop ceiling. To the right was the meeting room, which was about 20' x 40'. Three eight-foot wooden banquet tables made up a "U" shape for the officials to do business while seated on the navy-blue state surplus office chairs. Ten banquet chairs, lined in two rows of five, were placed for visitors on the south wall. Outdated carpet covered the floor, while table skirts that once were white, but now a faded yellow, like your grandpa's undershirt, aligned the front of the banquet tables. The room had two doors, one immediately to the right of the building entrance, the other was a little farther down the hall, accessible from the communal kitchen.

On the left side of the hallway was the Village Office. There was one computer and desk for the town clerk, and another computer and desk for the treasurer/water clerk (two positions staffed by the same person). There was a third desk for the mayor, but no computer. Historically, no one felt the mayor – the most important city official – needed a computer. That office room was a decent size, about 20' x 30'. The same outdated carpet covered the floor, illuminated by the same florescent lights in the drop ceiling. Despite the "retro look," the office didn't look too bad. There were three leather chairs, dirty and cracked, as if to match the skin of someone who fell asleep in the Sahara. I have to admit, the desks and shelving were a fairly new, elaborate wood concoction and looked very nice.

Beyond the hall was a small communal kitchen area with an oven, commercial sink, refrigerator, and microwave. This was used daily for staff preparing their lunches but was also heavily used for town banquets. The stove and sink were centered on the west wall of the kitchen. What was on either side of them? That would be a poorly located set of bathrooms! Each bathroom only accommodated one person, and each had the thinnest of doors which allowed you to hear EVERYTHING ... often during a board meeting.

Down the hall, the Village workshop was on the left, which housed much of the gear that the crew needed, as well as one of the two utility trucks. The second truck was used so frequently by the water superintendent that he kept it at his home.

To the right was the space rented by the local Fire District. The space included a meeting room, chief's office, and two large bays with around 20-foot ceilings and concrete floors. The first bay was used for housing gear and an emergency response pickup truck, the second bay housed two firetrucks. The back wall of the second bay shared the east wall of the meeting room. It wasn't uncommon to be in the middle of a board meeting when the roar of a firetruck siren came blasting through the wall, resulting in a needed underwear change! That bay had an attic above it, which was only accessed by uncomfortably climbing a 20+ foot ladder.

I arrived that night for my first day as our town's new mayor, and found Mayor Carl Donaldson in the office, going over his final paperwork and collecting the last of his things. As much as I disagreed on his policies and actions, I have to admit he was entirely courteous and professional as I took over what had been his spot for the last 24 years. That's not what I expected, considering how badly I beat him in the election. As we were preparing to start the meeting, he handed me the literal keys to the town.

I jokingly asked, "Do I have any idea what I've gotten myself into?"

He smiled and replied, "Nope. You're about to be sworn in to be sworn at."

***

The May meeting began with the clerk, Rhonda Brown, presenting Carl with a plaque in recognition of his years of service to the town. I was snickering as I watched Rhonda, who sported a typical short gray haircut and frail-ish figure that you'd expect from someone in their golden years, as she was. I laughed only because if I were him, my first thought would have been, "I gave you over 20 years of my life, and all I get is an engraved chunk of wood?" But, when you're a town of 500, the budget isn't quite there to enroll you in a wine club.

I was then sworn into office as my wife, Mom, and sister looked on from the cheap banquet chairs (Dad didn't attend because he voted for Carl Donaldson). I always wondered if those uncomfortable chairs were put there for the public with the goal of being too uncomfortable to sit on for an entire meeting. Maybe they held a meeting and decided, "These chairs are so bad, they'll leave because their back hurts, and that's when we can really talk business!" Once officially sworn in as mayor, I had to appoint a new trustee, since I had to resign my trustee spot in order to accept the mayorship. After a lot of begging and pleading, I was able to convince Barry Vance to take the spot, and the board voted unanimously to approve him.

I had known Barry since I was a little kid, because I grew up with his daughter, and his house was the cool hangout when we were in high school. Barry was the definition of a "Good Ol' Boy." He worked for the local grain elevator, was in his early 60s with thick salt-and-pepper hair and dark eyes, had a husky build, and a booming laugh. No one had a negative thing to say about him. Barry was absolutely hilarious, and he had already spent years as a trustee for the town. In fact, when he decided he had enough and would no longer run, I was elected to the trustee seat he no longer wanted.

Because of his knowledge and comic relief, I knew I needed him. I had to beg him to come back like an old desperate boyfriend. "Please, come back, I'll make sure you're happy, pleeeeeeaasse!" He also made things interesting because he peppered every sentence with added words like "Giddy-up," "Ayeeeeee," "Mmmm mmmm," and "Yee-haw." My favorite was when he'd press his lips together and make the actual sound you make when you pass gas. In a typical meeting, he may say something like, "We should ayeeeeee increase the budget for this giddy-up because it's not enough mmmm mmmm funding (fart noise)."

Just before the meeting another trustee, Rita Robins, re-signed. Although she was a nice older lady, I always felt she was simply there to vote however Carl told her to vote. So with her departure, I was a bit sidetracked as trustees were being sworn in. I had to consider who I would put in the seat. Getting Barry was goal number one and had been accomplished. I re-alized that getting Margie Baggio back was goal number two. Margie, Ed Quentin, and I were sort of the renegades of the group, fighting against what we felt were foolish decisions by the mayor. I felt like appointing her was easily justified since she finished fourth in the last election.

After Agnes Cobb and Ed Quentin were sworn in, Johnny Lynch was up. I had never heard of Johnny, but knew he was a younger guy interested in politics, which meant he was a threat to my seat. He was in his late 30s and about 6'0", fit and tan, with dark, thick, buzz-cut hair. If I was to be reelected and grow my political career, goal number three was to bury Johnny Lynch's political career. Isn't it amazing how fast poli-tics turns cutthroat?

At this point I was ready for my wife, Mom and sister to leave, since I wanted to be viewed as a leader, not as "Mrs. Nunes's son." I gave my Mom "the look," the same one my wife gives me at home. You know the one. My Mom read it loud and clear, and they left at that point, saying something like, "These chairs make your back hurt!"

As all this floated through my head, the meeting continued. It was my duty to appoint the treasurer, water commissioner, attorney, and engineer of our town. It was important to me that I surround myself with people that knew what they were doing, because I was smart enough to know that I had a lot to learn. If you think about it, I had been a trustee for two years, attending 60-minute-long meetings once a month. Technically, I had 24 hours, or three business days, of experience when I became the man in charge. So wisely, I reappointed all the same people to their positions. I figured if there was a bad apple, I'd sniff them out over time.

That night, two big concerns were being debated. The first was whether the town could use a website. Can you believe this was even a debate? This was 2013; how many towns don't actually have a website? In our horse-and-buggy town, this counted as big controversy!

The other big concern was that an area water district, Country Water Association, was rapidly growing and geographically approaching our water customers. I was aware that our system was almost at capacity, so I could have cared less what another district was doing. If they wanted to provide water to customers that are on well water, good for them.

Unfortunately our water superintendent, Ron Butcher, saw it differently. Ron was about 70 years old at the time, bald on top with some short white hair on the sides, about 6'5" with a medium build and blue eyes. Ron had a habit of strongly arguing his point and in this case, Ron wanted to fight it. Since I needed Ron on my side long term, I agreed with Ron and Village Attorney Reggie Phillips that we would form a committee to fight this "travesty." I knew Ed Quentin and Barry Vance had the knowledge, so I suggested they join the committee with Ron and me. Since I needed to know more about Johnny Lynch to continue my covert investigation, I asked him to join the committee.

"Ayeeeeee, if we need to mmmm mmmm shut 'em down, to yee-haw protect my town, then giddy-up, let's do it (fart noise)," said Barry.

Ed, scratching his unshaven face, chimed in, "I'd buy shrimp from the trunk of a car before I'd trust these guys."

Meeting adjourned.

***

In the days that followed my first meeting as mayor, I discussed my amazingly innovative ideas with my staff, such as having a carbon monoxide detector in our Village buildings and finding a way to test the storm sirens monthly. When I say "amazingly innovative," I'm being sarcastic, but that's what several people really thought.

A common complaint I heard when I was knocking on doors to get elected was that our water bills are sent out long after the meters are read. If you are a person who likes to sit and pay your bills all at once, you can do that, but you won't yet have your water bill. I asked our new water clerk and treasurer, Kara Gregory, why is it that when the bills are ready to be sent out, we just hold them. She said, "I guess that's just how we've always done it." I hated this answer because it's the go-to answer for every small town. I had gone to high school with Kara, so it surprised me that a younger person would have such an old-school answer. I changed the policy, and my approval rating skyrocketed.

***

It didn't take long for the first crazy thing to happen. Bill Murphy called and asked me to urgently come to the park. Bill was in his early 60s, a little overweight, with sun-spotted skin from his years of working outside. He maintained a five-day beard and was rarely seen without a baseball cap on. When I got there, I noticed Bill and part-time Village employee George O'Reilly standing near the back of the park where a bit of forest bordered the south side. George was in his late 60s and was almost frail looking, about 5'6" and thin as a rail.

"Well, Mayor," Bill said, tugging at his ball cap. "Looks like somebody is growing some marijuana at the park!"

"I guess we should call the police," I said.

"No, you don't want cops out here for that," George said.

"That's all we need," said Bill.

"What did you have in mind?" I asked.

"We'll cut it down and get rid of it. It's happened before," Bill said.

I wasn't sure why, if it had happened before and was not unusual, I was needed to be called urgently to the park. Bill Murphy then proceeded to mow over all that marijuana, put it into a pile, and burn it all. The whole town was in a good mood for a week!

***

It was this month that I received my first of hundreds of phone call complaints. The older man, Alfred Ziebler, was obviously frustrated.

"Were you part of the planning for that school prom parade?" he asked.

"No, that would have been the school," I replied.

"What about the police and fire trucks?"

"No, we don't have police, and the fire department is its own entity."

"You need to do something. Those sirens were way too loud!"

"There's really nothing I can do."

"Oh. I get it. You're a racist!"

"How? I don't even know who you are or what you look like."

"I'm one-eighth Cherokee! You racist!"

"I'll see what I can do," I said, as the guy angrily hung up. Of course, I had no intention of doing anything. I learned quickly, any time a politician says, "I'll see what I can do," that means it's not getting done.

***

As the weather heated up, so did the four-wheelers zooming through town. Aside from not being street legal, it was quite an annoyance to the older folks. One boy, about 10, was really moving quickly up and down the street. The use of four-wheelers didn't necessarily bother me. What bothered me was the numerous phone calls I got from people complaining about them. When the town has a problem, I have a problem. So indirectly, I had a problem with four-wheelers. After about five calls that day, I stepped outside and flagged the boy down. Before I could say a word, he started getting aggressive.

"You got a problem?" he said.

"Your four-wheeler is illegal. I need you to go home," I said.

"Why don't you make me?"

"I have the authority to make you, and I'm telling you to take it home."

"My dad says anyone who tells me to stop can come to our house and tell him to his face, 'cause he'll whoop ya' right there."

"Tell your dad I'm the mayor, and if he threatens an elected official, he'll get sent back to prison."

I had no idea who his dad was, but after raising a kid to say things like that, I was sure he'd already been to prison at least once! I was also very cautious not to upset anyone in order to be reelected, but I didn't care this time because I was sure this guy didn't vote.

***

On June 3, we held our next board meeting. Trustee Mike Madison didn't make it, which surprised me, because I had also gone to high school with him and saw him as part of the new era of the town. Nonetheless, business had to continue. We started with the board unanimously approving Margie Baggio to replace the recently departed Rita Robins. Margherita Baggio, or "Margie" as everyone called her, immigrated from Italy with her parents as a little girl. Margie was in her early 70s, had short gray hair, and packed all the fire that you'd expect from a 4'11" Italian woman. I saved her small-town political career by reappointing her, so I figured we had the unspoken agreement she would vote for a few of my proposals that she may be on the fence about. With Margie and Barry Vance now on the board with my appointment, I felt I had the team in place to get anything done. With a board of six, I had two hand-picked trustees. I only needed one other person to vote for my ideas to get them passed, because I would cast the tie-breaking vote in a 3-3 deadlock.

One lengthy discussion held that night was whether we would allow for water bills to be paid online through the website that we might create. But there's a problem: credit card companies charge a small percentage for the transaction. You probably already knew that, like most people. But that night, it was a shocking development for many in attendance. You would've thought I suggested we sacrifice a virgin in a volcano! There was no way the old guard of the town was going to let it happen! The most vocal, who helped end the debate without a vote, were Water Superintendent Ron Butcher and Village Clerk Rhonda Brown. It was frustrating when people like Ron and Rhonda argued against something I wanted to get accomplished, because they weren't members of the board, and therefore not eligible to speak during debates. Truth be told, they had the ability to be very persuasive, so I allowed it to continue because I knew it would benefit me someday.

We also had a brief discussion on why the eastern end of the town didn't have a storm siren. Several people on that end of town, including my very vocal father, regularly complained about it. The Village also hadn't updated its emergency plan in half a century, so that was one more thing to deal with.

Another mind-blowing idea I proposed was to actually have the trustees do tasks. Historically, they showed up once a month to the meetings, and that was it. That night, I had them in a situation in which they had to agree to do the tasks. No one in their right mind would speak up in a public meeting and say they preferred to not do anything. I was having them do projects, research, join committees, whatever it may be. I made sure they earned their hefty salary of $75 per month!

The meeting also involved a lengthy discussion about the upcoming Independence Day fireworks event. Many years ago, the Village stopped doing this event because it couldn't afford to. As a result, some residents in the town created the Dawson Town Team. The group raised the funds and organized the event entirely. It was always a point of contention, because many of the group's members were town employees and officials, while many other officials and employees who didn't participate in the group felt it was a waste of time and energy. The Town Team held their meetings in the Village Hall, and claimed they were all equal and had no leadership. But, it was clear that Rhonda Brown was the leader, and Ron Butcher was a close second, both affiliated with our Village government. With both of them in the room, they were clearly upset when, after much debating with trustees and input from our attorney, I made the final call that they could not have a bounce house at the fireworks event. Our insurance would charge us extra, I didn't want something bad to happen, and they'd never had a bounce house before. Ron was mostly quiet. As her gray hair fell into her eyes, Rhonda reacted with a flurry of expletives as if I set her cat on fire. Ed tried to stand up for me by saying, "Those bounce houses are riskier than a desolate Mexican restaurant!"

I also had my plate full because we had only three full-time employees: Treasurer/Water Clerk Kara Gregory, Maintenance Supervisor Bill Murphy, and Water Superintendent Ron

Butcher. Our two veteran full-time employees, Bill and Ron, were both nearing retirement. Ron was our only licensed water operator and was already in his 70s. Bill Murphy planned to retire within a year or two, and could operate the water plant; he just was never able to pass the licensing exam. I told the board I had to find someone eager to learn a physical job for minimal pay. And I had to convince Ron it was a good idea to hire his successor, something Mayor Carl Donaldson was never able to accomplish. Barry was on board, saying, "We've gotta ayeeeeee get this done, mmmm mmmm before its giddy-up, too late (fart noise)."

Before the night was over, I also brought up the fact that our new employees aren't granted sick days until they've worked for the Village for one year.

I said, "I think most people would agree that asking someone to work an entire year without so much as an hour off for a doctor appointment is, um –"

"Crazier than handing Gary Busey a loaded firearm!" Ed interjected.

At the time, Margie Baggio's grandson, Will Baggio, was being considered as the new water employee to work under Ron Butcher. The debate grew lengthy when Ron and Margie aggressively argued against allowing a sick day before an employee completed one year.

"Might as well give them a $10,000 bonus too! Unbelievable!" Margie exclaimed.

"Don't bankrupt our town! You're recklessly spending money on sick days!" Ron shouted from the public banquet chairs.

I couldn't believe it. Between saving Margie's political career, and her grandson being the one to benefit from this policy, I thought she'd easily be on board. But without Margie's vote, that likely meant I didn't have Agnes Cobb's vote, because they almost always voted together. They were the peanut butter and jelly of City Hall voting. With Mike Madison absent, that meant I had to have the remaining three board members vote with me, and willing to vote against the very vocal and intimidating Ron Butcher. Since I knew I needed all of these people to be on my side for more important votes in the future, I tabled the discussion for the night. With Johnny Lynch and Barry Vance both sitting silently during the debate, I didn't want to take any chances. After almost three hours of small-town board room debate, we called it a night. Meeting adjourned.

***

In mid-June, I found time to apply for a fully funded grant to replace all of the old street signs and stop signs throughout the town. It wasn't totally necessary, but if it was fully funded, it would be a step in the right direction toward my goal of beautifying the town. I would find out just a few weeks later that we got the grant. In just a few months on the job, I got our tiny little town its first grant in over 14 years!

***

That month I got a call from a middle-aged woman named Yvonne Barrett who had just visited the park and wasn't happy at all with what she saw.

"Aren't you going to clean up the graffiti at the park? No one wants to see that when they're trying to look at fireworks!" she said.

"I didn't know about any. What is it?" I asked.

"Someone drew a giant set of male genitalia on the slide!"

"Oh, we'll definitely take care of that right away."

"It's not the genitalia that offends me, it's just that it is offensively disproportionate!"

"I'll make sure it's cleaned up."

"I want you to launch an investigation!"

"I'll see what I can do."

***

We were just two days away from the Independence Day fireworks when we met on July 1, 2013 (our event was always held July 3). Don't worry, that graffiti was removed. This night, Barry Vance was absent. I wish he was there, because he and I would've laughed for days at what happened at the beginning of the night. I barely put my gavel down to start the night before Agnes Cobb started complaining that the meeting minutes were far too long and were more of a transcript. Rhonda Brown defended her minutes as being well detailed. I don't know their history, but these two worked together like cops and firemen. They got the job done, but neither really liked the other. Both argued that people in the town spoke up and expressed the same respective opinion that they were arguing.

Eventually, to end the 20-minute argument and to prevent these two older ladies from having any potential heart attacks, I asked that they compromise and have the minutes slightly less detailed. I noticed Rhonda roll her eyes, and I knew she wouldn't change anything. But again, I was new, and I wasn't ready to start making enemies until I accomplished my plans.

Prior to the meeting, I completed the simplest task that made me a hero. I asked the county to repair the giant pothole that surrounded the storm drain on one of our major streets in front of the post office. This is another one of those situations where people think I'm brilliant simply because I did a logical thing. Cars had bottomed out in that pothole for years. So, what did I do? I called the county, since it was their road, and asked them to fix it. The hole was fixed, and I could feel my reelection chances soaring.

In the board meeting, I made sure to announce the repair had been made, in order that this announcement would be seen in the meeting minutes. This is a tactic I used as a trustee as well. If the meeting was ready to be closed, I made sure that I made a motion to adjourn, or at least seconded the motion. That way, my name was in the minutes, and subconsciously the voters would be seeing that I was active in the meeting. You'll notice that just about everything I said was planned to be brought up again in the future, the same tactic every wife in America uses!

On this night we also had to approve the annual budget. I had written in a line item of $10,000 for "Special Projects." What did I have up my sleeve? Well, the board didn't seem too concerned, and it passed unanimously without any discussion. I was aware that our town had no formal plan written, and I knew that to have legitimate experts put one together would cost around $10,000. I also couldn't stand the beat-up, half-working flashing arrow at our town entrance on which announcements are posted. It was rusty, with faded paint and numerous dead and flickering bulbs. To replace that sign with a new, modern sign would also cost around $10,000. Privately, Ed Quentin had described it as, "Essentially a garbage truck with Christmas lights: flashing trash." Between the plan and the sign, I thought I could get one of each over a few years.

We also brought back discussion about developing a town website. Now, we are required to post an annual water report in the newspaper, which costs $400. Legally, we could post it on our own website instead, which was going to cost us under $200 annually. The website was going to save us money, plus provide all the benefits that a website can. The board then voted. Remember, without Barry Vance there, I needed three of the remaining five trustees to vote yes. Agnes Cobb voted yes, Johnny Lynch no, and Margie Baggio no. I was stunned that Margie voted differently than Agnes, because they almost always vote together, and almost always oppose change or modernization. Johnny Lynch was part of the new generation, so I was surprised to see him vote no, but not surprised since he may have his eyes on the mayor seat and wanted me to look bad. Nonetheless, I needed the final two votes to be yes, or this was a donkey in the ocean: dead in the water. Ed Quentin and Mike Madison each voted yes, and the website passed 3-2. Ed said, "I love this town, so please understand. Without a website, people don't know who you are or where you are. Our town is in its own witness protection program!"

Next up, I once again made the case that employees should not have to wait an entire year before we award them a sick day. I mentioned that sick days are not paid out upon separation, so there is no direct cost to providing sick days. The discussion was far calmer than the last meeting. It might have been because I privately lobbied Margie Baggio and reminded her that this would benefit her grandson, Will, should we ever hire him. I was stunned when, after a little more arguing from Ron Butcher, the board unanimously approved my proposal to grant sick days after two months. City Attorney Reggie Phillips would draw up the final paperwork, then we'd just need one more vote to make it official.

I was riding high. I just got two big votes through, and I was ready to push for a third. It was time to ask the board to approve a similar policy for vacation days. I said, "It's crazy not to give someone a paid vacation day until they've worked for you an entire year." I asked for the motion, and I heard what a lot of new comedians hear at open mic nights ... crickets. Not one person on the board agreed, and my high was gone quicker than an underage drinker when the cops bust a house party.

My final pitch was to fix a policy that Mayor Carl Donaldson had been operating for years. Previously, an employee had to submit a request to the mayor to take a vacation day, rather than to their direct supervisor. This made no sense to me, other than the fact that Carl must've liked to be hands on. Why would you submit a request for a day off to your company president, rather than to the supervisor who directly knows whether they can afford to have you gone? I made the pitch for this change, and the board approved unanimously. After getting three out of four of my proposals approved, plus the budget without any questions, I took it as a win. Meeting adjourned.

***

The next night, one of my favorite small-town complaints came my way. I got a frantic phone call from an older lady, Carol Washington, that started with, "We've got a huge problem, listen to this!" I was very concerned, because the annual fireworks event was coming up, and it always made me nervous. The caller told me it was about Riverton, the town that neighbored us about three miles to the west, straight up a country road called Dawson Lane.

"It's Riverton! They moved their residential speed limit sign about a quarter mile toward us on Dawson Lane."

"So..." I replied.

"Don't you understand?! They're moving their town border closer to us!"

"Maybe they're just trying to slow down the cars that were zooming down that country road."

"No, they're trying to overtake our town! You better not let it happen on your watch!"

"I'll see what I can do."

***

On July 3, the town hosted its fireworks event. Ron had asked me to give a speech to the crowd, which was written by his son Lance, about the greatness of America and Independence Day. The fireworks event was truly the "Super Bowl of Dawson." We packed hundreds of people into our three-acre park, maybe even 1,500 people, with many people standing shoulder to shoulder. On the north end of the park, we had two small basketball courts which doubled as a dance floor every July 3rd. There was a small stage where a band performed and, at this point, was also where I would speak.

Now remember, this is a larger park filled with people partying. So, although I'm about to speak into a microphone, the only people that could hear me or see me were the people around that concrete slab. About 100 yards from me, standing on our baseball field, was some guy who was hired to play videos on a giant screen. His video screen and sound system were designed for everyone in that park to hear and see. His video about how great our firemen were had just ended. The band playing on the stage stopped and handed the mic to me. However, the guy standing with his video board in center field kept talking. I asked Ron if I should wait, and he said, "No, he knows to be quiet when you start."

I began reading the speech that was written for me to the 50 or so people that could see me. I didn't so much as finish my first sentence when that guy continued speaking through his booming sound system, yelling, "Let's give it up for this awesome town!" The people watching me would look back at him, then back at me. I knew I was about to experience a hot mess. I then read the next line of the speech, saying, "Please stand if you're a veteran." I looked around. There were no seats, so EVERYONE was already standing. A few people looked at me as I noticed a few shoulder shrugs and heard a quiet mix of coughs and crickets, and then some high-pitched microphone feedback. Trying to think on my feet, I said, "Let's give a round of applause to all of the veterans here tonight." As soon as I finished the word "tonight," I heard our friend in center field yell through his monster sound system, "Let's give it up for all of our veterans! USA! USA! USA!" As the massive crowd started chanting, I just put the mic back in the stand and walked off. Although it felt like I failed, at least only a handful of people even noticed.

The fireworks ended without anyone getting hurt or anything blowing up, which was always my greatest fear. As I walked into my driveway alongside my wife and in-laws, we noticed a huge fire coming from Wayne Josten's house, two doors down and across the street. There was so much fire and smoke that burnt debris was raining down on us and on my father-in-law's new Corvette. I scrambled to call 911 but couldn't get a signal. I ran down to Wayne's house to help, as I heard many people leaving the park screaming and yelling things like, "Oh my!" and "Call 911!" As ash and burning debris fell from the sky, one pedestrian, who may have been overserved, yelled, "It's the apocalypse! It's the apocalypse!"

Wayne was close to 60 years old, with both legs amputated and hence confined to a wheelchair, so there was certainly concern that he was trapped. He had a detached garage that shielded my view of his house and the fire, so I could only see the rolling smoke and the tops of the flames just beyond the roof of the garage. As I got to his house, that's when I saw it. His house wasn't on fire at all. He simply had about 20 people at his house sitting around the biggest bonfire known to man. It looked like "Burning Man" came to Dawson!

Wayne Josten had always been a headache for Village leadership. Whether it was playing his music way too loud, or having all kinds of junk and debris piled all over his yard, or being suspected of running a drug ring, or in this case a giant bonfire, he was always testing our patience and the law. Since this was my first encounter with him as mayor, I wanted him to know I wouldn't be playing around. The next day, I issued him the minimum fine of $100 for improper burning. It was mailed to him by certified letter, with much enthusiasm from our Clerk Rhonda Brown, who couldn't stand him. I wasn't sure how he'd react, but I wanted him to know what my friends joked about me: If you mess with the mayor, you get the horns!

After inhaling lethal amounts of carbon monoxide, I soon decided to arrange a monthly meeting with my staff to check in on projects. Mayor Carl Donaldson would actually meet with them weekly on Friday mornings but, other than working as mayor, he was retired. I was working and traveling for comedy full-time and trying to carve out time to run an entire town. Typically, there were three staff members that joined: Ron Butcher, Bill Murphy, and Kara Gregory.

Ron not only oversaw the water system for Dawson, but also for the combined water system of the neighboring towns of Buffalo and Mechanicsburg, through which we had an intergovernmental agreement. Ron had been working for the Village for decades and loved it about as much as his own family. In fact, his family loved Dawson too. His son Lance served as volunteer fire chief for the Dawson Fire District. His daughter Melissa regularly helped out with the Town Team planning events, and his daughter Nora always volunteered at the Independence Day fireworks event. Lance, Melissa, and Nora had all grown up in Dawson and moved away but were all still close enough to come help the town.

Bill Murphy was known as Merf to just about everyone and served as maintenance supervisor, meaning he oversaw just about anything that wasn't related to the water system, but he also did a lot of work with the water system too. Like Ron, he too had grown up in Dawson and worked for the Village for decades. He even served as volunteer fire chief prior to Lance Butcher and Mike Madison. There happened to be a framed news article about Merf hung on the Village Office wall. Several years back, there was a rift in the fire department, and numerous members quit. Merf then became the fire chief of the short-staffed unit. Not long after, Merf and his team responded to a fire along with other area departments. As the story goes, Merf needed some help.

Merf asked someone from another department, "Would you mind showing me how to attach the hose to the fire hydrant?"

The man responded, "You should ask your chief to show you that."

Merf replied, "I am the chief, and I have been for two days!"

Merf, Ron, and I were big Chicago Cubs fans. I could always break the ice by bringing up the latest Cubs news. I had tons of respect for both of them for their years of work for the town. As I began to take over the mayor role, I did have some people tell me that Merf was a bit of a snake, and would make you feel like best friends to your face, but completely turn on you when you were out of earshot. Since Merf had always been nice to me, I had no reason to feel anything negative toward him. I always dismissed it as small-town people being, well, small-town people.

George O'Reilly had worked part-time for the Village for years, but for some reason never attended the staff meetings. His late wife had previously worked for the Village for years as well. Since he really had no reason to work, and Merf could relay important information to him anyway, I had no reason to rock the boat and mandate he be there.

Kara Gregory worked as the water clerk and treasurer. Kara was about a year older than me with sandy brown hair. She had only worked for the Village a short time prior to my becoming mayor. You'll remember the previous water clerk and treasurer, Tina Elton, had abruptly resigned one day. I was told that her rumored affair with Mike Madison was "discovered," though you know how it goes with small town rumors of rumors. I viewed Kara as an important member of the new generation of the town. Though she didn't live in the town, she had the ear of a lot of people in it. Kara's daughters played softball, so she always had a nice tan from her time in the sun, and plenty of conversations with our town's "Softball Moms." Carl Donaldson told me that he hired Kara and her predecessor, not for their resume, but because he needed some eye candy during the long days in the office.

Although we had a lot of topics to cover in our staff meeting, the main one was a little kicking of the tires on how Ron felt about hiring someone to learn his job. Many of the Village officials were concerned that if something happened to Ron, we wouldn't have anyone licensed to run the plant. Of course Merf could run it in theory, but without a license he couldn't legally do it for more than two weeks. Ron seemed receptive to the idea, but hesitant. Almost like when your wife asks where you'd like to eat dinner and you name the place, but you can tell that's not exactly what she wanted to hear. Sadly, this should have been addressed years ago by Mayor Donaldson. You must have three years of experience to be a licensed water superintendent. We knew that Father Time was catching up with Ron, but with training and development of a new employee, we needed him for about four more years. I almost needed some politician's reelection rally to follow Ron around, chanting, "Four more years! Four more years!"

Aside from dealing with all of this, late July is when I realized that I had booked a comedy show on the third Saturday of September, which had traditionally been the day of the All Town Garage Sale. My wife Sandra and I had planned to hold a garage sale, so I decided we'd push the date back to the fourth Saturday, no big deal. That's when I learned an important lesson in small-town politics: "Thou shalt not attempt to change the traditional date of any event!" I first talked with Rhonda Brown, who said the Methodist Church in Buffalo has traditionally sold concessions at the park, so that's something I should run past them. That group was led and organized by Opal Winthrop. Opal was an older widow, who was as spunky an old lady as you'd ever meet. I'd always been told that she could be your best friend or your worst enemy. She was also one of the "Blue Hair Club," as my campaign manager Matt Butler called them, a group of elderly ladies in the town that had their hands all over Dawson politics. They comprised about 25% of the voter block, so you certainly wanted them on your side. I called Opal and explained the situation.

She replied, "NO WAY! I have volunteers lined up already, and that's when it's always been. We're not changing it!"

I explained that the volunteers would have plenty of time to make arrangements, since this is still over two months away.

"NO! It's going to be the third Saturday, and that's final! GOODBYE!" she yelled.

And with that, Opal slammed the phone and hung up. Not wanting to lose a quarter of the voter block, I let it be. The third Saturday of September would remain the official day for low-ball offers on incomplete china sets.

CHAPTER 3

WATER-GEDDON

Like so many previous board meetings, the August meeting also didn't have all six trustees in attendance. This time, Agnes Cobb was missing. Without Agnes, I still needed three of the five trustees to vote for the official new sick policy. Reggie Phillips, who had been the city attorney for decades after taking over for his dad, had drawn up the paperwork. Reggie had thinning hair that was turning gray, and he always showed up in a suit. I never quite understood why Reggie felt that the board had to vote to approve him drawing up the paperwork, then vote again to approve the paperwork. But hey, he'd been around for so long, I didn't really want to question his knowledge of municipal law. But anyway, Reggie discussed the sick time policy that he'd written up. It was unanimously approved that he draw up the paperwork, so I was excited to see this get approved and make some progress. Ron Butcher got a little vocal, as usual, to oppose the policy. But that didn't concern me because he's an employee and can't vote. Margie Baggio made a motion to approve the policy. Then, nothing but silence and the sound of someone slowly passing gas. I looked at Barry Vance to see if he had made the noise with his lips, but he hadn't. It appeared that Margie's nerves got the best of her and she let one go right there in the board room.

I was disappointed. The same board that agreed to pay our attorney around $500 to draw up the policy is now refusing to approve that exact policy. I looked around as the remaining four sat on their hands. I thought for sure Barry Vance was with me, but no. His buddy that sat across from him, Ed Quentin, also did nothing. Both were approaching old-school age and attitude, so I understand that they may have mule-level stubbornness. Johnny Lynch just sat there. Mike Madison, who I also was beginning to suspect had his eyes on the mayor seat, also sat in silence. Mike was in his 30s, just a year older than me. He was handsome, and even when we were in high school he had no trouble getting girls. With him now also trying to make me look bad, I was starting to fear the worst. I can't get anything done if the people who have to approve changes don't want me to get anything done.

Moving on, I had recently learned that one of our storm sirens wasn't functioning. It was installed many years ago, and leaders immediately recognized that it couldn't receive the appropriate radio signals because it was surrounded by metal structures. Did our crew of officials have it moved? No, of course not! Instead, they just left a non-functioning $20,000 siren sitting there. Since the eastern end of town had no siren at all, I had my crew look into the logistics of relocating the siren. We needed a stable place to install it and the appropriate electricity had to be available. I discussed this with my board, and after all these years they agreed it should be moved. Ed said, "It's about time we did something with that siren. Right now, it's as useless as lady parts on a bore!"

Margie then asked why all the signs throughout the town had been replaced. "It looks nice but that must've cost a fortune, and I care about this community too much to allow it to happen," she said. "Why did you do that without the board's permission?"

"Well," I replied, "I don't need the board's permission if it's free. I got us a grant for it, fully funded."

"Whoa, maybe you know what you're doing after all. Maybe Rhonda should stick to her own business."

Rhonda's jaw dropped, and from that point forward I knew I couldn't trust Rhonda. Clearly, she'd been talking bad about me. I wanted to go after more grants, but I'd been so overwhelmed with other things going on that it would take me a while to get back to applying.

Ron Butcher quickly changed the subject before Rhonda could respond. He really pushed that we seek to expand our water system to some customers in a nearby rural subdivision before Country Water Association got to them. Ron was certain we had just enough capacity to do it. After a couple of our water committee meetings, I realized we'd be providing safe water to people who wanted it, and boosting our revenue, so I was completely in agreement. We drafted a letter to deliver to those homeowners, because we needed their participation in a low-income survey in order to receive the appropriate grant. Barry chimed in as his thick hair shuffled from the ceiling fan breeze. "I think ayeeeeee Ron is onto something, mmmm mmmm, giddy-up (fart noise)."

Ron's ability to pitch ideas seemed to work tonight as Barry defended this idea for the first time. Ron was incredibly skilled at two things: pitching ideas and finding a way to jerry-rig any water plant repairs. You could almost count on Ron to pitch a new money-saving idea, rather than a true repair, at every board meeting. This meeting he revealed that our wells had seemed blocked beyond repair, but instead of replacing them he had power washed them with acid!

We could have spent the money to fix whatever the problem was, but that's not what Ron stood for. I once heard Bill Murphy refer to Ron's spending habits as "tighter than tree bark." He was tight, but he'd also saved us tens of thousands of dollars over the years with his unique methods. I was starting to wonder how much longer all of this equipment would hold up, because you can only do a temporary fix so many times, especially when power washing acid was involved! But for now, it was time to go home. Meeting adjourned.

***

Something that I never quite understood is how people simply abandon a house. At this point, we had two houses that were abandoned (it would later grow to four), and our crew needed to mow their respective yards. The crew would keep a log of every time they mowed, and eventually we'd bill the new owners for the work we'd done. The mowing was done to make the property look somewhat reasonable, even though these houses were essentially falling in. In fact, one of those houses got so bad that a family of skunks had moved into the basement and was stinking up the entire neighborhood. In a town as small as Dawson, the mayor has numerous default titles. Although the county often helped out, I was labeled the Police Chief, Liquor Commissioner, Health Inspector,

Building Inspector, and in this case, Animal Control Officer. One angry older resident of the town, Lee Finley, stopped me at the post office to complain. He said it was my duty to crawl into the vacant house through a basement window.

He said, "You should take your gun, locate the skunks, and shoot each of 'em!"

I replied, "I'd rather have the Sangamon County Animal Control folks take care of the skunks."

"No, it's urgent. You need to get in there right away."

"I'll see what I can do."

***

When I later visited with my staff to check up on things, we brought up the Country Water Association. This time, it was because their water lines were now directly across the street from ours. Ron suggested that we chat with them about connecting the lines, in the event that one system was experiencing problems. Then, you could simply open up the line and allow the water to flow through to the respective customers. Of course, Country Water Association continued to ignore us. They were like a distant relative: you'd never hear from them unless they needed something from you.

As I continued chatting with Ron and Merf, I could tell they were not pleased when I gave them a policy on what to do if there was any sort of accident, whether it was an employee or a resident getting hurt on our property, like the park. Previously, there was nothing said, nothing documented, nothing done. When I'd mention something like this, the crew would always respond with something like, "But this is Dawson, we don't do things like this," or "We've never done it that way before." I'd always respond by saying that we have to be more modern in our actions, because everyone sues everyone nowadays. They'd just smirk and move on with the discussion.

We also talked more about hiring the understudy for Ron. Merf always agreed, saying it should've been addressed years ago. I could tell Ron still wasn't fully on board, but I kept being persistent, because I knew it was necessary and I could eventually wear him down. I was almost like a husband trying to talk his wife into letting him go on a weekend retreat with his old buddies. I knew the answer was no, but over time, I might just get a half-hearted yes.

***

Later in August, I had quite the incident with a dog running around near my house. Now, I had really believed that I needed to be strict on all the loose dogs in the town, which would help with my goal of cleaning up and beautifying the town. A new family had moved in just a few houses down from me, and their dog was regularly loose. On a few occasions, it would stop in my yard, and the owner would find it there and bring it home. "You need to make sure you're keeping your dog leashed up," I would say. One of the owners would always respond with, "I know, he just always finds a way to get loose." One Saturday, I was outside doing yard work when the dog trotted around my yard again. It made its way to my garage, where it defecated on the concrete floor! I ran it off and called the pound, using my authority as mayor to get a Saturday pickup. Within about 20 minutes, the pound grabbed the dog and off they went. Three hours later, the owners, a young couple in their 30s, with two little boys in the back, drove by slowly. They lapped the block a few times and the mother asked if I'd seen the dog. Before I could reply, the little boy with big tear-filled eyes asked out the window, "Mistah, have you seen our lil' doggie?" I felt terrible. I didn't want the boys to hear what really happened and break their hearts, so I told the mother that I saw the pound come through, so she may want to call them and see if they have it. They pulled away and drove back about 10 minutes later.

The mother screamed, "They said you called it in! What a total jerk of a mayor you are! You know what you are? You're Hitler!"

I replied, "Maybe you should keep track of your dog. If a dog takes a dump in the mayor's garage, it goes to the pound!"

They pulled away, giving me a one-finger salute as they zoomed down the road. From that day forward, any time that family drove by or walked past, I would give a friendly wave, even years later, hoping to ease the tension. Every time I wave, to this day, they respond with the one-finger salute.

I did, though, make it a point to treat people fairly and won an award because of it. The Illinois Municipal League gave me the award for "Illinois' Most Ethical Mayor." It was granted to me largely because I issued a fine to my parents! I still remember Dad calling me when he found out about it.

"Jeremy, why did I get this fine in the mail?" he asked.

"Your grass is way too high. You have to mow your grass," I responded.

"Jeremy, YOU MOW OUR GRASS!"

"Well, you should have called me sooner."

***

The next board meeting was September 3, 2013, this time missing Mike Madison. Every meeting started with the Pledge of Allegiance. I always had a good laugh because Margie Baggio was always the loudest person reciting the pledge. Margie also always said the wrong words, or forgot words, or mixed up words. Because she was so loud, she often tripped up others. She'd say something like, "And to the republicans or democrats, for which – whoops! Justice for all."

She was also notorious for receiving a call on her cell phone during the meeting, then taking the call. She'd start the conversation inside the meeting room, then step just outside the room to continue the conversation, while the rest of us waited for her to finish. Between the paper-thin walls and her loud voice, you could hear everything she said. She'd say something like, "I CAN'T TALK NOW, I'M IN THE BOARD MEETING," or "OH THE TEST CAME BACK POSITIVE, THAT'S NOT GOOD!"

Wayne Josten came to the meeting to complain that he had been fined for that big fire back on July 3. He said that if we pursued the payment of his fine, he would request a copy of all rules and regulations of the town, and he would travel around the town verifying that all rules were followed. He also said it was only a small brush fire that got a bit out of control, and this is either being blown out of proportion, or he is being singled out. He started to get loud and angry, saying he wasn't trying to be a jerk (using stronger language), but if we had to take this to court, so be it. At that point, Barry Vance erupted back at him, saying that he was clearly trying to be a jerk (again using stronger language), and comparing Wayne to a pile of dog excrement (but of course with stronger language), and ending his rant with, "Giddy-up (fart noise)." Remember, Barry had been serving the town for decades, and combined with the fact that he lived just a couple houses down from Wayne (in the opposite direction of me), Barry had seen enough.

Wayne continued saying that the upcoming Village bonfire would be after 8:00 p.m., which was the same violation he was cited for. He reiterated that this was obviously a case of him being singled out, and he was ready to go to court. I told him that the town's fire would be small, there would be no people panicking about a fire, and there would be no ash on any cars, as his fine notice indicated. He paused his rant, as if knowing I was about to fire back (pun intended), and I knew it was my time to shine. I said that if he wanted a copy of all ordinances, we could do so for 10 cents per page, and he would need to pay the total of around $80 before we'd make the copies. I added that Village ordinances allow recreational fires at any time, but brush fires must be extinguished by 8:00 p.m. I then said, "You, sir, have just admitted that it was a brush fire, so you did violate the ordinance, regardless of size of the fire." I continued to prove that fire was large as I offered photos of my father-in-law's car, covered in ash, as well as a photo of the screen grab of my call log displaying the 911 calls I attempted. I finished up, saying, "But if you feel you want to get an attorney involved over a $100 fine, then do what you have to do." I smirked as I was ready to drop the mic, displaying a sort of "In your face" attitude.

Then Agnes Cobb, already sporting a grandmotherly Christmas sweater, spoke up. "I was outside all night, and didn't notice any fire at all, so I think this is really blown out of proportion. Jeremy, you need to reconsider this." I couldn't believe it. I had just buried one of the town's biggest troublemakers, and she was letting him off the hook. Somehow, she didn't see the fire, and now my reasoning is vulnerable. In the interest of time, I agreed to reconsider the fine in the coming days.

We then moved on to yet another example of how simple, logical thinking made me look brilliant. In the 25 or so years since the Village Hall had been built, dozens and dozens, maybe hundreds, of employees, elected officials, and the general public had received keys to the building and offices. As those people moved on, their keys were never collected. I had the locks changed and supplied the current officials and staff with new keys. Brilliant! Also, the main entrance had a dead bolt lock that required a key to lock or unlock it on either side, which was no longer up to code. I had that dead bolt replaced with one that turned with a thumb lock. Brilliant! The Board was quite impressed as I informed them of the changes.

We also talked about the new website. Since I was very busy with all the things that a mayor does, I would need someone to supply information to the webmaster. He would need general information to put on the website, but none of the trustees seemed interested in helping. I didn't push them, because again, I needed their votes for other items. Luckily, Barry Vance finally agreed to lead the project with assistance from Clerk Rhonda Brown and Treasurer Kara Gregory.

The area sewer commission had a small building on the east end of our town. Remember, that's the same end of town in which people can't hear the storm siren. I worked out an agreement with the commission to allow us to move our non-functioning siren to a pole on their property. So long as that siren still worked after years of sitting out in the weather, the board approved the agreement. Ed helped persuade the board to my side, saying, "If the people can't hear the storm siren, they're a horse at a glue factory!" Of course, we would soon find out that after years of sitting in the weather and not being used, that siren simply didn't work. I was going to have to find a way to purchase a storm siren.

I had also recently discovered another problem that had been neglected. New employees were provided a handbook. The rules and policies outlined in the handbook didn't necessarily match what was written in the Village Code of Ordinances, which is the listing of rules, laws, and codes that govern the town. At this point, would you expect anything less? First, the handbook listed that employees were provided up to a 2% match of 401k, which wasn't in the Code of Ordinances. The handbook stated that employees are given a paid holiday for Columbus Day, but not in the Code of Ordinances. It was going to take a while to sift through the differences between the ordinance book and handbook, then eventually we could vote on the corrections.

Since the group seemed to be in a good mood, I capitalized on my opportunity. I pitched an improvement to the vacation policy and sick policy, both of which had failed previously. Without hesitation, the board approved the changes unanimously.

Next on the agenda was video gaming. At this point, it seemed like every town was approving video gaming, which was providing a nice boost to the revenue of these municipalities. If you aren't familiar with it, video gaming is essentially legalized slot machines, typically placed in taverns, in which a cut of the machine's earnings are returned to the municipality. It was our turn, and it passed 4-1. If you had to guess which trustee voted against it, and you guessed Agnes Cobb, you'd be right! She said, "We don't need those highway robbers coming in here!"

As you can tell, this meeting was getting long. But they kept approving anything I was pitching, so I had to keep firing away. I mentioned that I recently met with the Regional Planning Commission, who had informed me that many area towns recently collaborated to successfully be awarded numerous grants. And you'll not be shocked to learn: Dawson didn't participate. Not only that, but Dawson didn't so much as respond to any of the invites to collaborate. I mentioned to the Town Board that the Planning Commission informed me that our being awarded grants was very unlikely unless we had a 20-year comprehensive plan in place. Remember that $10,000 I had budgeted for special projects? I knew it would be needed for either a comprehensive plan or a new sign at the town entrance. I was planting the seed for both tonight.

Agnes Cobb fired back, "A plan? For the neighborhood I adore? That sounds uppity!"

"Yup!" said Margie Baggio.

I figured they wouldn't be interested in the plan anyway, so I didn't argue and moved along. I had just taken some photos of the flashing arrow sign at our town entrance. In my opinion it was an eyesore, and it just got worse. Or at least, I wanted the board to think it was worse. Someone had rearranged the letters on the board to list a bunch of swear words, so I showed the board photos of the arrow sign with these swears on it. I had hoped to upset the board enough that they saw the need to get rid of arrow signs altogether. Not only did the town's main corridor house our flashing arrow, but the flashing arrow for Mr. Ribeye Lounge sat right next to it. The Mr. Ribeye Lounge sat a block to the east of the town entrance, but since the majority of traffic flowed through the entrance, that's where they placed the second eyesore. The Sunset Bar, which was located on US Route 36, just south of the majority of the town, also had an arrow. I felt we had an epidemic of rundown arrow signs.

When I showed the board members the photos of the swear words, all five in attendance had a good heavy laugh. As athletically fit as Johnny Lynch was, he was laughing so hard his belly was shaking. I held my poker face (since I found it funny too) and reminded them that this is what visitors to our town see when they enter. We can't continue to give vandals the opportunity to greet our visitors with swear words on a beat-up arrow sign. The City of Springfield had recently barred flashing arrow signs citywide as part of a city improvement program. The north end of the city had a reputation for being, well, trashy. I mentioned to the board that if it was considered too trashy for the north end of Springfield, it should be too trashy for us. I remembered that Margie Baggio's son and daughter-in-law owned the Sunset Bar, so she would oppose a ban of the arrows, and could easily sway others to her side. I pitched restricting arrows to within a certain distance of the business to which it was advertising. This wouldn't affect the Sunset Bar whatsoever, and meanwhile force the Mr. Ribeye arrow away from the main corridor. I got a verbal consensus from the board, so I knew we could get something done in the future.

After Margie Baggio and Agnes Cobb agreed to organize the Halloween weekend wiener roast, I then asked to go into ·executive session, which removed everyone from the board room except the attorney and elected officials, to continue discussions on how we would hire an understudy for Ron

63

Butcher. It wasn't really necessary to move to executive session, but I wanted to keep Ron out of the room. If he disagreed with anything, he would be sure to argue vigorously against it, and sway the board to his side. This time, he erupted like Mount St. Helens, wondering why we kept hiding things in executive session. He eventually stormed out of the meeting room, which was the best thing that could've happened. Ron was a mountain of a man, and more than twice my age, so I surely didn't want to have to kick him out, but begrudgingly would've if I had to. There were no decisions made, just an update to the board that Margie Baggio's grandson, Will, was showing more interest in working for us full-time.

As the meeting ended, Barry Vance and Johnny Lynch told me not to let up on Wayne Josten. They had a good laugh at his threat to pay an attorney to fight our $100 fine. I agreed, because if there's any attorney willing to work for the $10 an hour necessary to fight the fine and sustain a profit, I'm sure that's not even an attorney! Meeting adjourned.

***

During the month of September, I had time to think about the fine to Wayne Josten. He lived just two doors east and across the street from me, so I didn't want to make an enemy of him or the "workers" he constantly had running in and out of his house. As I mentioned before, we always suspected they were dealing drugs out of there. Aside from that, because he argued against the fine in the board meeting, anyone in the town who followed the politics would read about it in the meeting minutes. The town, and Wayne, were now aware that I wasn't messing around. I sent Wayne a letter stating that I believed him when he said he wanted to improve the town, and I needed more people like him to help. I swallowed my pride, wrote to Wayne that I believed he could be an asset to the town (yeah right), and waived the fine.

***

Ever feel like that old cliché, "when it rains, it pours"? September was continuing to prove complicated as I received my first real test as mayor. Ron Butcher had let me know that there was a break in the water line (or "water main," to use the lingo), somewhere between the water plant and the town, a span of about four miles. There was no real advanced way to locate the leak without spending a chunk of money. Since Ron was described as "tighter than tree bark," and I was described as having "moths in my wallet," you might guess that this leak was going to be tracked down the old-fashioned way ... driving slowly along the path until it was noticed. Our crew spent a couple days driving along the path of the water line, looking for signs of a leak. Finally, one of our part-timers, Dan Jones, noticed some bubbling in the ground along the side of the road.

Ron called me and said, "Good news, Mayor, we found it!"

"That's great," I said. "Where is it?"

Ron said, "That's the thing. It's underneath the westbound lanes of Interstate 72."

I didn't have time to panic because it was time to get down to business. During that phone call, Ron and I discussed the plans for moving forward. His job would be to lead the crew to get the repair done, and I granted him spending authority to acquire any equipment or services needed. "Don't worry about the cost," I said. "I'll rewrite the budget when we get it fixed." Kara Gregory, with Rhonda Brown as backup, would handle any phone calls that came to the office with questions from the public. Remember, this was a small town of 500 people, so once word got out, everybody and their mother would be calling to get the full story like a bunch of *National Enquirer* reporters. Aside from rewriting the budget, my role would be to work with our engineers to get their assistance and be the liaison with any other government agency. With the leak under the interstate, we'd have to be in touch with the Department of Transportation to get the interstate shut down. Yep, the mayor of a town of 500 people is going to shut down an interstate!

What I didn't realize is that I was going to be needed to serve as a liaison for the media requests. I loved to talk to the media, so it wasn't a problem. Amid all the chaos, I didn't consider the fact that the local news media would be all over this story. And the thing is, it made for great TV in our small media market that typically had nothing to cover outside of the State Capitol shenanigans in Springfield.

Once the main break was found, we had to shut off the water being supplied to the town. The people of the town only had water for as long as the water tower maintained it. Once the tower drained, which at best was two days, the town was out of water. This meant our crews had a mere two days to completely repair a broken water line underneath an interstate. The local news was all over the story, with graphics such as "H2O-pocalypse" and "Water-geddon." From the numerous voicemails I received, I knew that they were seeking to interview town officials or employees, so I rushed to the scene of the leak to be sure I was the face the public would see. I wanted the people of our town to appear professional and knowledgeable, rather than some good ol' boys giving it their best.

I was interviewed at the scene, but my interview wasn't ever aired. What did get aired were two very unique interviews. The first was footage of our elderly Clerk Rhonda Brown. She was talking out of the driver's side window of her maroon minivan, with her 1997-esque Bluetooth dangling from her left ear. Her speech was calm, but appeared nervous as she allowed her minivan to slowly creep away from the interviewer while she kept talking. Her comments audibly faded off as she pulled away.

Then, they aired an interview with our part-time employee, Dan Jones. Dan was about 45 at the time, about six feet tall, aged high school athlete build, with a shaved head and an envious tan from his years of working outdoors. Dan was a great guy, and along with his wife and kids, was a tenant in my family's trailer park. Dan had even saved my dad's life by helping him get out of the house when it was burning down. In a way I felt I owed Dan, but that feeling quickly subsided for the time being.

After Dan's interview aired, just about the entire town was chuckling along with me. The interview footage of Dan Jones reminded you of an interview with a murder witness who was already in the witness protection program. His eyes were incredibly wide open, enough so that the largest of horse flies would be uncomfortable. As he spoke with those giant eyes, he'd look left, right, and behind him, as if someone was watching him. Why did these two get chosen to air and not my professional interview? I'll let you be the judge.

Luckily, as the mayor, I get to make new rules. No officials or employees were to do interviews. Any request for an interview would be directed to me. I handled a few radio interviews and a couple more TV news interviews. Aside from being the "Face of Dawson," this also got my name out there. With the idea of someday serving in the Illinois Legislature and needing the public to begin recognizing my name, it was a win-win.

Our crews ended up doing a great job, working nearly 24-7 to get the job done. With time to spare, they were able to get everything repaired and in working order before the town ever ran out of water. By this time, I had created a Facebook page for the town, in order to keep the public informed of what was happening in our community. I used this platform to heap praise on those workers for working such long hours to complete the task. The event taught me that we weren't prepared for a situation like this, and we would need to put a plan in place for future issues. I added this to my mental checklist of projects to work on, and knew I'd bring it up at our next board meeting.

***

Before that next board meeting could happen, I got an interesting phone call. It was a younger guy by the name of Xavier Dinardo.

"They cut my cable, and you need to fix it!" he yelled.

"You probably need to take that up with the cable company," I said.

"Nope, I don't deal with them. You come fix it."

"Fix what?"

"I ran cable from my neighbor's house, and he mowed over it. Now I ain't got no cable!"

"What am I supposed to do?"

"Come bring me a new cable!"

"I'll see what I can do."

***

In the October meeting, we were missing Barry Vance and Mike Madison. Barry was busy during the fall harvest since he worked for the local grain elevator. I was frustrated that he couldn't be at the meetings, but I understood. Mike, on the other hand, seemed to have just up and quit.

In most towns, the storm sirens are tested monthly. In Dawson, however, they just weren't being tested at all. I knew we needed to find a way to do it, but wasn't sure who to turn to. At Merf's suggestion, I had urged Mike, since he had previously been fire chief, to resume these tests. I chatted with the four board members in attendance, and none of them had heard the sirens being tested. I had called and emailed Mike to check in, but he wasn't responding. I was being ghosted by an elected official!

Barry, on the other hand, had agreed to work as the liaison with our website developers. My biggest fear was happening, though. See, I had delegated tasks because I was becoming so overwhelmed. Now, we were months into the agreement to develop a website, and nothing was being done because Barry wasn't responding to the web developer's requests. "When you care about your town like we do, well, sometimes you just gotta do it yourself," said Ed Quentin. "I tell my wife that right before I take over cooking her burnt dinner!"

As they say, the show must go on. As the meeting began, Ron took a moment to publicly apologize for erupting at me at the last meeting. He had apologized to me earlier in the month while I was at my office in City Hall. I was impressed that he was willing to do that without my urging, and he had my respect. I asked him to publicly apologize at the next board meeting, he agreed, and now followed through with the apology. He showed genuine remorse, seeming like a boy who just got caught looking at his dad's dirty magazines.

As the meeting continued, I mentioned the need for our water system to expand and add customers, thereby increasing our revenue, before other area water systems expanded to our area. The board voted unanimously, 4-0, to apply for grants to make this happen. Now is when I planted that seed once again. "The Regional Planning Commission tells me that chances are slim-to-none that we get any grant, so long as we don't have a written comprehensive plan," I said. I added that if we wanted to be serious about residential or commercial development, it would also be needed. I wanted to get them on my side, because I already knew that in the coming months the Planning Commission would be coming to our board meeting to pitch a 20-year comprehensive plan. Of course, my board didn't know that yet. You might say that secrets don't make friends. To that I say, "Secrets get things done." And one way or another, I was going to get that plan approved and written.

Something Carl Donaldson had started when he was mayor was to have a "Senior Dinner" in December. The Village would invite all of the senior citizens living in the town, plus one guest, and serve them lunch on a Saturday afternoon. We didn't really have enough space to serve the crowd, so each year we set up banquet tables and a portable heater in the Fire Department's dusty old garage. It was musty and an unusual setting, but "That's what we've always done."

Mayor Donaldson, who was retired and had plenty of free time, would do the majority of the cooking. The other elected officials helped prepare some of the sides, then helped set up and break down. It was such a large meal that it took a few days to prepare, and required giving up your entire Saturday to set up, serve, and break down. There was generally an array of food so significant that it would make a Golden Corral manager jealous! The Village shelled out enough money to serve ham, turkey, rolls, green beans, mashed potatoes, gravy, noodles, salad, and pie. They would also purchase a good amount of Christmas decorations and give them away as door prizes. The town's population was 500, and only about 50 residents would attend the event. In the two years I was a trustee, I didn't attend. As a stand-up comedian, I certainly couldn't afford to give up my Saturday availability for my $75 a month trustee job.

All these factors combined, I certainly didn't want to continue doing this event. However, with reelection and a political career in my future plans, I certainly couldn't outright eliminate this event, so at our board meeting, I pitched the idea of having the event catered. This way, we wouldn't have to spend days preparing, and would be able to reduce our total time spent at the event on that Saturday. Agnes Cobb and Margie Baggio both seemed to be opposed to the idea, but didn't argue too much. As a man in his late 30s with a wife and two young boys at home, Johnny Lynch seemed to be in favor of catering. Ed Quentin seemed indifferent, though he was typically difficult to read. Agnes and Margie had been around the town for decades, and liked change about as much as cats liked dogs. But, until we had an accurate RSVP total, we couldn't get an accurate catering quote to make a decision, so this concept was tabled for a month.

I then brought up the fact that although we cannot know when a water main break will happen, we can at least plan for the scenario. I had received a lot of positive feedback about how well we handled the communication of the Interstate 72 main break. I took the positive feedback to mean that I did a good job in "winging it." But, that's not something I wanted to make a habit of. As I began to discuss the need for planning, I could see Ron Butcher growing frustrated. He'd been winging it for 40 years, and wasn't about to change things.

"We've never had a plan for these things, we just fix it when we need to fix it," he said.

Rhonda Brown chimed in and said, "That's just how we've always done it."

You know by now that I hate that phrase. I told them that just because something had been done a certain way for years didn't necessarily mean it was being done the right way. As Ron and Rhonda continued to oppose the change, I dropped the argument, knowing they could sway the board to their side, and I didn't want them to recognize that power. If there was a plan or procedure in place, Ron would be responsible for handling it at ground zero, while Rhonda would be responsible for handling it in the office. I had no authority over Rhonda, since she was elected to be the Village Clerk. I had authority over Ron, but he'd been around 40 years. I was starting to learn that since I couldn't be around to make sure my crew was doing their jobs, I had to choose my battles. Ron was more than capable of handling the water main breaks on the fly, so I made like a Disney princess and "Let it Go."

With the water main break comes the responsibility of alerting the town to a "boil order." That boil order is just in case the water now flowing from their faucets is coming from the river. Despite an abundance of notice, there were still some residents in the town who complained that they weren't aware of a boil order. I would say, "The boil order was announced on the radio, TV news, and newspaper, as well as being listed on the town's Facebook page and the classy flashing arrow at the town entrance." These people would still argue that it wasn't enough. I arranged to have small signs made to be placed at the lesser used corridors which announced boil orders. Ed, still wearing camouflage from some hunting trip, said, "If they want to be hermits and stay away from everything, let 'em drink the river water!"

I then asked the board to create three subcommittees that the trustees would represent. None of the subcommittees would ever meet; it was simply a way to assign smaller tasks to trustees so I could unload some of the burden. We currently had six subcommittees: ESDA, Health/Safety/Drainage, Parks, Water Works, Finance, and Streets. When I explain this, the next two questions are, "What is ESDA?" and "Why is Drainage combined with Health and Safety?" ESDA is an acronym that means "Emergency Services Disaster Area," aka, the organized response when something bad happens. To answer the question about Drainage being combined with Health and Safety, I have no idea, but "That's just how we've always done it!"

I felt this grouping of subcommittees didn't cover all aspects of the town, so I created three "catch-all" subcommittees: Employee Relations, Internal Affairs and Residents, and External Affairs. To my surprise, the board approved these unanimously with no arguments whatsoever. They were going to have to take on some responsibility, and surprisingly they were up for it.

The last item on the agenda was whether or not we'd continue to have a Christmas lighting contest. Traditionally, our town would pay out a small cash prize to the top three decorated houses. I have to admit, some folks could really put on a display. If you don't believe me, just drive by Dawson any time of the year, because most of those lights are up year-round! But anyway, some of our trustees had become a little hesitant to continue the prizes because participation was down. But I really wanted to get the community working together to clean things up and make the town appear nicer. I lobbied the board to approve the prizes that we've always paid, which was a whopping $50 for first, $30 for second, and $20 for third. Considering that only a handful of houses had been participating, you could set up a handful of broken-down candy cane displays and have a decent shot at third place. Meeting adjourned.

***

On the fourth Saturday of October, our Village hosted the wiener roast at our park pavilion, as it had done for years. This was another event that I really didn't care for, but I continued because I wanted to keep the older folks happy and increase my chance of reelection. Since Agnes Cobb and Margie Baggio had done the organizing, planning, and cooking, my effort was minimal. To keep my trustees happy, I showed up early and stayed late to set up and tear down. To keep the town happy, I mingled while folks visited, ate hot dogs and chili, sat around the bonfire, and snacked on candy. I basically just needed to shake hands and kiss babies, or as we small-town mayors joke, "Kiss hands and shake babies."

The event ran smoothly, largely because of our resident party planners Agnes and Margie. They were both retired grandmothers who had the time and ability to pull it off, without me even worrying that something would go wrong. Village Clerk Rhonda Brown was also a retired grandmother who would help plan, though she never got entirely involved when Agnes and Margie were in charge. For whatever reason Rhonda couldn't entirely get along with them, and they literally fought "like two old ladies." We also had Bill Murphy and his wife, along with Ron Butcher and his wife, who all hung around and visited after setting up. The only other elected official to come to the event was Johnny Lynch, who arrived with his wife and two young boys, about ages eight and six at the time. Johnny and his family were late, with his wife saying they had just gotten back from the Halloween event in the next town east, Buffalo. That was all it took for all three of our older ladies to absolutely lose it! "Those no good (expletives) over at Buffalo, they know we do this every year on this Saturday," Rhonda said. Agnes said she thought Buffalo was moving the date so we wouldn't have a conflict. "Well apparently, they're a bunch of lying (expletives)," Margie added. As the crowd of about 25 Dawson residents looked on from under the pavilion, some shocked, some nonchalant, I didn't know whether to laugh or hold my poker face. I compromised with a smirk.

We knew Buffalo well. We and they, along with Mechanicsburg, make up the school district for Tri-City High

School. When all three towns consolidated their schools, Buffalo was chosen as the site for the school because it was the central town of the school district. Ever since, the older ladies have held a grudge against Buffalo. Plus, Buffalo's Halloween event didn't truly cause a conflict. It ran from 3:00-6:00, while ours ran from 5:00-8:00. With the towns only two miles apart, and both events "come and go as you wish," anyone could easily attend both events if they wanted. Later, Johnny and I had a good laugh about it all. I was starting to recognize that he saw the humor in a lot of the same scenarios that I did, and he was growing on me.

With the park only about a block north of my house, I was walking back home when lifelong Dawson resident Eddie Von pulled up next to me in an old minivan.

"Boy, you guys sure like to do those boil orders, don't ya?" he asked.

"This was the first one since I've been mayor, I think," I responded.

"Ol' Carl Donaldson did 'em all the time. Looks like you're gonna too!"

"It's a safety thing."

"Nope, I'm tired of it! I just started drinking it anyways! It's my right to drink the water, so don't try to take my freedom!"

"I'll see what I can do."

CHAPTER 4

OFFICE CHRISTMAS PARDON

As you can guess, we convened on November 4; once again Mike Madison and Barry Vance were absent. Kim Kirk, the new pastor of the local church, stopped in to introduce herself. She was a kind, older lady, who said that if the church could be of assistance in any way, to let her know.

Discussion then moved forward about the consistent absence of both Mike and Barry, but more specifically Mike. I told the board I had continued to reach out to him by email and phone but had no response. He had also assured us he would be testing the storm sirens, but it simply wasn't getting done.

We discussed whether an ordinance could be written to address the situation, or if impeachment was a possibility. As this discussion lingered, I heard someone snoring, and recognized that Pastor Kim Kirk had fallen asleep, draped over a couple of the banquet chairs she was sitting on.

Switching subjects, Agnes Cobb stated that a dog was loose in the trailer park, and someone had trapped it in a shed.

People were nervous because it was growling at people, so she called animal control and had it picked up. Why was it important to announce this in a board meeting? It wasn't.

I then mentioned that the Regional Planning Commission was continuing to write 20-year plans for multiple area towns, including neighboring Riverton. I added that they were interested in writing a plan for Dawson and also guiding us on getting a walking trail on the abandoned railroad passage, which ran between our town and Buffalo. This was something just about everyone in town had an interest in, so I knew it was important to plant this as another seed before I sought the financial approval to fund the 20-year plan.

Agnes, with her gray hair freshly permed, then presented some catering quotes for the senior dinner, saying she was excited to "literally serve the town we love." If you recall, I wanted no part of cooking for this thing. Agnes pitched the prices, which were far more than the cost of cooking it ourselves. I knew that with our tight, small-town budget, I stood a snowball's chance in Qatar of getting that thing catered. As you would expect, everyone agreed we needed to continue cooking and serving the meal ourselves, as long as everyone would help out. Ed said not to worry about him, and that he was "feminine enough to cook noodles." Margie Baggio was especially opposed to the catering, though I wasn't sure why. Everyone agreed not to cater the event, and she continued to argue as to why we shouldn't cater it. I couldn't put my finger on it, but I'd figure it out in time.

Another hot-button issue in our meeting was ... drum roll ... what restaurant we'd choose for our annual Christmas party. Traditionally, it was at the Boston Steakhouse in Springfield. In recent years, Mayor Carl Donaldson switched it to the Mr.

Ribeye, here in Dawson. He stated that it was to support the local business, but many others thought he did it simply because it was the bar he liked to drink in, and he was trying to help his buddies that owned it. Meanwhile, the other bar and grill in Dawson, the Sunset, had never hosted a Village Christmas party. Since I've been described as being so cheap that I have cobwebs in my wallet (the moths have since flown away), the board wondered if we'd even have a party. Or, if we did, if I'd be so frugal about it that we'd be eating fast food cheeseburgers. As the board argued over which place we should go, I simply said we needed to move on, and I'd let everyone know my decision later. They'd been arguing for 45 minutes!

We concluded with the annual salary review, which was mandated by ordinance to be done in November. Everyone agreed with my suggestion to give a raise in the same percentage to each employee, and we concluded. As we started packing things up, I noticed Johnny Lynch poke Pastor Kirk to wake her up. She looked a little confused when she woke up, but like all of us, was ready to go home. Meeting adjourned.

***

The funny thing about wanting to bury Johnny Lynch was that as I got to know him a little better, I realized he was an all right guy. He asked if I was willing to come speak to his children's Boy Scout troop. Johnny was the leader, and they needed someone from a political office to talk to the kids. I agreed and gave a brief speech to about a dozen little boys who were oddly intrigued at my position. During the question-and-answer session, they asked questions like, "Are you

Illuminati?," "Are you involved in any Quid Pro Quo?," and "Are you allowed to kill people?"

***

In late November we got some significant snowfall. Rhonda Brown called me and asked if I wanted to declare a snow emergency.

"Isn't that just to prevent parking on snow routes? We don't have snow routes," I said.

"Then I guess there's really no reason to," she replied.

I took some time to think about it. With one of my primary goals being for people in the surrounding area to have actually heard of Dawson, it made sense to get the free publicity. When the news stations listed off the area towns under snow emergency, Dawson would be announced. From that day forward, even if we got just the slightest of flurries, I declared a snow emergency!

***

As I was enjoying Thanksgiving dinner with my family, the doorbell rang. One of Dawson's senior citizens, Teddy Frederickson, stood in the doorway as snow swirled around him.

"Are you OK? Do you need to come in?" I asked with concern.

"This will just take a second," he replied. "I'm sorry to bother you on a holiday, but we've got a big problem."

"What's going on?"

"Did you see that the high school football team got eliminated from the playoffs?"

"Yes, I saw that. I've got company over. What's our big problem?"

"I just told you! The quarterback is terrible and he'll be back next year! What are you gonna do?!"

"Umm, it's not really my place."

"You better get to recruiting, that's all I can say. Good day."

"I'll see what I can do."

***

On December 2, we met for the final time in 2013. This time, we had five trustees in attendance, as Barry Vance made it. Mike Madison was missing once again. The first big item for discussion was brought up by our engineer, Gene Winters. Gene was about 65, a short, slim man with a bald head, who reminded you of the stereotypical local farmer. He was soft spoken and seemed to address every idea we had for him. The firm that Gene worked for had represented our town for years and was the official firm of many other local towns. Gene said that our plan to extend the water system to the rural subdivisions before the Country Water Association got there wasn't looking good. We ran an income assessment, and the residents there made too much money to qualify us for a low-income grant. We'd have to foot the $300,000 bill ourselves, or at least ask the 75 households to split it, neither of which would happen. Gene went on to say that he was retiring, and that Joe Hulvey would be taking over for him. Joe was in his early 40s, more of a medium build, with thick, black hair. I'd only had minor interactions with him, but that's all it took for me to label him as an arrogant punk!

We then unanimously approved an ordinance which would allow the Town Board to remove an elected official for abandoning their position. Two weeks before this meeting, I had finally gotten Mike Madison on the phone. He told me that with his own three children, and recently married to a woman with three more children, he just didn't have the time to continue while he lived a real life *Brady Bunch* scenario. I told him I understood, and that his resignation would need to be in writing, which he agreed to provide. This relieved me a bit because I knew he likely didn't have interest in my mayoral title. By the time the board meeting rolled around, he had yet to provide the written resignation. Bill Murphy had agreed to do the storm siren testing each month, since Mike never actually started the process. I wasn't sure why Merf tried to defer to Mike in the first place. But nonetheless, I said that since Bill had been the fire chief in his younger days, remembering how to test the storm sirens would be like riding a bike for him. An unshaven Ed Quentin said, "It'll be like riding a bike, or a pony," then the 50-year-old proceeded to dance while singing the words "Like a pony" to Billy Idol's "Mony Mony." Margie and Agnes both laughed hysterically while also seeming semi-attracted to Ed.

Without actually coming right out and saying it, there was a lot of concern for Ron Butcher's health. It was clearly going downhill, and he was still the only person we had that was licensed to run the water plant. During the past month, I had taken Ed Quentin and Johnny Lynch to the Riverton Village Hall. Their leaders expressed interest in helping us out if Ron were unable to fulfill his duties. For now, we at least had a band-aid plan in place, but I still needed a long-term solution. Barry pulled me aside later and said, "Jeremy, you're a (fart noise) good leader and ayeeeeee a smart guy, mmmm mmmm, you'll figure it out, giddy-up, save our town."

We then discussed the findings from our annual audit, which is an audit mandated by law. They didn't find anything unusual but urged us to consider additional checks and balances. I had run that past Rhonda Brown, who told me they mention that in the report every year, and there really isn't much else we can do. We only have two people in the office, which is our Water Clerk and Treasurer Kara Gregory, and our Village Clerk Rhonda. Kara has access to the funds because she pays the bills. Rhonda cross-checks Kara's work. These two could pull off a heist if they wanted to work together. Rhonda had been affiliated with the town for decades, so I trusted her not to steal. I didn't know Kara that well, even though I went to high school with her, but I figured with Rhonda cross-checking there wasn't much to fear. I took Rhonda's advice, and left the process the way it was. I figured that in time, I could address it. For now, I had a hundred other things to worry about. Meeting adjourned.

***

I had decided that the easiest way to avoid controversy with the location of our Christmas party was to avoid both Dawson restaurants altogether. We might have been able to alternate years, but both were typical hole-in-the-wall bars, and I wanted something at least a little classier for the staff. I had recently asked the employees to pull back on spending, largely due to the budget constraints that the water line break had caused. I felt that it wasn't right for me to fund a high-end dinner at the Boston Steakhouse when I had just asked everyone else to tighten their wallets. I called the trustees and staff, and notified them all that we'd eat at Edzo's, a low-budget Italian restaurant in Springfield. Agnes Cobb told me that Edzo's was a bad idea because she has a gluten allergy and Edzo's doesn't have a gluten-free menu, whereas Boston Steakhouse does. Likewise, Ed Quentin said his wife has the same allergy, and also suggested Boston Steakhouse. "Otherwise, she's popping like a firecracker on the Fourth of July," he said. After all that, I called everyone back and told them we'd go to Boston Steakhouse.

When we had the party, I couldn't help but notice that Ed's wife didn't attend. As I chomped on my New York strip, I noticed that Agnes Cobb's choice for dinner was fettuccine alfredo and garlic bread. Clearly, Agnes and Ed both used gluten as an excuse, or at least Agnes didn't care that she'd be – as Ed put it – "popping like a firecracker." My wife comforted me by stating that the employees and trustees work hard, so it was a well-deserved treat. They all seemed to enjoy themselves, so I took solace in knowing that Sandra was right (as usual).

It was also the time for the senior dinner that Margie and Agnes largely planned out. I was impressed that with the exception of Mike Madison and Barry Vance, all other trustees helped cook and serve. We had about 45 seniors attend. As they made their way through the buffet line, Ed whispered to me, "Look at that lady's hair! It's bluer than a smurf in the ocean!" I smirked toward Johnny as I tried to maintain a straight face before examining the buffet. Margie Baggio had purchased a whopping 15 pounds of turkey and 15 pounds of ham. Rhonda Brown then mentioned to me that Margie buys that much meat every year. I wondered why she would over-purchase, and continued to wonder why she argued so hard to avoid catering the food. As the event wrapped up and we started cleaning up, Margie quickly claimed the leftovers. After another quick chat with Rhonda, it all added up. Margie is the matriarch of a large Italian family. The common tradition is for the entire extended family to have lunch on Sundays at the matriarch's home. Aha! It thus was an annual tradition for Margie to serve her family the senior dinner leftovers the following day. I let it go for now, because I knew I needed her vote for that all-important comprehensive plan funding, which was right around the corner.

***

About this time, I got a phone call from an angry resident from nearby Mechanicsburg. As part of an intergovernmental agreement, our crew ran their water plant which also supplied Buffalo. This guy was mad because he watched our crew sit at the Mechanicsburg convenience store, sipping coffee and eating donuts for hours every morning. He eventually confronted the crew, who mostly laughed him off. He was mad, stating that although he doesn't live in Dawson, his water rates pay their salaries, and it wasn't right that they just sat around. It sounded to me like our guys didn't have enough to do.

I decided to meet with Merf and the crew to discuss the situation. I had picked the brain of Barry Vance as to what he thought because I really respected him. I also ran it past Riverton Mayor Red Tomko. Every time I chatted with the 40-something Red, he always wore a "Village of Riverton" polo shirt, which somehow always highlighted his fading freckles. Barry and Red both said it was probably best just to talk to the crew about proper use of time, because they're good guys and will understand.

As we sat around the table, I looked at Merf, Ron, and Dan Jones. As usual, George O'Reilly didn't attend. They all sat with their heads down, like kids who just got caught throwing rocks at a girl. I asked the crew about the incident. Merf quickly spoke up before the others, saying they were on break when the incident happened. The crew doesn't actually get breaks, but I understood in cold weather it was important to go inside now and then, especially guys the age of Ron and Merf. I told them just be aware of the perception of whatever you happen to be doing, because the whole town feels like they need to watch you.

"THAT'S EXACTLY RIGHT!" blurted Merf. "WE'RE ALWAYS DOING WHAT WE'RE SUPPOSED TO, AND THEY WATCH FOR US TO SLIP UP SO THEY CAN TATTLE LIKE LITTLE PUNK KIDS!"

At that point, my only thought was, "Thou doth protest too much."

I informed him that the water line break caused enough financial damage that I was going to have to slightly cut the hours of his two part-timers, George O'Reilly and Dan Jones. The two guys who were typically working 32 hours a week would be cut to 24 each. I had run the numbers, and aside from a few other budget cuts, cutting those sixteen total hours every week for the rest of the fiscal year would keep us in the black.

"HOW ARE WE SUPPOSED TO GET EVERYTHING DONE?!" he shouted.

"You're just going to have to figure it out. We're making several other budget cuts too."

He was mad, but trying to hold it in, almost like my little boy when he's told he can't have any more cookies. I felt bad to cut hours, but there really wasn't anything else I could do. As I recall, this is the first inclination I had that I was paying for a lot of guys to do a lot of sitting around.

See, I regularly got a call from someone complaining that the crew was sitting around their workshop at the Village Hall at the beginning of the day, or at the end of the day. This crew is responsible for responding to water emergencies 24/7, and occasionally is working long hours in the middle of the night, often in the freezing cold or blistering heat, often in snow or rain. I really had no problem with the crew slowly easing into or out of their day for about 15 minutes or so. Plus, this had been their habit for 20+ years under Mayor Donaldson, so the idea of shaking things up over something so minuscule didn't interest me.

***

I did get an interesting voicemail from Rhonda Brown late in the year. She left a message saying, "Hi, Jeremy, this is Rhonda. I just wanted to let you know that Opal Winthrop just called me. She was cleaning up the Village Hall for us, and there's plaster dust and a bulge in the wall of the meeting room where one of the fire trucks backed into the wall and broke it again."

Did you notice the word "again"?! It had happened once before when I was trustee. The issue is that the garage that housed the fire trucks was only about six inches deeper than the length of the fire truck, so those massive machines have to be perfectly parked. Luckily, Chief Lance Butcher got after his crew and they fixed it up, so the fire department got a mayoral "pardon."

***

My doorbell rang a few days before Christmas. Gus Sheffield, along with his wife and teenage kids, stood on the front porch, each holding white sheets of paper.

I smiled and yelled to Sandra, "Honey, come quick! We've got carolers!"

Gus looked back at me disturbed and said, "We're not carolers. What are you talking about?"

"I thought you were carolers."

"No, we're here to complain about the tree limbs that scratch our camper roof when we drive by!"

"They're ten feet high, and that's the ordinance requirement. Besides, I can't really have my crew trim them in the middle of winter."

"You better do something quick! And we're offended that you called us carolers!"

"I saw the sheets of paper and – "

"We have four pages of petitions to get the tree limbs trimmed."

"I'll see what I can do."

I looked down at the petitions as I closed the door. Each of the four pages had only one name on them: the specific name of which Sheffield handed me their "petition."

***

The meeting on January 8, 2014, was my most important one yet. Unfortunately, Mike Madison and Barry Vance weren't there. At this meeting, Rob Dellomo and Mia Ryan of the Regional Planning Commission had come to explain the importance of a written, comprehensive 20-year plan for the town. Rob was in his early 40s, a bald Italian man who was part of a prominent political family in the area. Mia was about 23, fresh out of college, with an incredibly impressive mind for public administration.

Rob explained (as I had previously mentioned to the board), "It is nearly impossible to be awarded a grant without a written plan in place." The two handed out copies of plans they had written for dozens of towns in the area. Mia explained that they first conduct a survey of the townspeople, gathering the thoughts, concerns, and ideas that the residents have. They explained the topics overviewed in the plan and the objectives for each. Margie Baggio and Agnes Cobb, representing the senior demographic, largely argued against the plan. They said it wouldn't do much for us, and no one would follow through completing the survey. I reminded the group, "We have already approved the line-item funding for the plan and we need the written plan in order to receive a grant. Without a plan we would be left behind by all the other area communities moving forward." As a town dwindling in population, this was a necessity; we could no longer just "wing it" as had been done for the past several decades.

Someone should create a sign that says, "Everything takes longer in a small town." How long would this discussion take in your meeting? Well, it took over two hours in Dawson that night! I'd had enough and asked for a vote. With only four trustees in attendance, I needed two votes for a tie, in which case I'd cast the tie-breaking vote. Johnny Lynch voted yes, then Agnes and Margie both voted no. I held my breath as I anticipated Ed Quentin's vote.

He said, "If you wreck a truck for the insurance money, but forgot that you let the policy expire, you've got nothing. Without a plan, you've got nothing. I vote yes."

With that joke falling flat, I cast the tie-breaking vote of yes, and a plan was in the works. I knew that meant I couldn't replace that flashing arrow sign just yet, but I had at least accomplished one of my two big purchases that night.

It was getting late, but I still had a couple other things to address. Ron Butcher's hope of extending the water system any farther was dwindling even more. The area residents that would tap on to the water system were no longer showing interest, and our new engineer Joe Hulvey wasn't sure much else could be done.

We were looking at some sidewalk replacements as part of the "Safe Routes to School" grant. Rhonda Brown said that she didn't believe anyone from the town had ever done a safety assessment of the problem sidewalks in the town. Imagine that. Just a week before, Ed Quentin had done an excellent job of touring the entire town and mapping the problematic sidewalks. However, Joe Hulvey insisted that he come along with Ed and me to view the sidewalks personally. "I want you to show me," Joe said. Ed quipped that Joe must be from Missouri.

With Mike Madison still not attending, I announced that everything was in order to officially remove him from office at the next meeting. I had continued to reach out to him to come back or resign, but he never responded after our last chat. Ed said, "I bet you haven't been rejected like that since you partied at a college bar!" Agnes Cobb said she hated to do a forceful removal, so she would try to knock on Mike's door and explain what was happening.

We ended by discussing the need for some new Christmas decorations that could be placed along Route 36, the main highway that passed along our town. No decorations had ever been put there, and I thought that since the majority of traffic passes along that route, it would be a nice display for travelers to notice our town. Once again, I was preparing them for the pitch I'd be making in the coming months. Meeting adjourned.

***

In late January, I met with the staff to discuss a few things. I asked if the playground equipment at the park is regularly checked for safety issues. Merf told me that they check them at the beginning of spring, but that's it. I asked for them to do a monthly inspection, except for during the winter. I'd hate for a small child to get hurt because of something we could have easily prevented. I tell you that to tell you this: I started hearing from a few folks in the town, and part-timer Dan Jones, that Merf had been complaining I was working him too hard. I wasn't sure whether to believe the small-town rumors. After all, was asking for a monthly task to be done considered working someone too hard?

Merf called me a few days later. It seemed that after confronting him about those long breaks at the Mechanicsburg convenience store, he'd have a complaint for me almost every month.

"I know you're doing all these budget cuts, but I'd appreciate it if you spent a little more on toilet paper," he said.

"I didn't cut spending on toilet paper," I responded.

"I know, it's been like this forever! Early settlers would opt for leaves instead of this stuff!"

After ending the call with Merf, my phone immediately rang. I could hear a lot of noise in the background and recognized the voice as Robby Hanson, an area millennial.

"You need to come to Mr. Ribeye right now," he said, sounding like he was crying.

"What's wrong?" I asked.

"I ordered a cheeseburger, and they didn't put lettuce on it."

"Could you maybe ask the waitress?"

"And create tension? No way! I don't need conflict!"

"I'll give them a call and *I'll see what I can do.*" I never called.

CHAPTER 5

YOUNT AND THE RESTLESS

Our next meeting was in early February. Every meeting seemed to be an elementary classroom roll call and someone was always missing. I am sure you could guess who was absent: Mike Madison and Barry Vance. But this time, it was different. Agnes Cobb was able to contact Mike Madison, who put his resignation in writing. I felt bad for Mike, especially since he was an old classmate of mine and part of what I called "The New Guard." Agnes was almost the town grandma and had a way with comforting and guiding us younger leaders. I had already spoken to several people whom I would have liked to appoint to the seat, but none were interested. Many in the town were aware that if you were on the Town Council, you were Public Enemy Number One. And for $75 a month, that was as desirable as a colonoscopy. I had my work cut out for me.

I had recently noticed that we were paying taxes on our telephone bill, which didn't make sense, since we're a government entity and tax exempt. I asked Kara Gregory to look into it, and she said we'd been paying taxes on those bills as far back as she could review the bills. I called the phone company, discussed the issue, and by the time the next bill rolled around those taxes were gone. I had saved the town hundreds of dollars annually by simply asking a question.

Margie Baggio asked why previous leadership never addressed that. Ed Quentin said, "Why didn't Village leadership address a lot of things? It's like the licks to the center of a Tootsie Pop. The world may never know."

Agnes Cobb said, "Speaking of not addressing things, the Village has been sued in the past for the broken sidewalk from that tree root on Ledlie St. The tree causing the issue is on our right-of-way, and so it's our responsibility to fix it."

I said, "You're saying we were sued because of that and it was still left that way?"

"Yes," she said.

I told the board we would address that tree as soon as the winter weather passed through. Right then, Johnny Lynch had enough. "What has even been done for our town the past 24 years?! Nothing!" I smirked because I knew that Johnny was officially now part of The New Guard. He understood exactly what I was dealing with. Have you ever taken over a job in which your predecessor seemed to have done nothing for the past several years? Johnny just learned what I already knew: I'm living it.

To fan the flames, I notified the board that I was working with our engineer, Joe Hulvey, to work with another government agency that does water rate analysis for free and would have the results shortly. That analysis was one more thing that had never been done. I've watched enough shows on TV about saving restaurants and bars to know that you have to know what your costs are! We really had no idea. The water rates had been the same for a long time, and it had never been reviewed to understand if it was even profitable.

The only work that had been done was a research project I did myself. Every town's formula for billing water is a little different. Typically, they bill one amount for a minimum usage, and that minimum varies by town. Then, they charge an additional rate for usage on top of the minimum, and that usage increment also varies by town. Some charge administrative fees, some don't. So, the only real way to compare prices to other towns is to take the average household water usage and plug it into each town's formula. Doing that, I discovered that Dawson had the second lowest rate in the county, behind only neighboring Riverton. Ironically, it seemed more people complained on Facebook about high water rates in Riverton and Dawson than anywhere else. This proves once again that the social media warriors really have no clue what they're talking about.

We then moved on to discuss the issue of overgrown shrubs that had grown onto public streets, a slightly different issue than what those "carolers" were complaining about. It violated ordinance, but guess what, was never addressed. Over the years as drivers drove around those big hunks of foliage, the straight roads were now developing into slight S curves because of the traffic pattern. I'd had enough, and was ready to address it. The only problem was, how would we dispose of all the brush that we were asking our residents to cut down? Agnes suggested that we collect all the brush and burn it in a giant pile down at the park. You might think this was a crazy idea to everyone sitting in the room, but it wasn't. As I started to wonder how I could shut down this idea politely, Ron

Butcher spoke up and said, "You're going to have a giant brush pile on fire in a city park? With kids playing in the same area? That's dumb!" I held in my laugh as I remembered why Ron was such an asset to have when he's on your side of the argument. I asked if there were other ideas. Hearing none, I decided to just let this one go. If the people needed to dispose of limbs and brush, they would have to figure it out on their own.

I then brought up all of our efforts to receive a "Safe Routes to School" grant. If you recall, we'd been paying our engineers to head that effort, and had been doing so for years. I had learned that to qualify for the grant, the location of the project needed to be within two miles of the school. Dawson sat 2.5 miles from the school, which if you recall was in Buffalo. We'd been wasting our time and money for years, and our engineers either didn't care to tell us, or simply didn't know a basic fact of their jobs. In addition, Joe Hulvey sent us a significant bill for his ride-along through the town, investigating sidewalks, that he insisted he be a part of. During his ride-along with Ed Quentin and me, Joe contributed such thought-provoking statements as, "Yeah, that one looks bad," and "Oh that's a nice sidewalk right there." Joe was also getting less and less responsive to my calls and emails. When I had become mayor, I reappointed everyone, because I wanted that knowledge base surrounding me, knowing that I could make changes later as necessary. I was starting to think I recognized the first appointee I'd be letting go, though I didn't tell my board just yet.

I pitched another task for the trustees to address, and surprisingly they didn't decline it. I had started to notice that many of our town ordinances hadn't been updated in decades. The ordinance book was around 750 pages, so I knew there was no way I could review it all. I started assigning two trustees each to read about 10-12 pages per month, and at the next meeting bring up anything that might need revising. There were plenty of rules about where to tie up your horse, how to properly use a spittoon, and wiping muddy boots outside.

I then reintroduced my idea to put nice Christmas decorations along the highway for those passing by. I felt it would create a nice image for the town.

Margie Baggio quickly let her Italian fire out as she argued against my request for $1,600. "The Village Hall needs a new roof, and the crew still needs a new tractor," she said.

I reminded her and the board that I had written both of those into the budget, as well as the Christmas decorations. Plus, if we postponed the decorations, we'd no longer be paying the after-Christmas price of half off. Agnes argued that the majority of our traffic enters through one entrance, so this made no sense. She added that the old gas station closed years ago. I have no idea what relevance the gas station had, but Agnes regularly brought up old businesses and buildings that had closed. I again reminded the group that we need to worry about our image. The town had gradually changed from a beautiful bedroom community to, well, trash. There were still plenty of nice homes and lawns, but those were becoming fewer and fewer. I couldn't let it go any further, and improving our image was a top priority. Then, Ron Butcher once again came to my rescue. He said that on Memorial Day, the flags look far better when they're all posted on the major roads, rather than a few here and a few there. Of course, I use the term "major roads" very loosely. But as soon as Ron said that, it was like a light bulb went off over everyone's heads. They got it, and the motion passed unanimously.

To continue improving the image of the town, I wanted to address the stray cats running around town. I described them as strays, knowing that a lot of them are owned by people in the town who just let their cats roam . . . especially Agnes Cobb. I mentioned that we already address dogs, but need to do something about cats. Who do you guess would argue first? Not Agnes, but her tag team partner Margie Baggio. "I've never seen a cat chase a kid on a bike," she said. "Plus, I haven't seen stray cats in a while." I told the group they aren't all strays, but several owners of cats just let them run around. Agnes straightened up in her chair, and resident jokester Ed Quentin decided to have some fun with me. With a smirk, Ed said, "Who specifically is just letting their cats roam?" We both knew exactly what he meant. Ed lived only a block from Agnes and me, and had even chatted with me about 80-year-old Agnes and her cats. Not wanting to open a can of worms, I just said, "I'm not sure but I see collars on them. Maybe we should table this until I can learn more." Ed chuckled as I seemed to be the only person to know what was amusing.

Agnes then asked if I had found someone to take the place of the recently resigned Mike Madison. I told her I was working on it. I told the board that if they know anyone interested to let me know. In reality, I had roughly a week between his resignation and the board meeting. In that time, I had received a hard no from 12 people. No one wanted any part of the small-town politics or the Facebook roasting that came with it. We all know that there was truly only one person who wanted the job, and that was Sharon Yount. I didn't want her, no one on the board wanted her, and after finishing last in two straight elections, it was clear the town didn't want her. Meeting adjourned.

***

As we walked out of the Village Hall, Agnes pointed to a light bulb that was out under the entryway awning. Without that motion light bulb, it was a little dim, and you had to rely on just the streetlight's illumination. She said, "At my age, I need to see the sidewalk clearly, especially when we've got snow or ice. I'll fall down to Chinatown!" She was funny and right. I hadn't really ever noticed the light being out, but agreed I would talk to Merf about getting it fixed.

As February rolled on, I started noticing that the salary report wasn't matching what I had budgeted. When I looked into it, I noticed that our part-timers were still working the same number of hours they had been prior to my cutting the hours. In some cases, they were even working more. I had a short meeting with Merf to see what was going on and to also bring up the light bulb.

"It's bright enough just from the streetlight. Agnes can deal with it. That's her problem," he said.

I said, "We need it changed, and what's going on with our part-timers' high hours?"

"We just can't get it all done without those guys here!"

"We don't have the money to keep doing this, Merf."

"You've been asking a lot of us, and there's just not time. I don't even know how I'll find the time to change that light bulb! You ask me to do something that's gonna take 15 minutes, and I've got 30 minutes left in my day? You're rushing me! There's no way!"

A few days later, I had been outside my house doing some work when Dan Jones stopped by. He told me that Merf said, "I'm not cutting hours, and there's nothing the Wonder-Boy can do to stop me." If this was true, my suspicions that Bill Murphy had grown jealous of me were true. Of course, I once again didn't know if I could believe a small-town rumor, so I uniquely addressed it. The next morning, all part-timers and their supervisors were notified in writing that the part-timers would not be paid for any work they did beyond the hours limit I had in effect. Merf was right, I couldn't stop him from working guys more hours than I wanted. But he forgot that I sign the checks, and I'm sure he was hotter than a firecracker when he saw that memo. The Wonder-Boy had outsmarted him.

***

After two more people declined the trustee position replacing Mike Madison, I asked Agnes Cobb to look into what her friends thought about bringing in Sharon Yount. I needed to know what the "Blue Hair Club" thought. Agnes told me that after chatting with her friends, they all felt it was the right thing to do. If you recall, Margie Baggio had finished fourth in the trustee election, and I appointed her shortly thereafter. There is no rule that says you must appoint the next highest vote-getter; I simply wanted Margie back. Of course, Margie was part of the "Blue Hair Club" also, so it certainly helped my status among them. Remember, Sharon Yount had finished fifth and last for the second election in a row. It was clear the people didn't want her, but I was out of options.

Aside from her recent failed campaigns, I also had a bitter taste in my mouth from a recent story. Sandra and I were wrapping up a date night and decided to stop at the Sunset Bar for a drink before heading home. We were enjoying our time when we noticed herds of patrons rushing out of the bar, as if to watch a fight outside. Since I was the mayor, I didn't want to be around if a fight was going on and the police showed up. I stepped out to ask some onlookers what was going on. With cleaned up language for the purpose of this book, one guy said, "Sharon is drunk and showing people her breasts!" Now, why anyone would want to see that is beyond me. Even back when I was single, I could name 500 people whose "sets" I'd rather see than Sharon Yount's. But that, my friends, could be your next Village trustee.

In mid-February, I begrudgingly reached out to Sharon Yount. We sat at the Village Hall while I explained to her why I needed to appoint someone to the seat. Sharon was in her mid-late 40s, portly, with stringy black shoulder-length hair. She and the trailer she called home both looked low-income and worn out. Her teenage son and husband Harry were both notorious for stirring up trouble all over town. They even had a miniature junkyard in their backyard. They didn't have a junkyard business, they simply had junk covering their yard. All three of them had the attitude of "If you disagree with me, we'll throw down right now." I try not to judge a book by its cover, but I already knew their story. You've heard the phrase, "Don't be that guy." But, they were THAT family. I hated the idea of appointing her, but there seemed to be no one left in the town to so much as gauge their interest.

After chatting and learning about her thoughts and ideas, I got a feeling that she may be a good fit as part of The New Guard. Despite the fact that the junkyard behind her trailer had become a miniature wildlife sanctuary, she felt the need for the town to clean up, improve, and make changes for the better. We ended our chat with the agreement that I would appoint her at the March meeting. We stepped out of the Village Hall. As I turned to lock the door, Sharon mentioned that the extra $75 per month would come in handy. She told me she had recently won $100 on a lotto scratch-off ticket and quit her job, thinking she could retire. "Maybe I'll have her write the budget," I thought.

The next step was to let each of my current trustees know that I'd be appointing Sharon at the next meeting. Agnes and Margie were on board, feeling it was right. Johnny Lynch was fairly new to town, so he wasn't aware of her reputation and really didn't care. Then I discussed it with Barry and Ed. They were certainly reluctant, but also understood I was out of options.

"There's no one else you can ask?" asked Barry.

"Even a dumpster would call her trashy," added Ed.

I told them that she wanted to help make changes for the town, and maybe the idea of being a town official would inspire Sharon and her family to clean up their acts. And with that, I knew I had a 5-0 consensus to approve the appointment. The last thing I wanted was someone to vote against her, then have that person have to work with her over the next few years.

***

Another member of the "Blue Hair Club," Iris Pagnozzi, called me in late February to raise a concern.

"Have you been to a basketball game at the school?" she asked.

"Not this year but I've been there," I said.

"Those bleachers are terrible on your back."

"Yeah, they're hard, I guess."

"You need to make the school replace them!"

"I don't have a relationship with the school."

"You better do something. I pay taxes to have the school up to code!"

"I think it's up to code. They're just basic wood bleachers."

"Something needs done. It's unacceptable!!"

"I'll see what I can do."

∗∗∗

We met on March 3, 2014, for the next board meeting. This time, all five current trustees were there, including Barry. Sharon sat in the old beat-up banquet chairs for the public guests, alongside her husband and son. With no debates or discussion, Sharon was unanimously approved as the trustee appointment. Sharon was sworn in as her family watched, looking like stereotypical junkyard employees.

My first order of business was to provide updates on behalf of our engineer, Joe Hulvey. I told the board that we were charged excessive amounts for the sidewalk tour he insisted on being a part of, and also for attending our board meetings (which used to be a free service). I announced that our water rate analysis had been completed by a government appointee named Max Woodrum, and we were simply tied up trying to schedule the meeting with Joe, which was getting frustrating. I was planting the seed among the board; I was ready to switch engineers, I just didn't know who would replace him.

We got the estimates back from Joe Hulvey as to the cost of running a trail on the old railroad to Buffalo. This trail had been a goal of the people of the town for years, but it just wasn't going to happen. Even if we were to get a grant, the cost of our share would be about a third of our annual budget. Even with financing, it was far too great a cost. If we were to get a grant, we were required to have a surface that could be driven on by an emergency vehicle, including a bridge over a small creek that crossed under the path. Even though the path sat about 15 feet from the highway, the rules are the rules, and I gave up on pursuing this. Ed Quentin added, "Maybe if the Illinois Governors would stay out of our business, things would run a lot smoother, and they would stay out of jail!"

In between board meetings, our fire chief and Ron's son, Lance Butcher, had reached out to me about visiting a fire-house in Mt Zion. He felt that Dawson's firehouse, which oc-cupied about half of the Village Hall building, was old and outdated. He wanted to show me what a nice firehouse looked like and suggest some improvements. Not wanting to upset anyone affiliated with Ron, I happily obliged. Lance looked just like his father, only larger and stronger. I hopped into his gorgeous pick-up truck while the 6'6", 300-pound man drove us 40 minutes down the road. We talked about sports, mutual friends, and how great his dad is. The Mt Zion firehouse was immaculate and shimmered like a fairy-tale palace.

On the drive back, I pitched a four-phase improvement to our firehouse, since I had a four-year term. We'd paint certain areas over a couple years, then add concrete slabs outside the Hall, then finish by adding a nice clear enamel floor. It was in our best interest to improve the firehouse garage, or "bay," to use the lingo, since we regularly held public gatherings in there. Lance agreed with the plan, so I asked the Village board to authorize $400 in paint and supplies for phase 1. The vol-unteer firefighters would do the labor for free. The board approved it unanimously. Barry added, "Well, yee-haw, if they're gonna risk their giddy-up lives to protect us and our friends for free, the ayeeeeee best we can do is get 'em (fart noise) some paint." I couldn't agree more. Giddy-up!

The last item of business was a good bet to make some voters turn on me. Over the years, Mayor Carl Donaldson hosted an Easter Egg Hunt Extravaganza, giving away prizes such as new bicycles, iPads, iPods, and big cash. Kids from all over the county would come to win their big prizes, then return back to their own towns in celebration. Though I loved the concept, we were a town of 500 people. With so many neglected expenditures on the horizon, one of the first things I sought to eliminate was giving big prizes to kids that were typically from other towns. A handful of kids were from Dawson, but in general, most winners were the outsiders (stay golden, Pony Boy). I explained this to the group of trustees and got a little resistance. Agnes and Margie would chime in with things like, "But my granddaughter from Riverton really wants to win another bike," and "My grandson from Pawnee went through the $100 he won last year in a month. He wants more!"

"If that four-year-old boy burned through $100 in a month," said Ed, "then I'm glad he's not writing our budget! I'm with Jeremy. We need to stabilize our funds."

"I ride a bike every day. Even I don't need a new one every year!" said the athletic Johnny Lynch.

The board then approved reducing the Easter Egg Hunt budget from thousands of dollars to $150. I guess now you know why they call me frugal. Meeting adjourned.

***

Later that month, I had a brief one-on-one meeting with Merf. He had seemed to put aside his recent frustrations with me, being overly nice, so I figured he wanted something. I was right. He explained why our utility tractor needed to be replaced, why a new roof was needed on the Village Hall, and why a few other purchases were needed. When I told him I had already been budgeting for all of those things, and planned to address them before he retired, he was giddy as a school girl. "I'm gonna get a new toy . . . ahem, I mean tractor??!!" he shouted. If I could get him motivated to be at work, I was in. I just needed the Town Board to approve a new fiscal year budget and we were on our way.

Although he needed something, Merf still found a way to bring up yet another unusual workplace complaint.

"You know I made those copies of all those fliers for you," he said.

"Yes, thanks again for that," I replied.

"Kara told me that I should have refilled the copy paper when I was done! She was mad!"

"I guess that's standard office protocol."

"You're telling me I need to make copies AND refill the copier?"

"It's common courtesy."

"Unbelievable! You just keep adding jobs!"

***

Since it was mid-March, I had some friends over to sit and watch the opening round of March Madness on a Thursday afternoon. I was interrupted by a front door visit from Otis James, an older man who had lived in the town forever.

"Did you know you've got an unlicensed business operation going on in this town?" he asked.

"No, what's that?" I said.

"Just down the road, two little girls are running a lemonade stand!"

"Are you joking?" I said as I laughed.

"I'm serious! They can't do that! Go shut them down!"

"I'll see what I can do."

***

I also took the time to meet with Gary Whitcomb, who was an engineer that previously worked for our current engineering firm, but had since broken off and started his own firm. After discussing my engineer troubles with numerous area mayors, they all directed me to Gary. After exchanging a few phone calls and emails, I suggested Gary and I have dinner in downtown Springfield. I figured if my mayoral status was going to get me anything, at least I'd get a free meal out of it! As we talked, I realized that Gary was genuine, professional, and a funny guy—the exact opposite of engineer Joe Hulvey. He also charged less, or even nothing, for the same services for which Joe Hulvey was charging us excessively. I told Gary to come to the next board meeting and I'd appoint him the new engineer. I made a few calls and emails to the board to forewarn them of what we'd be discussing, to which all seemed to agree.

***

Rhonda Brown left me quite a voicemail that March. She said, "Hi, Jeremy, this is Rhonda. We kind of have a situation over here on Walnut Street at the house next to the trailer court. Umm, there's a raccoon, I had the guys go look. They don't want to mess with it because, uhh, the animal is sick, and Merf says he doesn't know if it's having convulsions or what. It's stuck in the fence, under the fence, between that house and old man Dilbert's house. And we need to have animal control come out. I, umm, I'm not at the office. I'm not where I can do anything about it. We need for you to take care of that for us if you will."

Being the good mayor that I am, I called her back and said, "Rhonda, get a gun, shoot it."

***

When we gathered for the April meeting, Barry Vance was absent. We kicked things off by discussing Gary's qualifications and peppering him with questions, to which he was quite impressive in response. He was about 40 years old, 6'2", with an athletic build, and dark hair and eyes. Being a veteran, he stood erect as he addressed the room. To add to the verification that Gary should be the guy, I even had a statement from Merf that he felt Joe Hulvey had taken advantage of us during the I-72 water main break and that we should consider other options. The board was starting to recognize that Merf and I didn't always see eye to eye, but when we did, you could count on it being the right decision. All five trustees present, as well as Ron Butcher, were clearly in agreement to make the switch. But, in typical Dawson fashion, we had to debate for 60 minutes before the unanimous approval was given. Ed Quentin, wearing his usual college sweatshirt, said, "When it's time to let someone go, you gotta let 'em go, just like my high school girlfriends did to me." It was official; we had a new engineer. I later dismissed Joe Hulvey in what was possibly the giddiest phone call I've ever made.

When it was time to discuss our budget needs the trustees sat silent with no suggestions. Previously we had paid our attorney Reggie Phillips to write it but I felt that was a waste of money. At the very least, we could put together the budget as we felt it should be, then allow Reggie to finalize it. The trustees all knew this was coming. I laughed a bit when I asked if anyone had any suggestions for items we needed to fund, and I saw a room of adults looking around and twiddling thumbs like a group of school kids hoping not to be called on.

Speaking of, our recent water rate analysis was complete. Approaching one year into my tenure, the analysis discovered that our operating costs were actually exceeding our income. No rate analysis had ever been done and water rates hadn't been increased in 20+ years. With the growing cost of labor, supplies, equipment, etc, it was clear that I was going to have to increase the rates. Even though at the time we had the second lowest rate in the county, I knew there would be an uproar from the townspeople. I feared it would hurt my reelection chances, but bankrupting the Village would do far worse. I explained it all to the board and let them know we'd take a vote next month.

The only other item of note is that we had begun work on the comprehensive plan. The next step was the community-wide survey, so I urged the board to encourage residents to complete the survey. It was important for us to know what people liked and didn't like, and what people truly cared about versus could care less about. Agnes and Margie clearly didn't want to help with this.

Agnes said, "I told you no one would do the survey and Dawson doesn't need the plan anyways."

I said, "With that attitude we'll just have a town full of grouchy old ladies!"

She had regularly referred to herself as a grouchy old lady, so I smirked as I made the comment, and she laughed back. Maybe I'd won over a policy vote or two. Meeting adjourned.

***

As the April rains approached, I got a phone call from Katlyn Norris, a college-aged girl who I'd never even spoken to before.

"I use a very specific hair product and the dollar store in Riverton doesn't sell it!" she said.

"Okaaaaaay," I replied, not knowing where this was going.

"Don't you think you could address it?"

"Umm, how?"

"You call the manager and tell them that you know someone that needs a product and they better find a way to get it!"

"Did you talk to the manager?"

"No, that's your job!"

"I'll see what I can do."

***

I was headed out of town for yet another comedy show when my phone rang. Merf was calling so I suspected it was something urgent.

"Does Opal Winthrop still get paid to clean the Village Hall every month?" he asked.

"Yes," I replied.

"She hasn't been here in quite a while; it's frustrating."

"She goes in once a month. She was just there a couple weeks ago."

"That's the problem. I ate peanuts at the break table and there are shells all over it. They've been there for at least a week and I can't eat at the table again until someone cleans them up!"

"You want Opal to clean up the peanut shells that you left on the table?"

"It's not MY job to clean them up!"

CHAPTER 6

RESIDUES AND RESI-DON'TS

On May 5, we held the public forum that was required prior to voting to raise water rates. Ed Quentin, whether wisely intentional or simply unable to attend, was absent. I wondered if I'd get hammered with questions from angry residents, but also knew that no one really ever cared about Dawson politics. I walked into the meeting room, one year after being sworn in, and saw only one person in the banquet chairs: Opal Winthrop. By now she seemed to like me, but with her spunkiness, you never knew what was coming next. I sat nervously as I waited for the appropriate time to start the forum. I pounded the gavel at 6:30 and started the meeting. Max Woodrum explained the need for the rate increase and then opened the floor for questions. Max came across as a good ol' boy, wearing farmer attire, standing close to 6'5" and 300 pounds, with a buzzed head and a booming voice with a drawl. Opal, unafraid of the large man next to her, spoke up and said, "First time visitor, first time complainer. I don't think it's right, but you're going to do it anyways. That is all. Opal Winthrop. Dawson." I thanked her for her input, restricted my smile to a smirk, and closed the forum at 6:40.

Since the actual board meeting didn't start until 7:00, we all just sat there making awkward small talk. The room was full of people who weren't much more than casual acquaintances. We certainly were not friends, and each person in there only liked about half of the other people in the room. I did my best to guide this rocking house party for the next 20 minutes. Fortunately, I was rescued by Barry Vance's reciting of 17 minutes' worth of offensive yet hilarious Polish jokes. Without Ed there, Barry was easily able to carry the room. Of course, each joke ended with Barry's trademark, "Ayeeeeee!" or "Yee-haw!"

I had recently instructed Merf to fill me in on anything he directly saw at the park that needed to be improved or replaced. That's why it was surprising to me when Sharon Yount proudly stated that Merf invited her to the park and showed her several items needing improvement. She, rather aggressively, stated that the improvements needed to be done right away. I reminded her that we first needed an estimate of cost of the specific improvements, so she'd need to chat with Merf about that. I wasn't entirely positive whether I could trust Merf or Sharon, and their new partnership had me wondering if a pair of bad apples had just partnered up. I thought that at least early on, Sharon would be on my side since I gave her what no one else could: her oh-so-coveted seat on the Town Board.

While contemplating that in my mind, Barry Vance announced that he had not been contacted whatsoever by the website developers. This was just one more thing I started to realize I was going to have to address on my own. The older folks in the room seemed to think that just because I was college educated I could build the website on my own. I told them I'm lucky to build Lincoln logs on my own! This was, of course, hilarious only to the seniors in the room.

It was now time for the big vote. Would we continue to operate our water system at a loss every year and pay fees out of savings? Or would the board do the right thing and approve a small rate increase? Even with the increase, we'd remain one of the least expensive water systems in the area. What was frustrating to me was that typically water systems do a small rate increase every 1-2 years to keep up with rising costs and inflation. Of course, Carl Donaldson hadn't raised the rates in over 20 years. That meant it was time for me to be the bad guy and do what was right. I brought up the need for a vote. Barry Vance made the motion to approve, simply saying in his booming voice, "Well ayyeeeeee what else do we (fart noise) need to say, giddy-up, we can't keep yessir paying from savings, my town will go bankrupt, yee haw." Johnny Lynch made the second, and the resolution passed unanimously. Though I knew this could hurt my reelection chances, it needed to be done. Plus, the vote that would decide my reelection was still 2½ years away, so I figured most folks would forget it even happened. Remember, the biggest demographic of voters is all over 75!

As we were wrapping up for the evening, I reminded the board to encourage their friends to complete the comprehensive plan surveys, which were recently mailed out. It is difficult to write a plan based on the views of the public if the public won't tell you their views. My announcement was received with a pair of eye rolls from our resident seniors Agnes Cobb and Margie Baggio.

I then told the group I had discovered one more thing that Mayor Donaldson had neglected. I was reviewing our written emergency plan, which hadn't been updated in 50+ years. It read like the King James Bible, with phrasing such as, "In such a matter, thou shalt communicate thereforeto with authoritative delegates." This plan would be used to guide officials from various levels of government, as well as volunteers, as to the processes, contacts, etc, needed to restore both the town's infrastructure and government, so it needed to be updated and understandable. There were several names listed, with specific roles, who were no longer affiliated with our town. In several entries, the person listed was dead! For instance, if a tornado hit the town, you'd review the emergency plan and each person would take on their respective role. Except of course, the dead guys, who wouldn't pull their weight.

Sharon agreed to work with our Clerk Rhonda Brown to update the emergency plan. Over the years, anything typed up had been done by Rhonda. My theory is that between her and Mayor Donaldson, she was the only one who knew how to use a computer. And with the board not having been previously involved in tasks, that left Rhonda as my go-to. With Rhonda helping, I knew the plan was in good hands. Meeting adjourned.

***

With the weather turning from spring to summer, lots of people had been out walking and riding through the town. This was the subject of my next phone call complaint, which was from Manuel Lopez, an older man who I believe was the lone minority in the town.

"Some lady just let her dag-gum dog poop in my yard!" he yelled.

"Was it even on a leash?" I asked.

"It was on a leash, but it pooped!"

"Do you know who it was? I'll see if I can get her to come back and pick it up."

"She don't need to come back to pick it up, she need to clean it up!"

"I don't know what you mean."

"She picked up the poop when it happened. But now, there's a little bit of residue left on some blades of grass! My yard has been tainted!"

"I'll see what I can do."

***

Speaking of residue, that's the sort of thing Bill Murphy was unhappy about. I stopped in the Village Hall to take care of some paperwork before heading out for a comedy tour. Merf stopped me in the hallway, wearing his signature ball cap and t-shirt, to raise a concern.

"Is it true that Kara is responsible for ordering the office supplies but Ron has final say on what gets ordered?" he asked.

"Yes, that's correct. What's going on?" I countered.

"My tape dispenser got lost, so I needed another. Ron said he'd get me one."

"Then what's the problem?"

"Kara said he never ordered one, but somehow I got a 'new' one (using finger quotes)."

"I'm not understanding."

"He didn't get me a new one! I know it's not new! It has tape residue all over it! How am I supposed to feel respected, after all my years of service, if I'm forced to use a tape dispenser with residue on it?!"

"I'll make sure to get you a new one."

***

Our next meeting was June 2. Barry Vance and Agnes Cobb were both missing, but we still had a quorum to continue. Sharon Yount arrived with a newly prepared emergency plan (with help from Rhonda Brown) and financial figures from Merf about the park repairs. I was impressed that she was working hard and proving she wanted to help our community. Since she seemed to be willing to take on challenges and get things done, I removed the delegation of website development from Barry and handed it to Sharon. I knew if she failed, we'd still be in the same boat. If I could avoid taking it on by giving it to Sharon, I was all about that. To the tune of Kool & The Gang's "Celebration," Ed Quentin, wearing a college hoodie, started singing, "Delegation! We're gonna delegate and have a good time!"

I was proud to announce that the surveys for the comprehensive plan were returned at the highest response rate that the Planning Commission had ever seen! I wanted to gloat about it since Agnes was so vocal in saying that no one would respond. Since Agnes was conveniently absent, I only bragged a little to Margie, who I knew would secretly pass it on. Metaphorically, I wanted to celebrate with a boatload of mortar fireworks but settled for a single sparkler.

It was now time to address the abandoned house problem. In fact, one of the houses was in such bad shape that our fire department refused to enter it should there be an emergency.

We had four houses in all that had simply been abandoned and the Village was mowing the grass at all of them. We needed to be reimbursed for the labor costs but no one knew where any of these homeowners now lived. Our attorney Reggie Phillips was going to investigate. I always wondered, though, how does anyone just up and leave a house? I never understood that. "Our grass is high and I don't feel like mowing. Let's pack it up!" "This floor is getting beat up and needs fixed. We're outta here!" Meeting adjourned.

***

Between meetings we had the "Super Bowl of Dawson," the fireworks extravaganza, on July 3, 2014. My wife hated this event because I was a nervous wreck every year. I knew if anything went wrong, I'd be on the news trying to defend the town. "It's always been a quiet event, except for the big explosion this year. Didn't expect that." Fortunately, my second fireworks event concluded without a hitch.

As you might imagine, though, not everyone saw it as a success. As the late-night partiers stumbled through the streets that July 3, I got a knock at the door. There stood Mildred Kincaid, pushing 90 years old, at 10:00 p.m. She was wearing a nightgown and was obviously up way past her bedtime.

"Do you know what time it is?!" she asked me aggressively.

"It's ten. What can I do for you?" I said.

"Those fireworks are too loud! Why must they be so loud?"

"I think that's just how they are."

"Why are they so loud at this time of night?"

"I'm not sure."

"Can they lower the volume?"

"That's not really an option."

"Then maybe they should move them to earlier in the night so they don't wake me up!"

"They start them at about 8:30. That's really all the earlier they can do it."

"No, they can do them at 4:30."

"It would be way too bright and no one would see them."

"I would!"

"I'll see what I can do."

***

As successful as I thought the night was, there was still one more person to complain: Merf. He called me on July 6.

"I got paid a full day when we were closed for Independence Day, right?" he inquired.

"That's right. You're paid a full day for any holiday in which we're closed," I said.

"Then why is it that Ron got paid time and a half?"

"He worked all day on July 4 to operate the water plant."

"You're telling me that it's fair for Ron to get paid time and a half, but me only regular pay?"

"He worked and you didn't."

"That's so wrong. You're singling me out! I should get time and a half too!"

***

I was still happy that another "Fireworks Spectacular" ended with no casualties when we met on July 7. This time, we barely had the quorum, with only the left side of the room attending: Margie Baggio, Sharon Yount, and Ed Quentin. After some frantic phone calls, we convinced Agnes Cobb to come, who arrived about 10 minutes late. Barry Vance and Johnny Lynch were out.

I was excited to hear what Sharon Yount had done with the website developers. I then got an inkling that maybe Sharon was what many in the town thought she was, when her response to how things were going was, "I didn't do nothin' with the website. I'ma need that guy's contact info again. I lost it." And with that, we were going to have to wait another month. The good news is that I had a feeling this would happen, so I had already sent the web developer quite a bit of information when I had some free time.

Agnes Cobb, wearing a Christmas sweater in July, then stated that she learned in her ordinance reading that there are several permissions required to operate a junkyard, and we may have to go after Harry Yount if we were to properly represent our town. With Harry being Sharon's husband, a shocked silence came over the room as every face turned to me. Even Sharon, who supposedly had an aggressive personality, reserved her response as she stared at me, mouth agape. The future of the board hinged on my statement, so I had to get it right. "I am going to have to review the rules and go from there. I can't react to something without fully understanding the entirety of the situation," I said.

Ed chimed in, "You've barely been married a year and already have the skill to calm two angry women at the same time!"

Honestly, if nothing else, I bought myself some time. See, the fact is that the Yount's backyard wasn't truly a junkyard by definition. Harry collected scrap metal which he piled up around the backyard and side yards. However, it certainly wasn't a typical yard either. It was a giant eyesore in the middle of our town and people complained to me about it all the time. On the other hand, if I needed to get things accomplished in our Town Hall meetings, I was going to need Sharon's vote. I privately told Sharon a few days later that as long as I could count on her voting for my proposals, I wouldn't challenge the yard. She agreed, knowing full well that somehow they were surviving off of scrap metal and that lotto scratch-off ticket.

We then discussed that if we were going to get our ordinances posted on the new website, we needed them in electronic format. With our attorney Reggie Phillips modifying or creating every ordinance, we figured he would allow us to use those. After months of Reggie denying that he had electronic copies, which we knew wasn't true, he finally produced a CD of all ordinances. However, it wasn't an updated version. It was the original that he had been provided when he took over as Village Attorney some 20 years ago, so it needed a TON of updating. For whatever reason, Reggie just did not want to give up those documents. Since I wanted no part of the project, I told the board that maybe we could forgo that project unless someone really wanted to take it on. To my surprise, Ed Quentin volunteered, saying, "I can do it, and I'll charge a lot less than the attorney that already did this!"

I told the group that we were required to send someone to the natural hazards meetings at the county building in order to be eligible for certain funding in the event of a natural disaster. Knowing the importance of this, I decided to take this on myself. However, Sharon Yount spoke up and said that she really wanted to handle it. I knew she might blow it, but she also just seemed so eager to do it. Not wanting to rock the boat, and also wanting to enjoy at least some free time, I agreed that

Sharon would attend the meetings. Ironically, trusting Sharon for this was as risky as buying a $100 lotto ticket.

Ever since I took over as mayor, Merf had pushed and pushed about every week to get a new utility tractor. The tractor they were using was 20-plus years old, regularly broke down, and was legitimately held together with duct tape in several spots. It was clearly time for an upgrade. I knew getting the new tractor would make Merf happy, so maybe he'd work a little better for me. Just to help him remember that I was in charge, I delayed purchasing the tractor for the first 14 months and finally brought it up for a vote this night. With no concerns, the board members unanimously approved the purchase of Merf's new toy.

The last thing I brought up was announcing that the Riverton officials had no concerns with assisting Dawson's water operation in the event of an emergency. Now behind closed doors, "emergency" meant if Ron Butcher passed unexpectedly, which was our biggest fear. Remember, Merf had the ability to run the plant on his own; he just couldn't pass the licensing test to allow him to legally run the plant. With Merf planning to retire in the near future, we needed a contingency plan in place until I could get Ron's understudy hired. We would have an intergovernmental agreement written for approval shortly. Meeting adjourned.

***

In late July, I once again stopped by the Village Hall to check in on the staff. I had simple discussions with Kara Gregory and Ron Butcher. Merf, though, was not too happy when I asked him if he could clean out the Village garage that morning.

"I'm going to have a few folks meeting me here tomorrow, so I'd appreciate if you could have the garage cleaned up," I said.

"Jeremy, I haven't even been here ten minutes and you're already coming at me with projects," he said.

"I don't think that's a big deal. And weren't you supposed to start 40 minutes ago?"

"That's not the point! Don't come at me like that!"

"Like what?"

"You can't come at me with projects first thing. It's rude!"

"Okay, Bill, please get it done."

I had a one-day comedy tour planned, so I was driving out of town when I left the Village Hall. I was frantically flagged down by Nikki Johnagin, a single mom in her early 20s.

"Did you track down those guys snooping through yards last night?" she asked.

"I wasn't aware of them," I responded.

"I hope you catch them. That's scary!"

"Did you call the police?"

"No, I posted it on Facebook."

"Maybe next time you should call the police instead of posting it. I'm not usually going to see that."

"You should be in tune to social media! How else would you be aware of an emergency?! You jeopardized my safety by not calling the police for me!"

"I'll see what I can do."

CHAPTER 7

STINK TANK

On August 4, we were back in the Village Hall. To my surprise, all six trustees were present. What was also surprising was that Sharon Yount stated she had been gathering information for both the website developers and the upcoming natural hazards meetings.

Ed Quentin stated that he was working on updating those electronic ordinances but it was going to take a while. Our attorney Reggie Phillips, dressed in his usual business suit, said that his office has a fully updated electronic version and would be happy to print it out for him.

Ed said, "It would be much easier if you just provided an electronic copy of those ordinances."

Reggie responded, "We don't have that."

I resisted laughing at Reggie contradicting himself. Again, I have no idea why Reggie didn't want to give them up, because it was obvious he had exactly what we wanted. But Reggie was Reggie, and with the support of the townspeople behind him, I had no real reason to move on from him.

Ed then spouted back, "I don't know why you think those ordinances need guarded like Fort Knox!"

About this time, I started putting a little more pressure on those four abandoned houses. We knew they were abandoned and that we had to continue to mow their grass. Some of them even had abandoned cars in the yards. One abandoned house happened to be right next door to Ron Butcher's house, and he was all about getting it cleaned up. Unfortunately, we have to follow all the protocols to the T, so it was a long process. I knew we'd get these houses addressed one way or another, I just didn't know if it would be before the voters went back to the polls for my reelection bid. We could get reimbursed for our labor, attorney fees, and other costs by putting a lien on each house, so that's what we did. I hated to do it, but as Ed Quentin reminded me, "If you pack it up and go, up the creek you row."

I brought up the need to back up our electronic files on something besides thumb drives, since those become corrupted over time. Plus, if the backup drives are kept in the same area as your computer, it does you no good if there's a fire, water leak, tornado, etc, because your primary and backup files would both be destroyed. Barry Vance chimed in, saying, "We better (fart noise) ayeeeeee have those things mmmm mmmm backed up, giddy-up." I suggested an external hard drive to back up files at the water plant and the Village Hall. Each drive would then be stored at the opposite facility for safekeeping. Reggie insisted that since this wasn't a line item in the budget, I needed to get the board's approval before making this $300 purchase. I said that office supplies are in the budget, but he urged that it wasn't specific enough.

I said, "Under that reasoning, I need board approval to buy ink pens!"

Reggie replied, "Yes you do."

I held in my eye roll as I asked the board for approval for the hard drives. They agreed. I didn't say anything more, but knew that going forward, there was no way I'd be asking for board approval to purchase ink pens. Ours would just magically happen to work for all four years of my tenure! Meeting adjourned.

***

A couple days after the water bills went out, a younger man by the name of Paul Isringhausen stopped by my house. When I opened the door, I noticed his wife waiting in their beat-up Buick LeSabre.

"Are you lining your pockets?!" he asked me rather aggressively.

"Umm, no," I replied with a confused tone.

"We just got our utility bill and it's ridiculous!"

"We can check to see if you've got a water leak. That's no problem."

"Not water, the power! It's always the highest in the summer and winter!"

"Then you'd need to talk to the power company. I have no connection to that, but it's probably because you use your air conditioner and heater during those months."

"I think you've got a collaboration to line your pockets! I'm on to you!"

As he backed out of the drive, his car backfired and died three times before he finally got onto the road, where he squealed his tires and drove off in anger.

"*I'll see what I can do,*" I shouted.

***

One hot summer day in late August, I stopped in the Village Hall to take care of a few things before heading off on another comedy tour. As soon as I opened the door, the worst smell imaginable hit me. In all my years of changing diapers, I have never again come across such an odor! I held in my gag reflex as I moved forward down the hall. I looked left into the office, where Kara Gregory mouthed, "I know." She had the lone window open and fans blowing. Before I could ask what happened, Merf, sweating through his t-shirt, grabbed my attention and escorted me into the kitchen.

"Kara is really at it today!" he said.

"What's going on?" I asked.

"She told me I can't boil fish in the microwave!"

"Is that what I smell?"

"It's not her business what I cook for my lunch!"

"Maybe you could cook it at home. You do live right across the street."

"That would take five minutes off my lunch period! Why can't I just cook my lunch in the office microwave like every other American?"

"It smells terrible, though."

"I'm gonna keep doing it. I don't work for you when I'm at lunch."

***

I was finally starting to feel that I had all of the projects under control when we met in September. Also seemingly under control was the Town Board, of which all six members attended this night! That's two in a row!

Rob Dellomo and Mia Ryan returned and presented the survey results that the Planning Commission had compiled. My plans for the future were validated when the biggest concern of respondents was lack of property maintenance and unrestrained dogs and cats. Between those two factors, I thought that made us look like a one-horse town more than anything. It had to be addressed if the town were to improve and be open to development, and luckily the people of the town were behind me. Agnes Cobb and Margie Baggio sat there like a couple of lost puppies, recognizing that the people had confirmed my plans. Merf happened to be at the meeting that night to talk about staffing. Upon hearing the news, his shocked face confirmed him as the third pup in the litter. I knew Ed Quentin was on my side when he joked, "We better start cleaning things up, or this town's gonna be mistaken for the set of *Deliverance!*'"

Otherwise, there wasn't much to discuss. Ron and Merf lobbied to get Will Baggio and Dan Jones hired full-time. Will had worked part-time reading meters in the past but had since moved on. Dan still regularly worked for us part-time. Both seemed to be knowledgeable and good fits. Barry, wearing a flannel shirt tonight, said in a booming voice, "We better ayeeeeee do something, (fart noise), or mmmm mmmm we're gonna be without giddy-up anybody." With Merf and Ron getting older, it was time to train their understudies. I completely agreed that it needed to be done, I just didn't know how we'd fund it. Meeting adjourned.

***

After the meeting, I sent an email to Sharon Yount telling her she shouldn't continue to let her dog run around outside her house. We had a leash law, and if I was going to ask regular residents to keep their dogs leashed, I should try to make the Town Board follow the same rules. I needed to ask Sharon to leash her dog anyway, because the town always complained about her in some way, whether it was the junk piles in the backyard, their trailer falling apart, or the dog running around. In my email, I warned her that people with concealed carry could shoot her dog and simply say the dog charged them. So, it's best for the town and the dog's safety that it be restrained, as the law requires.

The next day, I was mowing the grass when Harry Yount, Sharon's husband, pulled up in his truck and waved me over. I pretended like I wasn't sure what he was there to talk about, but truth be told I anticipated he'd be angry and want to talk. Harry had a notorious temper. He was about six feet tall with short buzzed black hair, dark eyes, always unshaven, sweaty, and overweight. The name Harry was very fitting for the immense amount of body hair he regularly revealed wearing cutoff t-shirts. He was always driving around in his beat-up red pickup looking for scrap metal. Harry's scrapping and Sharon's trustee pay was their only income, unless you count that lotto scratch off.

"Why'd ya' make my wife cry?" he said.

"I don't know what you mean. I haven't talked to her today," I responded.

"You sent her that email saying you was gonna shoot her dog!"

"No, I said someone else might shoot her dog, so she should follow the law."

"I'm hot over it! You can't tell us to leash our dog!"

"I can. I'm the mayor."

"I'll fight ya' right now and settle this!"

"Harry, I don't think we have to fight to settle this."

"That's what I thought. All you guys walking around with guns, this is all the gun I need" (pointing at his flabby bicep).

"For the record, I don't walk around with a gun."

"Good, then you won't shoot our dog. I'm glad we talked, I feel much better. Bye."

Not knowing what just happened, I walked back to my lawn mower and got to work as Harry drove off in his pickup, which was so loud that people in Riverton could hear it coming.

***

I started to notice a pattern in the complaints I was receiving. The majority of the complaints were simply issues that had nothing to do with me or the town. When I ran into Haden Quisenberry at the post office, it was no different. Haden was about 40 with a wife and two teenage kids.

"Do you know about this Mr. Sampson at the high school?" he asked.

"I know of him I guess," I said.

"The guy is giving my boy trouble and I wondered what you might be able to do."

"I'd suggest you reach out to the school. It really has nothing to do with me."

"All I know is he's a total jerk! Same as he was back when he was my teacher!"

"I'll see what I can do."

Small towns are notorious for having teachers that educate two and even three generations of families. We're also known for being able to bend the rules a little. On Labor Day weekend, I let everyone go home two hours early with pay to thank them for their efforts and boost morale. Of course, I should have known that Merf would find a reason to complain. I was working on some paperwork in the office when he approached me the next week, adjusting his ball cap.

"What's all this about needing overtime?" he inquired.

"I let you guys leave a couple hours early, so I need someone to do a few hours of paid overtime to help catch up. It'll be a nice extra bonus for someone," I countered.

"You need work done, huh? Maybe you should have thought of that before you sent us home early! Count me out!"

***

Even Merf's rant couldn't bring me down that month. My first child was born the morning of our October meeting, so I was sky high. I had originally planned to miss the meeting and have Johnny Lynch serve as chair, since I was beginning to trust him and develop somewhat of a friendship with him. Since all went just fine at the hospital, I made myself available. Barry Vance was the only board member absent this time.

Sharon Yount, wearing a faded t-shirt, assured us that she had been working hard to get information to the website developers and also attending those monthly hazard mitigation meetings. I was thrilled that two projects were off my plate and seemingly in good hands.

Agnes Cobb was impressed to see that the abandoned vehicles left in the yard of one of those abandoned houses had been removed and the yard cleaned up. The property was then sold and the house demolished. And just like that, our issue with four derelict houses was reduced to three.

At this point, I needed to notify the board of some troublesome news I'd been given. There were cases and cases of old documents piled in the attic of the Village Hall. Someone from the Secretary of State's archive office has to approve of the destruction of any of these documents before we can actually do so. The oldest documents were over 60 years old, and the required inventory review had been done under then Mayor Carl Donaldson about 15 years ago. Were the documents removed from the attic when Carl got the approval? No way! Carl left them up there like a forgotten stepchild. Ed Quentin, wearing his usual college sweatshirt, joked that "Some of those documents are so old they were notarized by Jesus." But anyway, it was now causing some structural issues to the building. Our first step would be to get those documents sorted. I'm told they were just slew around up there as if a tornado hit a small-town insurance office. Once we knew what was in the boxes, we could get approval to shred them like the feds were coming to investigate! Meeting adjourned.

***

When we reached late October, it was time for the town bonfire and weenie roast. Neighboring Buffalo once again held their Halloween festivities the same night. Rhonda was furious.

"Those no-good jerks in Buffalo did it again!" she said.

Margie Baggio added, "How can we draw a crowd in our town if they're doing an event too?! You know they must have a problem with us!"

"You know, a lot of people here tonight are saying they went to Buffalo first, so I think people can go to both events," I said, hoping to calm the nerves.

Rhonda responded, "Are you standing up for them?!"

I ended the discussion, saying, "They are allowed to have an event too, so we shouldn't be arguing about this every year. But *I'll see what I can do.*"

***

Halloween night was especially cool but by no means frigid. I think that evening it was in the high 30s. In the early morning of November 1, a young mother by the name of Rhea Oglesby knocked on my door.

"I can't believe you didn't cancel Halloween!" she yelled.

"It's on October thirty-first every year," I countered, playing dumb.

"It was way too cold for little kids! My son had to wear three layers under his Superman costume!"

"Don't you have to wear layers to bulk him up like Superman anyways?"

"That's not the point! Cancel it next year!"

"I'll see what I can do."

***

As I prepped for the November board meeting, Merf happened to catch me in the Village office. He seemed to be a little sore for some reason.

"What happened?" I asked.

"Lumbar!" he replied.

"Did you hurt your back?"

"I'm gonna if you don't do something! I need a chair with better lumbar support!"

"I don't mind doing that, but you're on your feet almost all day, so maybe it's a different issue."

"No, when my day starts and my day ends, we spend a good chunk of time sitting and chatting in the shop. That's when I get hurt."

"You're getting hurt sitting around the shop?"

"That's right!"

"Maybe you should do less of that then."

"Don't even start!" he yelled as he stormed off.

CHAPTER 8

SANTA'S BURP-SHOP

On November 5, we met again, and once again Barry Vance didn't make it. I could tell he had given up. But of course, we had to move forward.

I had learned something interesting in the time between meetings. We were required by law to have a generator available to the water plant. If there was a power outage, the water needed to keep flowing. Did we have one? Of course not! So, I worked with Mayor Red Tomko in Riverton, who was willing to provide one to us when needed, because he had a spare that didn't work for their upgraded water facilities. Our outdated facility would handle it just fine, though; all we had to do was upgrade some wiring. Just in case that wasn't clear, we needed to upgrade to the level that Riverton just upgraded beyond. We were two steps behind. For the cost of a small electrical job, we were going to have a generator. The 50-year-old Ed Quentin joked, "We need to protect our community and get this fixed before Y2K hits." Of course, Y2K happened more than a decade earlier, but only Johnny Lynch and I got the joke. The others agreed that Y2K could be a problem!

Ron didn't want to have a generator on site. He had a shop in Springfield that he liked to lease the generator from when it was needed. The issue was that if there was a major catastrophe, the shop could be out of generators. Without a generator, we couldn't pump water during a power outage. He was dragging his feet a little to find an electrician for the upgrade. He knew that once the wiring was upgraded, I was taking him out of the good ol' boy network.

On the abandoned houses front, we received payment for our yard work at one of the houses. Someone had bought the property and was looking to fix it up. Our list of abandoned houses just dropped again. From four, we were down to two.

With December on the horizon, I knew it was time to start planning once again for the senior dinner. Luckily, Agnes Cobb and Margie Baggio were very excited to do the prep work and planning again. If I could be hands off, then just show up and serve, I was all for it. It was going to cost us a little more to have Margie involved, since she would be buying enough food to feed her army-sized family, but I really didn't care. At this point, I was a parent, and had learned you have to choose your battles.

Speaking of choosing your battles, I wasn't about to have another huge argument over where we would have our Christmas party. I told the group that we'd be at the Boston Steakhouse, knowing that everyone would be content with it. In a town this small, my willingness to spend that kind of money on a Christmas party was a bombshell worthy of coverage in the tabloids. Meeting adjourned.

***

As Thanksgiving rolled around, I debated whether I'd let the crew leave early on that Wednesday to get an early start on their four-day weekend. Since Merf had really complained about catching up on work with overtime after Labor Day, I decided against it. Now, Merf saw it differently and called me on Thanksgiving.

"Why didn't we get to leave early yesterday?" he asked.

"You were upset that I did it over Labor Day, so I figured this was best," I countered.

"You're telling me that I get paid in full for Thanksgiving and Black Friday, and you can't even let me go a little early the day before?"

"Yes, I guess that's what happened."

"What kind of a sweatshop are you running?!"

***

In late November, we had a string of about three days' worth of snow and ice. The roads were pretty bad and many people were encouraged to stay home. I got a call from Sheri Garrett, a woman in her mid-40s.

"You need to get a handle on traffic. I just saw someone blow a stop sign!" she yelled through the phone.

"Who was it?" I asked.

"I don't know but they're driving like a maniac!"

"In this weather?" Something didn't seem right to me. "Did they roll through the stop, or zoom through it entirely?"

"They tried to stop but slid through the intersection."

"If they tried to stop, I'm not sure what else they could have done. The roads are slick."

"They should have backed up and stopped properly!"

"I'll see what I can do."

***

It was December 1, 2014, when we met again. This time Barry was there but we were without Johnny Lynch. Maybe Barry hadn't given up after all. Things seemed to be going smoothly with the crew and the trustees, and the recent survey for the comprehensive plan showed I had over a 90% approval rating. I wanted to keep the momentum going to ensure I won my reelection bid roughly 2½ years away. That's why it caught my attention when Sharon Yount said that she'd been at a standstill with the website development and the hazards mitigation meeting. "I ain't done did it," she said. She added that her email has been down for a while, so she's been unable to communicate. She has a standard yahoo email account, so to say email has been down for a long period of time made as much sense as a one-legged karate instructor.

The annual audit was complete, and once again they recommended more checks and balances. With only one office employee, there wasn't much else we could do. Rhonda Brown continued to serve as clerk and cross-check the details of Treasurer Kara Gregory's work. As mayor, I was the second set of eyes that reviewed the payments. Johnny Lynch had previously agreed that we needed more accountability, but try as he might, just couldn't figure out how to do it. If we were to have an additional person review the transactions, that was a fourth person with access to funds and our financial data. It seemed riskier to have another person involved. Likewise, Rhonda continued to say that there's never been an issue with our current process, so why change it. Barry said, "Ayeeeeee, we've been (fart noise) trying to figure that out mmmm mmmm for years, there's not much giddy-up, that can be done, other than saying a prayer for the town, yee-haw." With seemingly no alternative, we left the process alone.

At this point we officially hired Will Baggio into a full-time role. Will was about 23 and in the National Guard, with the lean physique to prove it. He always sported a buzz cut and clean-shaven face that you'd come to expect from a soldier, and the dark hair, eyes, and skin that you'd expect from an Italian. The plan was for this young man to learn under Ron Butcher and eventually take over. Ron's health was starting to turn and his years of hard labor were taking their toll. We just kept hoping Ron could work three more years, which is the length of time required before Will could be licensed to run the plant.

In the meantime, Riverton Mayor Red Tomko had agreed to an intergovernmental agreement which would allow the licensed Riverton operators to legally operate our plant in the event that Ron retired prior to Will getting licensed. Privately we all still feared that Ron could pass away, but we couldn't say that publicly.

I was proud to announce that the third of our four abandoned houses had the lien paid, so our list was down to one. Ron Butcher happened to live next door and had bought the property and house, if you could call it a house. He was considering either tearing it down to expand his yard or simply renting it out. Ron adjusted his flannel shirt while he coughed and explained to the board that the lady that had lived in there was definitely the "cat lady." They found dozens of cats, along with plenty of cat "presents," left behind throughout the house.

Ron showed us some pictures, and it was so disgusting that people on the TV show *Hoarders* would have been appalled by it! Ed said, "Even a dumpster would call her trashy." I told Ed I thought he'd used that joke before. He looked slightly to his left at Sharon Yount, then looked back at me. "No, I don't think I have." Meeting adjourned.

***

In the middle of December, two of the three events I managed went without a hitch. The senior dinner and the staff Christmas party went great. I made no changes to the senior dinner, although everyone seemed to want to cut back next year except Margie Baggio. Margie made sure once again to take all the leftovers to her family for a Sunday lunch. I avoided the drama and didn't say anything when she claimed the food. The staff Christmas party at Boston Steakhouse went great. The third event of December was Santa's workshop, organized by the Town Team, where the kids got to come meet Santa. I never attended since the Town Team always had it under control.

This year, for reasons unknown, the man who typically played Santa Claus was unavailable, but Sharon Yount was able to find someone to play Santa. I got a frantic call from Margie Baggio on the day of Santa's workshop. "Jeremy, you gotta get down here. Santa ruined Christmas!"

I rushed down to the Village Hall to get some clarity as to what happened. To make it even more memorable, Santa showed up quite drunk. He hadn't shaved, so his dark facial hair was easily noticeable beyond the fake white beard. When Margie's five-year-old granddaughter sat on his lap, he burped directly into her face. That's what prompted the phone call. I was told that even earlier, a little girl was about to sit on his lap when he said, "I don't want you on my lap, tell your mama to sit on my lap. 'Cause she's been bad! Or if she hasn't, she's gonna be!" Margie told me I had to get Santa out of there. I went into the room, not yet knowing who was playing Santa Claus. At that moment, I had to tell Sharon's husband, Harry, that he couldn't be Santa anymore.

***

Merf walked into my office at the Village Hall in mid-December and asked if I had a minute to chat. He seemed really uncomfortable.

"What's on your mind?" I asked.

"This is a hard thing to bring up," he said. "I felt it was appropriate to take down the Christmas tree."

"Why?"

"It could be offensive to people."

"Did someone complain? It's not even in the public's view. Only the staff can see it."

"I asked everyone individually and they all love it. But it's the right thing to do. Christmas is canceled in this building due to political correctness."

"What about all the decorations we hang from the streetlights?"

"That's different. I don't want to climb up there."

Maybe he should have. On December 26, just the day after Christmas, a concerned elderly lady by the name of Frances Thompson called me.

"The town doesn't look so good anymore. We're in bad shape," she said.

"What's in bad shape?" I asked.

"The Christmas decorations are still up and Christmas is over!"

"It was just yesterday. I'm not going to make the guys do it in this snowstorm."

"Maybe they should. Back in the day, men in this town would've had it done! They're too soft nowadays!"

"I'll see what I can do."

***

It was now January 5, 2015. This time, Agnes Cobb was absent. It was starting to seem like having all six trustees at the same meeting was about as likely as seeing Halley's Comet. I informed the group that the web developers were growing frustrated with the lack of information being provided. I would have to take over for Sharon Yount and handle this myself. She mentioned that her email was finally up and running and assured everyone that she could handle it. Silently I knew I would have to take this over but I didn't reveal my intentions just yet.

I thanked everyone for their hard work at the senior dinner. Margie thanked everyone for allowing her to claim those "accidental" leftovers.

Ed said, "I'm just happy I'm still feminine enough to cook noodles."

Agnes and Margie then volunteered for their next project to be sorting all those documents up in the Village Hall attic.

Johnny Lynch discussed the audit findings and what we could do to keep our finances more secure. The answer, of course, was nothing. Johnny was sharp and had a budgetary background. Still, he agreed that with our personnel situation, it was as secure as it could be. With the clerk reviewing every transaction that the treasurer made, then in addition the mayor also reviewing all payments made, it seemed lots of eyes were on the funds. Any directly wired or transferred money out of our bank required three authorizations: the treasurer, the clerk, and the mayor. We had a lot of stopgaps in place, though I knew we were vulnerable to someone who knew their way around the system. But with no other personnel, the best we could do was hope for honesty.

I was excited to announce that I had single-handedly gotten us a grant to replace the numerous outdated bulbs and ballasts in the Village Hall. Many of the bulbs we were using weren't even made anymore, so the grant made perfect sense to pursue. We would receive 90% funding to upgrade to energy efficient lighting. It all made perfect sense, except to Sharon Yount, who argued we should just keep replacing the old bulbs. I reminded her that those bulbs are no longer manufactured, to which she replied, "I don't understand." Ed joked, "Clearly the light bulb didn't click on for some of us!" Sharon laughed, having no idea the jab was at her expense.

With the survey results including several people concerned about the dogs and cats running around town, I brought up that I'd soon be creating an ordinance to hold irresponsible pet owners accountable. The group seemed a little hesitant but I wanted to address this. Stray dogs and cats were one more reason our town was so "redneck." Agnes reached out to me later and expressed her concern with the same argument she always had.

"You can't do anything about stray cats because they're an animal of prey and help our community," she'd say.

"No, Agnes. That makes no difference," I'd reply.

The reason she'd defend those stray cats is that she had a good five or six pet cats that she would let run freely around her yard. They mostly stayed on her property, but once in a while crossed into mine. I never made much of a big deal about it because our house never once had a mouse and I knew why!

This was also the moment I chose to pitch Dan Jones as a part-time employee. For the sake of clarity I've been referring to him as part-time in this story, though technically until this point he had been an "extra help" employee, as they called it. He was doing work for us as an independent contractor and was therefore not one of our employees. Merf really felt that Dan was the guy to take his place and I agreed. With Merf's retirement on the horizon, we needed to get someone acquainted with the systems, the machinery, and the drama that is working in a small town. Aside from that, town policy paid the "extra help" crew only minimum wage. I knew Dan was a great guy; after all he did save my dad's life. With my urging, the board unanimously agreed to make Dan an official part-time employee and welcomed him with a nice raise.

Finally, we addressed the first complaint that I received regarding what would become one of the biggest headaches of my tenure. Someone had complained to me, and I honestly don't remember who, about the significant damage being done to the alley behind Agnes Cobb's house. The Green family had recently moved in, who happened to run an asphalt paving business. Many in the town were starting to raise their eyebrows because the family had begun driving their equipment in and out of our town, and storing it at their house, which of course was zoned residential. With all the big trucks and heavy machinery moving in and out of town daily, the roads were starting to get torn up. And with a town the size of Dawson, there was no budget to replace or even repair roads that quickly. This needed to be addressed right away. Barry said, "You gotta ayeeeeee, get 'em now, (fart noise), before they mmmm mmmm make a habit of it, giddy-up." Meeting adjourned.

***

After the meeting, I got Ryan Green's phone number from our water customer information. He didn't answer when I called, so I left a message explaining the situation. Shortly after, I got a text that said, "No worries. We will stop tearing up the roads and fix what we tore up." This was quite the relief to me. The only problem was that after a couple of weeks, nothing changed. I called and left another message. This time I got no response. We did get a message on the Village Hall voicemail the next morning. "Ya dumb (expletives) down there need tuh (expletive) figure out how tuh (expletive) get yer (expletive) together!! This is Deb Green. Bye." She was obviously a very posh lady.

I talked with our attorney Reggie Phillips about what we might do to address this. He said the first step is to track down the landlord. I tried, but Rhonda Brown hadn't been able to find a name. Every utility seemed to be under the Green family. The county records showed the property had been sold but didn't have a name of the new owner. It seemed that we were going to have to go directly after them. And by "we," I mean me.

***

Another older lady in the town, Urma Edwards, knocked on my door on New Year's Day. It was quite cold so I was surprised to see a woman of her age out and about.

"There were too many booms last night," she said.

"I know. I think some people were shooting off fireworks for New Year's."

"Well, I couldn't tell if it was fireworks or meth lab explosions!"

"I'll see what I can do."

***

The next week, Merf knocked on my door. He tugged on his ball cap, a bit nervous. "We've got a problem with Will and Dan," he said.

"What's the problem? Their work ethic?" I asked.

"Exactly. It's terrible."

"Sounds like we need to sit and have a chat with them. I'll encourage them to work harder."

"No! No! No! That's the problem! They work too hard and make me look bad! How am I supposed to impress anyone when these two guys work circles around me? Tell them to slow it down!"

CHAPTER 9

A PICTURE IS WORTH 1,000 DOLLARS

Both Agnes Cobb and Barry Vance missed our February meeting. This was the one time that flexing my political muscle had paid off. The house that my wife and I purchased was previously owned by a contractor. The company-issued garbage bin that we inherited was an absolute mess. It was covered with paint, caulk, spackle, some unidentified substances, and looked like it got dropped along the edge of the Grand Canyon. Sandra and I called the garbage company for a new bin, but they wouldn't replace it without us paying a gigantic fee. I called Denny Stevens, who was the town's account rep. I explained the situation, then casually mentioned that the waste removal contract was up for renewal and I was the mayor, so we should get a meeting scheduled. I never mentioned anything like "this for that," but Denny knew what I wanted. The next morning, a brand spankin' new waste bin was delivered to my house free of charge. At this February meeting,

Denny was there to speak about renewing the waste removal contract. The discussion began, but we withheld a vote for the time being.

Rumors had begun to circulate that Sharon Yount had already placed her eyes on the mayor seat. Can you imagine? I was hearing that she had been spreading some bad news about me. Since she was largely unpopular among the voters, I didn't have much to worry about. When the time came for the trustees to update us on any projects, I waited for Sharon to bring up the website, and that's when I'd send her a bit of a warning shot. When it was her turn to speak, she said that there was nothing new to report as things were still stalled. "We ain't been able to do nothin'!" she said. I casually added that I had taken over the website responsibilities because the developers were growing frustrated with the amount of time it was taking Sharon to handle their requests for information. I named off several items that I had assisted with getting onto the website, then thanked Rhonda Brown and Kara Gregory for all the help they provided. Rhonda and Kara sent no more than two emails, but I wanted to make it known who was getting things done and who was causing delays. My statements were now in the meeting minutes, which the town voters loved to read. I made Sharon look embarrassed and angry simultaneously, almost like a high school freshman after being depantsed in gym class.

As the meeting continued, I was ready to make my pitch to enact an ordinance to fine pet owners whose pets, such as dogs and cats, were loose. I had planted the seeds of my concerns at earlier meetings in hopes of warming the board up to the idea. For the ordinance, the first time in which a Village official directly sees the pet loose would result in a written warning. The second would result in a $25 fine, the third a little higher, and so on. I was happy that Agnes Cobb was missing, because she would definitely oppose this. With her cats running around all over her yard, she'd never support an ordinance that would force her to change her "cat lady" way of life. To be clear, your pet would have to be loose fairly often in order for you to be fined, because remember, a Village official has to directly see it. If your dog is out, and you get it back inside without a Village official seeing it, nothing happens. It's not like we were even driving around looking for stray pets. We'd have to coincidentally see it when we drove by. I just wanted to make an example of one or two owners and figured the problem would fade away after that.

I had known that the dogs were especially a problem because several people were constantly complaining about them. The outrage had gotten so significant that one person even complained that a county cop let his K-9 loose on someone. It wasn't a K-9; it was someone's dog attacking a pedestrian!

There was even a jogging club that had formed which would no longer jog in Dawson because they were so often chased by dogs. The four trustees in the room seemed to concur. I called for a vote, to which Johnny Lynch and Margie Baggio voted yes. Sharon Yount and Ed Quentin voted against it. With the vote tied at two each, I broke the tie to put this into law. Of course, with our attorney Reggie Phillips' weird rule interpretation, the vote we passed was to simply have Reggie write the ordinance. We'd have to vote on the actual ordinance next meeting.

To get some clarity as to why the opposition, I asked Sharon why she opposed, and she said she lets her dog run loose to use the bathroom. In that sentence, she made herself look worse than earlier in the night. I was already aware of what she was now stating publicly, which I made sure made the meeting minutes. She acknowledged that her dog is one of the problem dogs running loose. I've told so many people that it's not so hard to simply attach a long leash to your dog and tie the other end to a stake near the door or the door handle. Meanwhile, Ed Quentin scratched his bald head as he seemed to be evaluating his choice to take a side with Sharon. "Call me Germany, 'cause I might be on the wrong side of history," he said. He added that his concern was the ordinance was too strict and some people's pets just happened to get loose. I thought I'd covered that with the written warning and also that a Village official had to actually see it. Nonetheless, he was at least honest.

After quite a bit of work, we had finally sorted out the differences between the employee handbook and the ordinance book. If you recall, no one seemed to even know where the employee handbook came from or who wrote it! A lot of information in the handbook contradicted the ordinance book and vice versa. After a discussion that lasted way too long, we finally got board approval to make the corrections to match the two and update some policies to the benefit of our staff. It was unanimously approved, with Sharon Yount casting a very hesitant "yes" vote.

Ed added, "You've gotta match it all up for our town. If you're inconsistent, you're not 'in' consistent."

I didn't know what that meant, or even if it was a joke, but oh well, meeting adjourned.

***

The people of the town were really starting to get frustrated with the equipment and hazardous materials that the Green family had around their property. I talked to our attorney Reggie Phillips, and he suggested I reach out to government agencies such as the EPA and Department of Public Health to see if they could assist. In the meantime, he would try to research alternate options. I knew that meant we'd be getting a hefty legal bill next month!

I called the government agencies but none felt it was their responsibility to address. I was going to have to wait for Reggie to find a way to put a stop to this, but it seemed like we'd just have to keep waiting. And if you've ever hired an attorney, you know that means you'll be waiting a long time.

***

We got a heavy snow that February and I thought our crew did a great job of keeping the roads plowed and safe. Not everyone would agree though. Derek Viola, a younger millennial, called me to voice his concern.

"Your crew plowed in my driveway!" he shouted.

"Everyone's driveway gets plowed in. There's just no room for all the snow when the plow comes through," I said.

"They need to only plow where no houses are!"

"I'll see what I can do."

***

It wasn't long after that when Merf called me with another issue.

"Will Baggio rubbed me the wrong way!" he said.

"Why? What happened?" I asked.

"He had to go home sick. And when he was leaving, he asked if I'd finish up his work!"

"I thought that was pretty common practice."

"I don't think so! You're saying I need to do my work AND finish his? No way, Jose!"

***

We held our next board meeting on March 2, 2015. This time, Johnny Lynch and Sharon Yount were missing. The first order of business was Ron Butcher's request to raise the water rates again. Ron sat in the banquet chairs, as he did every meeting, sadly seeming a bit older each month. He described a few purchases that were needed and explained how a rate increase could pay for them. He also slipped in there that he'd yet to find an electrician to get that free generator set up. I'd worry about the generator later, though it was a priority. With the rates recently being raised, I certainly didn't want to raise them again so soon as Ron suggested. That would bury my reelection chances. I stated, "We've already budgeted for those purchases and the funding is already available. There's no need to raise rates at this time." With that being said, Ron concurred. I couldn't believe someone with so much power to persuade simply let it go, but he did. With that, I felt like my reelection chances were roaring louder than my overloaded washing machine.

Next up was to vote on the stray pet ordinance that Reggie Phillips drafted. With Johnny Lynch and Sharon Yount missing, one vote from each side of the argument was out. I was certain that Agnes Cobb would oppose it, but suspected Barry Vance would be in support. If Margie and Ed voted like they did last meeting, the vote would tie 2-2 and I'd break the tie to enforce the new ordinance. When Reggie finished explaining what he'd written up, he said all that was needed was a motion and second, then a vote.

With that, Barry said, "Giddy-up, this has been yee-haw needed for (fart noise) a long time, and I'm ayeeeeee glad to see it. I motion to approve yessir."

I looked at Margie for her to second the motion, but she stared down at her papers on the wooden banquet table. I looked down to my right at Agnes, who also looked down. I looked to my left at Ed, who was seated next to Margie, who just smirked. Reggie said the motion had failed.

Ed added, "I guess we can call that ordinance the Hindenburg."

I found his jokes less funny when they were at my expense, but it did make me chuckle anyway. I'd have to find a way to get this thing passed one way or another but it wasn't happening that night.

I mentioned to the group that we all agree we're here to represent the residents of the town, not necessarily our own interests. I reminded them that the recent town-wide survey indicated that nearly 70% of the residents considered stray pets a problem, and nearly 70% also stated that they felt the Village needed to strengthen its animal control policy. I also reminded them that the County Animal Control, which we use, was raising rates. The simplest way to cover those costs would be to have fine money available. After all, it wasn't quite fair for the law-abiding taxpayers to be footing the bill for the same handful of people whose pets regularly run loose. I also reminded them that the jogging group decided to no longer run in Dawson because of stray dogs, which should embarrass all of us.

For those in the town who defended dogs being loose in their own yard to simply go to the bathroom, I addressed that also, saying, "To the owner it may be a friendly dog. But a kid riding his bike nearby may get chased or someone walking a dog nearby could be attacked. We don't know what is going to set off a dog. We need to treat them all the same. It's not that hard to tie up your dog to let it do its business."

Agnes said that it's been an issue a long time and we've just ignored it.

I told the group, "If we know it's a problem, there's no reason to keep ignoring it." Then I joked, "Paying my taxes is a problem but I can't ignore it year after year!"

I asked the group what their concerns were and I could then address them in the ordinance. No one said a word. One of the most frustrating things as mayor was knowing people had thoughts or opinions but wouldn't share them.

Barry wrapped up the discussion by saying, "It ayeeeeee needs addressed. Mmmm mmmm you all are (fart noise) wrong on this one, giddy-up. Let's yessir talk to the people we represent and yee-haw revisit."

Margie and Agnes had continued to sort through all those old documents in the Village Hall attic and were making progress. The other trustees were working their way through those old ordinances and proposing changes to make the codes more modern. Johnny Lynch had finished sorting the discrepancies between the employee handbook and the ordinance book. We were making big strides; we just couldn't seem to make progress on the stray pets.

While the group was grumpy, it wasn't the best time to ask if we'd like to make a small donation to the Tri-City Public Library, but I did anyway. The library folks had reached out to see if we'd donate some funds which would allow them to purchase items for their silent auction fundraiser. Any time this came up, the group always seemed very hesitant to help, and I'm not sure why. We typically donated $50-100, and as tight as I am, I didn't see the big deal. I chalked up the hesitancy to some sort of small-town feud I wasn't aware of. Reggie Phillips and Kara Gregory made cases as to why we should donate to our local community library, even though they weren't supposed to be weighing in on the decisions since they weren't part of the actual board. I didn't really care, because at this point we were two hours into this circus, and the board had already declined to pass my top priority regarding the stray pets. With the influence of two unelected officials, the elected board then voted unanimously to donate a whopping $100 to the library.

With the Easter holiday around the corner, I asked if Margie and Agnes would again like to be our official party planners. Since I wanted no part of it, I even suggested they could take a break from sorting documents in the attic in order to plan. Luckily, they agreed. They even proudly announced, and somehow the official meeting minutes record this, that they located the bunny costume for Margie to dress in. Every year Margie would dress as the Easter Bunny for the kids, and by the grace of God, that tradition would continue! Ed even added, "It's a good thing you all found that. Those kids would've been confused if the old Italian-accented Easter Bunny wasn't there!" Meeting adjourned.

***

With the mid-term election right around the corner, I had been lobbying several people to run for a seat on the Town Board, but none were interested. Barry Vance had told me that he was no longer interested in continuing, having served out the final two years of my term as trustee. Three seats were up for grabs: Barry's seat, Margie Baggio's seat (which had been Rita Robins's seat), and Sharon Yount's seat (previously Mike Madison's). As much as the town complained to me about Sharon Yount being on the board, no one seemed to be willing to take her seat. The only two names on the ballot to fill those three seats were Sharon Yount and Margie Baggio. I'd have to find yet another person to appoint to the remaining seat. Seventy-five dollars a month wasn't exactly the best bribe to open yourself up to social media mockery!

***

About a week after the board meeting, I noticed a business card wedged inside my front door. I took a look and it was Ryan Green's business card. A note was handwritten on the back, which said, "Just letting you know I know where you live. This is our town now." This was quite disturbing, so I called the police. Since we don't have town officers, a county sheriff's deputy arrived. I told him this was a threat against a public official. He disagreed, saying that there was no specific threat, so nothing could be done. He gave me some tips on when it was okay for me to use deadly force but advised me to be smart and get the police involved as soon as possible. The Green family had just elevated the situation. At this point, I kept a loaded gun on the shelf next to the front door, the shelf next to the back door, and one on my nightstand. I taught my wife how to shoot because we feared we were going to have to do it. All of this because I did nothing more than enforce the law in this tiny town.

***

I soon got a frantic phone call from Ron Butcher and Merf. The two were on speakerphone. I was used to getting a complaint from Merf, but Ron rarely complained. I sensed something big.

"We need new computers!" Merf yelled.

"I thought ours were just fine," I responded.

"Not anymore!" Ron shouted.

"What's going on?" I asked. Suddenly, Rhonda Brown was on the call too.

"I got an email that said 'click here to download your pictures.' I didn't order any pictures, but figured I should probably click to see them," she said.

"Oh no!" I replied.

"Now the whole network is out!" she said.

Merf jumped back in, "So I guess we're all going home early."

"You don't even work on the computer," I countered.

"He can't hear you. He just left," said Rhonda.

***

In early April my doorbell rang. I prepared to defend myself, thinking it may be a member of the Green family. Instead, there stood middle-aged Wes Chapman, obviously angry.

"My neighbor has done it now! You need to go after him!" he yelled.

"What happened?" I replied.

"He told me that he was tired of my free-range chickens wandering around his porch!"

"Wait – you have chickens?"

"Yeah! And it's not his business if I let them run around on his porch!"

"Actually, it is, and you can't have them anyways. They're illegal here, so you need to get rid of them."

"OK, Mussolini!"

"I'll see what I can do."

***

It was April 8, 2015, when we met again, this time with Agnes Cobb and Ed Quentin absent. Sharon Yount and Margie Baggio were celebrating their soon-to-be successful unopposed reelection. With new terms officially taking effect at the May meeting, it would be Barry's last night.

Our first item of business was how to go about repairing the alley that the Green family had absolutely destroyed with their trucks and machinery. Now that the weather was starting to turn, we were ready to start planning road repairs. I knew that fixing the alley wouldn't be the only problem, though. As Barry Vance mentioned, "Ayeeeeee, you gotta keep those yee-haw, yee-haws, off that giddy-up alley, and yessir, park their trucks somewhere else." I wasn't looking forward to that interaction, but knew once we had a plan, I'd have to address it.

This meeting involved discussing a lot of items that had lingered or were just ready to be tied up. I snickered when

Ron Butcher said that he had yet to arrange for the generator setup to be installed at the water plant. He was going to keep his buddies as his contact for generator needs for as long as possible. Margie said that the Easter event went well and that she and Agnes would soon get back to sorting all those documents in the attic. She mentioned that when the Easter decorations were taken down, they discovered several more cases of documents hidden behind those decorations! The website was just about ready to launch. I had worked with the developers to get it to about 95% completed. The governor pulled the funding for the grant that we were to receive for replacing all the old light bulbs. Barry added, "Ayeeeeee, I guess we can giddy-up, turn off the lights on that idea, yessir."

Moving on, I got the board to approve an ordinance to improve the vacation time for our staff. Although they still wouldn't receive a single vacation day until after a year of employment, I did get one significant change. Previously, employees annually received one week of vacation after one year of service, two weeks of vacation after two years of service, and three weeks of vacation after 15 years of service. The board agreed to change the increment of 15 years of service down to five years of service, with years one and two remaining the same. This was a no-brainer for me. Since we didn't pay out unused vacation time, this did nothing except give an underpaid and overworked staff a reason to be happy. With Ron and Merf nearing retirement, it was important that our younger employees had a reason to stick around. The motion passed unanimously, with Sharon Yount hesitantly voting in approval. By the way, it was hard not to laugh at Sharon that night. She looked and smelled as if she hadn't showered and was wearing a faded "Police" concert tour short. With the 'P' and 'O' missing, the shirt read, "LICE."

I was ready once again to argue for fining irresponsible pet owners. With only four trustees in the room, I thought I might have a shot at getting it passed. With Barry on his way out, I was sure he'd vote to help me. I just needed one of the three to flip, resulting in a 2-2 tie, and allowing me to cast the tie-breaking vote. It wouldn't be easy, because they all certainly had their strong feelings about it. I made my case again, arguing those same old talking points over and over.

As I wrapped up my final point, Barry Vance jumped in, saying, "Yee-haw, this needs done, giddy-up, I've been around long enough, yessir, to know this town's ayeeeeee in trouble if we don't pass this, mmmm mmmm."

And with that ringing endorsement from the most respected person in the room, the board passed the ordinance unanimously, entirely forgetting about what they were opposed to in the first place. I finally got one more goal knocked off my to-do list. Meeting adjourned.

***

We sent the Green family certified letters requiring them to move their vehicles and equipment. They were obviously experienced in legal battles because they never picked up any letters we sent. I called Ryan Green twice, leaving messages both times. He never called back either time. When I happened to be outside, and the 30-something Ryan or his teenage son Roman drove by, they'd give a middle finger in my direction and drive away. I'd ignore them, but it was seeming more and more like an escalation was brewing.

***

Beth Ziele, a married mom with three little ones, called me in late April.

"Mr. Mayor, do you know what you get paid?" she asked.

"Umm, yes," I replied with a confused tone.

"And those trustees! They get $75 a month! Ridiculous!"

"I'm glad you think that. We're all underpaid for what we endure."

"Underpaid?! You should be forced to work for no pay!"

"That would make it slavery, ma'am."

"I want you to consider it!"

"I'll see what I can do."

***

I stopped by the Village Hall in late April to prepare for the next board meeting. I heard some activity from the workshop area and made my way back. There sat Merf eating some fast food.

"I wondered if you were here today," I said.

"Yep, just ran some errands on my lunch hour," he responded.

"Your lunch hour is over though, right?"

"Yeah, it ended about ten minutes ago. Now is when I rest and eat my lunch."

"Merf, that's what your lunch hour is for. You can't just bring food back when your lunch hour ends and then not work. I'm good with you doing it today, but I don't want it to continue."

"Are you serious?! Unbelievable! I must work in a Taiwanese factory!"

CHAPTER 10

OUT LOOKING FOR
A FIRE FIGHT

As we gathered on the first Monday of May, we had a new face on the board. After Margie Baggio and Sharon Yount were sworn in, the board – without Ed Quentin in attendance – approved my appointment of Kyle Langley to fill the third seat. Since the seat would be for a four-year term, it was my job to appoint someone to fill the seat temporarily for two years. At the next municipal election, the seats of Ed Quentin, Johnny Lynch, and Agnes Cobb would all be up for reelection, as would the remaining two years of the seat that Kyle now occupied. Every time I needed to appoint someone, Kyle was one of the first people I would reach out to. He grew up in the area and absolutely loved it. He was now around 40, working for the same company he got his first ever job at. In high school he started working part-time for a national tuxedo rental chain, eventually becoming the manager of that same store, and in recent years had become the regional manager. He was intelligent and obviously loyal, so I knew he'd be a great fit. He was a good ol' boy who loved to hunt and fish, but always dressed as sharp as you'd expect someone in his profession to dress. After the board approved him, the lanky 40-year-old with a thick head of hair sat down in Barry's old seat, which was also once my seat.

The first thing discussed was that Ron Butcher still hadn't worked to get the generator set up at the water plant. I just smiled and kept the meeting going. Without holding Ron by the hand, he was going to do what he wanted, and after some 40 years of service to Dawson, he felt he'd earned it. As I mentioned before, I had to choose my battles with Ron, because he could up and retire at any minute and we'd be in big trouble. Our backup plan was still in the works.

We had postponed the vote for renewing our waste removal contract long enough. Denny Stevens reminded us that the contract was set to expire. If we postponed another month, no one would be picking up the entire town's garbage. Denny stood about 6'5", weighed about 350, and had a booming voice that matched Barry's. When he was trying to be stern and make known the urgency of the situation, it was certainly recognizable! However, this was Sharon Yount's time to step up and be, well, Sharon Yount. I had just explained that I had reached out to several garbage removal companies for alternate quotes, but they either weren't returning my calls, or requested more time to collect data to provide a quote. We were out of time. Sharon, though, suggested we delay the town's garbage removal.

"Someone from another company is interested in puttin' in a quote, so we should wait on this to save our people some money," she said.

"Which company?" I asked.

"I don't remember."

"Did they speak with you?"

"No. They talked to my husband."

"Did they speak with any town official?"

"No."

"I guess they didn't want it too bad then. Let's vote."

Sharon Yount angrily cast her 'yes' vote while everyone else was happy to approve, and the contract was officially renewed. Although she voted yes, she continued to argue that we should let the contract lapse until we found a better deal.

"If we did that, people would just have to stack their garbage outside somewhere for at least a month," I argued.

"So! That's what we do at my house!" she said.

Our attorney Reggie Phillips then brought up the need to approve the new vacation policy. Last month it had been approved to be written with Sharon Yount seeming to oppose it. Somehow, with no discussion, the board approved it unanimously. He also brought up the fact that somehow, with a lien on one of the abandoned properties we fixed up, most of the land was sold by the county at a tax auction. Ron Butcher and Agnes Cobb both seemed to remember a lien being placed years ago and they were right. But now, we wouldn't get paid, because it slipped through the cracks, as a government worker must have dropped the ball. I was waiting for Barry to drop a great joke, but he was no longer on the board. I looked to Ed's seat, who wasn't there. The group all looked at me. "I guess that's what we get for thinking a government employee had it under control!" The group mildly chuckled. The house had long been demolished but the land was still there. We agreed that rather than spend thousands on a lawsuit to get ownership of those plots of land, we'd sell what was left of it to the neighboring property owner for whatever they'd pay us and be done with it.

Now we had one vacant lot that we needed to maintain and one abandoned house left to address. We learned that the company Kara Gregory had been dealing with to collect the lien from the remaining abandoned house was still dodging us. The woman who was working with Kara had left the company and our correspondence was left on her desk. I quipped, "She probably left to work for the government."

I took a moment to recognize that Dawson and Riverton were provided an award for efforts in efficiency by the county's Citizen's Efficiency Commission. Mayor Red Tomko and I had partnered up to assist each other's towns in the event of a water emergency, and I wanted to be sure the minutes that would be in the newspaper reflected that. I had that reelection campaign on my mind.

Speaking of, I made sure to also announce that after all of my efforts on the website, it would go live this very week. Likewise, the Village had an area for a soccer field at the park, and had even purchased soccer goals several years back. They were recently discovered, still in the unopened box, so we would work on adding a soccer field "at no additional cost to taxpayers," as the minutes read. I concluded the night by saying after years of wondering what to do, our new roof on the Village Hall has been completed. I could smell that reelection! Meeting adjourned.

***

Later that month, Sandra and I woke up in the middle of the night to some loud bangs near our house. I looked outside and about five people were gathered in front of the Green family's house, shooting full-size display fireworks at my house! They had the pyro box turned on its side with the fireworks shells zooming down the road and hitting the side of my house as they exploded. I immediately called the police. The county sheriff's deputy arrived right away and asked for an explanation of what was happening. He said he would go talk to the Greens and come back. I recognized both Ryan Green and his teenage son Roman in the group, but since the group was a few hundred feet away, illuminated by only streetlights, I couldn't tell who the others were. I knew they were quite drunk though, because I saw one hefty guy fall across a lawn chair and land hard on the ground. The teenage Roman yelled, "Come on, man, you spilled my beer!"

When the officer returned, he said there was nothing he could do because the Greens denied they did it. Would you expect a drunken family like that to be truthful? I showed the officer the burn marks on my siding, pointed out the empty fireworks box in front of the Green's house, stated that clearly no one else is awake to have done this, said that I specifically saw them shoot the fireworks, and reminded him of the threatening note in the doorway. Again, the officer said that since they wouldn't admit to it, he couldn't do anything unless it escalated.

I felt hopeless. These people were going to burn my house down, or hurt me or my wife or my child. The police seemed to not care. I even felt like the Greens had been wandering around my yard and peeping into windows the past few weeks.

Things just felt different. I knew if anything would be done to scare them off, it'd have to be done by me.

***

In mid-May, Jamie Knox called me. Jamie was a millennial mom who lived in our town with her husband and two young kids.

"You've gotta do something about the farmers!" she yelled through the phone.

"What do you mean?" I posed.

"When I go to the gas station in Riverton, they're sold out of donuts every morning! The farmers clean them out before I can get there!"

"I would talk to the gas station about that. And why do you think it's the farmers?"

"Who else would be up that early in the morning? I know it's not the bankers!"

"I'll see what I can do."

***

I stopped in the office the day after Memorial Day. I found it odd that Merf hadn't arrived yet. As I considered whether or not to call him, he slowly and gingerly made his way through the front door of the Village Hall.

"Whoa, are you okay?" I asked.

"Yeah, just partied a little too much on Friday night," he replied.

"Man, that was four days ago!"

"I know. I haven't eaten anything but crackers since Saturday!" he said with a smile.

"Yeah, I'm learning too that I just can't party like I used to," I responded, thinking we were finally going to have a cordial conversation.

"You saying I'm old?! What I do on the weekends is my business, so stay out of it!" he said as he stormed off down the hall.

"There's bottled water in the fridge!" I shouted to him across the building.

***

In June, we met without Margie Baggio or Agnes Cobb. We chatted about the feasibility of adding water lines to various subdivisions out in the country and what grants we could seek. We considered areas that we'd already addressed and areas we hadn't. I didn't expect any of it to happen, though I certainly wanted it to. And with Ron Butcher fighting to get it done, I certainly wouldn't count it out.

There wasn't much going on this month, so I made it a point to brag about the newly launched website saving us money. If you recall, we used to have to pay to publish our water report in the newspaper. But, if you have a website, you're allowed to publish it there instead. The annual cost of our website was less than what it cost to publish the report in the newspaper, so I had saved us money AND made us more modern. I reiterated this so that the voters would be reminded. Reelection, here I come!

Ed Quentin's gray whiskers were showing since he omitted shaving from his daily ritual that day. He shouted, "Dove! Zest! Irish Spring!"

"What are you doing?" I asked.

"Trying to figure out what soapbox you're on!" he joked, while the other three trustees and I laughed.

He turned to his left and high-fived Sharon Yount, then had an uncomfortable look on his face. He clearly regretted touching hands with her. With no hesitation, Ed pulled a small bottle of hand sanitizer from his pocket and scrubbed his hands vigorously.

I had also finally figured out a solution to not having a siren on the east end of town. The mayor of the nearby town of Spaulding, Clint Daniels, took a liking to me and offered to give me their old siren for free. He said I could find a way to make it up to him later. As long as that siren still worked, and the leaders of the sewer commission were still comfortable with us hooking into their electric at the substation, we had this solved. This is a small town we're talking about, so it was going to take some time to make this happen. Meeting adjourned.

***

After the meeting, I chatted privately with Johnny Lynch and Kyle Langley about Merf's bad attitude and unwillingness to work. I had given him numerous warnings over the past several months to be nicer and put in an honest day's work. He would soon have a heart procedure done, so any punishments I enforced could be construed as due to his health. Knowing Merf, he'd find a way to spin it as such. I had stopped asking him to do projects altogether unless something drastic needed done because he just wasn't going to do what I asked. He would tell me he was going to do it, then a week would go by with nothing getting done. I'd ask him about it and he'd say that there was too much going on at the water plant. This excuse was given over and over.

I had made a few surprise pop-ins at the Village office in the late afternoon, and Merf had shut everything down. His time sheets would say he had worked, but he had lied about it and gone home. I'd drive by the Village office in the morning, and 45 minutes after the crew was to start, they'd all be sitting around sipping coffee, contributing to the government worker stereotype. I didn't really hold the subordinate crew accountable, since Merf was their supervisor. I would sit around too if my supervisor told me to!

I started to get calls that the entire crew was hanging out at a store or restaurant in Riverton or Buffalo. It was so tough to enforce anything because I wasn't around town much. Merf had worked for the town for so long that I felt bad dismissing him, but I certainly considered it. I even talked things over with our attorney, Reggie Phillips, and developed a plan for termination. We were going to start with a suspension and see if that would fix things. Merf was incredibly popular with the town because of his "good guy" image, and I knew if I terminated him, the town would be in an uproar. And if I upset the town that much, there was no way I could be reelected. I updated Johnny and Kyle about all of this. Plus, I let them know of a recent discussion I had with him. I told Merf that I was going to install security cameras in the workshop, as well as a "punch-in" time clock. Historically the staff had simply handwritten their weekly time sheets. Not that I had the time or energy to check up on those things, but it would serve as a deterrent.

When I brought it up to Merf, he responded by saying, "The day you put those in here is the day I retire!"

"YES!" I thought to myself.

My problem would be solved. When I chatted with Johnny and Kyle at the office, they seemed to agree, so I planned to bring this up at the next board meeting for spending approval for the cameras and punch clock.

One of the nearby firefighters must have overheard and leaked our discussion, because in a matter of days, all four remaining trustees called me, saying something like, "You can't do anything that would make Merf retire! We need him!"

I felt that Dan Jones and Will Baggio had learned enough to take over, and Merf was getting ridiculous. But now, with four trustees opposed to termination, if I went forward with it, I'd never get anything approved by them again. With Merf having an upcoming heart procedure, with the town behind Merf, and four trustees behind Merf, my hands were tied.

While this was going on, I still had the Green family to deal with. Sandra and I were increasingly suspecting that the scrawny 16-year-old Roman Green, and maybe some teenage friends, were wandering around our fenced-in backyard and peeping into our windows. On a couple occasions we had seen dark figures that appeared to be Roman and another friend or two sneaking around. I wasn't sure what they were up to, whether they were just trying to be intimidating or considering how to get in. It's possible I was wrong altogether and this was just some creepy Peeping Tom wondering what I looked like in the shower!

I ran some fishing line across several spots in the yard to act as a trip wire and attached small bells to the wires. If this intruder hit the trip lines, I'd hear the bell, wake up, and be ready to defend my house. We were in the middle of a drought so I didn't have to worry about moving anything to mow, because the grass just wasn't growing. In the next several days, I heard those bells, quickly looked out, and recognized Roman running off on a few occasions. He wasn't going to be deterred by trip lines. I then took several 2 x 4s and spray painted them green so they'd blend in with the grass at night. I put numerous nails into each board, then laid the boards just beyond the trip lines. About a week later, I heard a loud teenage boyish scream from the backyard. I quickly looked out the window and saw Roman sprinting back to his house. The next morning, I looked and noticed a large amount of blood on a board and the surrounding blades of grass. This time, I think the message was received. I picked up the board and shouted triumphantly, "Gotcha punk!"

No one was around to hear me, so I awkwardly looked around as I put the board back down on the dew-covered grass. But at least now the Greens would have to find someone else to mess with until I figured out how to get them out of the town altogether.

***

I got a knock on my door in late June from Leo Irving, a recently retired long-time resident of the town.

"Do you know how hard I work on my yard?" he asked.

"You're encouraging me to not impose water restrictions?" I confidently said, thinking I knew where this was headed.

"What? No! I saw a lady let her dog pee in my yard! She's killing the grass!"

"In this drought isn't everyone's grass already dead?"

"Not mine, she killed it! That dog murdered my yard!"

"I'll see what I can do."

***

On July 1, 2015, it was almost time for the fireworks extravaganza! But first, we'd meet without Agnes Cobb and Sharon Yount. We learned that even when we tried alternate methods, we weren't going to get a grant for the water routes through the country. But, if the homeowners in those subdivisions were willing to split the cost, we could make it happen. We determined that we could keep costs down by doing the labor with our own employees. We'd send out letters right away to gauge interest. Ed Quentin chimed in, adding, "If you want something bad enough, you'll pay big money for it. My stepson learned that in Vegas."

In other not surprising news, Ron mentioned that he had yet to find time to get the generator set up at the water plant. I was still working hard in the background to groom a replacement for Ron when he was ready to retire, still assuming Will Baggio wouldn't yet have the experience. But, at this time Ron was the only licensed person to run the water plant, so I didn't want to pressure him so much that he'd get frustrated and up and retire.

My goal to clean up and beautify our town was still ongoing. I had budgeted money, built over two years, to replace the old and worn-out picnic tables and garbage cans at our park. Kyle Langley, wearing a sharp vest and slacks combo, supported the idea. "Our town's park is right across the street from me. If you want to beautify my front yard, I'm all for it!" he joked.

To my surprise, with no debate, the group unanimously approved the purchase of eight picnic tables and three garbage bins, which would replace all the old ones at the park. My mistake was just casually asking, "Does anyone care what color we get?" That launched a two-hour debate! Do you know what color we decided on? Wood. Meeting adjourned.

***

As we began walking out the door, Roman Green sat in the parking lot on his dune buggy, which of course was not street legal. I knew he was looking for an altercation with someone. There had been a lot of recent vandalism at the Village Hall ever since we put pressure on the Green family to clean up their act. Because of this, we had recently installed cameras around the building. Knowing any interaction would be on video, I chose to ignore Roman and instructed the board members to do the same. As we walked past him, he'd rev the engine, and say things like, "Isn't anyone going to stop me?!" or "I shouldn't be doing this, should I?"

Later that night, I got a call at home that there was an incident at the Village Hall. Merf, who still lived across the street from the Hall, took exception to Roman being there. Merf approached Roman and told him he needed to go home since it wasn't legal for him to be on the dune buggy. Roman responded by saying, "Shut up, old man, before you get hurt!"

At this, Merf walked over to the fire department that was having a meeting of its own. As the story goes, several members of the fire department approached Roman and had some words. Roman then challenged some of them to a fight, which was accepted, and didn't turn out well for Roman! Police were called and talked to Roman, encouraging him to stay away from Village officials and Village property. The police asked me to pull video of the incident, especially since Roman was a minor and the firemen were of age. Unfortunately for Roman, I was unable to pull the video, as I must have "accidentally" deleted the video. No firemen would be getting in trouble that night.

Merf called me the next day.

"You jeopardized my safety!" he yelled.

"What do you mean?" I asked.

"That kid on the dune buggy could have really worked me over!"

"I didn't tell you to approach him, Merf."

"But you didn't NOT tell me to approach him either!"

***

We got through the fireworks extravaganza with no issues. With the event on July 3rd, it meant many people celebrated a second night on July 4. On Independence Day I was called by Hal Manning, an older man who'd had enough.

"I read that as mayor you're the chief of police. I'm turning in Ron Butcher!" he yelled.

"What? What do you mean?" I asked in complete confusion.

"He's got his whole family, grandkids and all, playing at his house. They've got sparklers and those little poppers that the kids throw on the sidewalk!"

"So why are you angry? Those are tiny things that hardly make noise."

"Do you think they have a permit for those fireworks? I'll answer for you. No! So arrest him and take him to jail!"

"I'll see what I can do."

CHAPTER 11

ROCKS AND ROLLED

We met on August 3 without our resident jokester Ed Quentin. I was still in a great mood a month after the fireworks because it was my third straight year of no pyro mishaps. Merf just had the heart procedure done, so he was resting in the hospital and would be out of work for quite some time. Since he was out, we weren't going to be able to move forward with extending our water routes to those rural subdivisions using our own labor. Ron suggested, and I agreed, that we should wait until Merf came back to work and we understood his physical abilities. That didn't stop Sharon Yount from chiming in, though.

"If the people want water, why don't we just do it anyways?" she asked, adjusting her smudged glasses.

I responded, "To break even, using our own labor, the cost per home to contribute is around $7,000. If Merf comes back as limited as we think he'll be, and we have to hire it out, it would be around $12,000 per home, which is a big jump and would make a big difference on homes willing to participate."

Sharon replied, "Can't we just make Merf do the labor anyways?"

"No."

The group had worked hard and the ordinance book review was completed. A nearly 800-page book of rules had finally been reviewed after years of sitting dormant. We were able to address outdated laws, including one that prohibited pig wrestling after sundown. We were making progress!

With our website now active, we had a bit of a debate. Ron felt that the Village employees should have full access to the site in order to put up and take down anything they felt necessary. I had given Kara Gregory limited access so that she could post information or announcements in the event of something urgent or any emergencies arising. Ron fought and fought but I just wouldn't give on this one. No business allows their entire staff access to modify its website. And as hard as I've fought to clean up the redneck image of the town, I certainly wasn't going to let anyone post any time they felt it was necessary. I just knew I'd pull up the website and see an announcement reading, "A small black lab has been seen at the corner of Park and Main. It pooped at 301 Main, then peed on the fire hydrant at 303 Main. Would the owner please get the dog?" I truly believed that would actually be posted. Although Ron was mad, I wasn't giving anyone full access except the webmaster and me.

I told the board that it had been several months since the problems began with the Green family and things seemed to be getting worse. The piles of asphalt and oil dumping were more frequent. The family was getting more and more rude with anyone who challenged them. They were ignoring the warning letters we sent them. Since they weren't willing to talk it out, the only way to get this resolved was by court order. And with a town the size of Dawson, that was going to be a huge dent in our budget. I again called the health department, the EPA, and any other agency I could think of, but none felt it was something they were responsible for. We would have to do this on our own.

Kyle Langley joked, "Should our town enforce vigilante justice?"

"Maybe," I replied with a smile. Meeting adjourned.

***

A few days later, I was mowing the grass when Hank White, a nearby neighbor, had a fantastic run-in with Roman Green. Hank was in his early 70s, still in decent shape, and a retired Marine. Roman was recently expelled from the Tri-City school for shooting the bus driver with a BB gun – while the bus was driving down the highway. You can see how these two guys wouldn't quite mix.

Roman slowed the truck down as he approached his house. When he parked, he parked the truck ACROSS the street, so that it was blocking traffic from going either direction. I am cleaning up the language for what happened next. Hank, who lived across from the Greens, wasn't happy.

"What are you doing?" he yelled.

"What's wrong?" said Roman.

"Move your truck!"

"Buzz off, old man!"

"I'll come over and show you what this old man can do!"

"Shut up, old man, before you get hurt!"

I recognized that as Roman's line to scare people off. After he said it to Hank, though, Hank started making his way toward Roman at a steady pace. Roman jumped out of the truck and started heading inside.

He yelled back over his shoulder, "I'm gonna go tell my dad!"

Hank mocked him, in a childish voice, "Oh boo-hoo, you gawta go get yah daddy?"

"I'm telling him!"

"Go get your dad! I'll whoop his butt, then I'll whoop your butt, and when your mom comes out crying, I'll whoop her butt too!"

At this, Roman slowly walked to his truck and appropriately moved it to the side of the road. He slowly walked back to his house in defeat, and had no response when Hank yelled, "Yeah, that's what I thought, you little wuss!"

That scene had ended, but from what I had gathered about this family, it was far from over. The people of the town had enough, the Village leadership had enough, but this family wasn't about to just give in.

***

Merf called me to let me know he was home from the hospital. He wasn't happy with how I handled his heart procedure.

"You never came to see me in the hospital," he said.

"You might not have known, but I was on a comedy tour while you were in there. I sent flowers, though. Did you get them?" I asked.

"I got 'em. But I heard you were on vacation."

"We were three states away. I had one night off on the tour that we spent as a family day."

"Why couldn't you have canceled your tour and come to see me? I see where I stand!"

***

As August turned to September, I was met at my door by Ned Gossage, an older man who'd lived in the town for years.

"You've got a big problem at the park," he said.

"Oh no, is something wrong?" I asked.

"Oh yeah! There's way too much shade. The grass isn't growing evenly!"

"Shade?"

"You better cut down all those trees at the park or you're gonna have uneven grass! You'll be the laughingstock of the county!"

"I'll see what I can do," I said, as I looked at this man's grossly uneven flat top.

***

On September 8, 2015, we met without Kyle Langley. The first thing to celebrate was that we received the signed contract for painting the water tower, which the board had approved. The water tower painting was just another long overdue task that there simply had not been funds set aside for. I planned it, I budgeted it, and it was going to get done.

I couldn't be excited for long. Ron Butcher, still seeming to grow older by the day, said that we're still not bringing in enough funds in the water system and a rate increase is necessary. We had already increased the rates once and I reminded him that I certainly didn't want to do it again. If we raised rates a second time, I'd really have a hard time getting reelected if someone chose to run against me.

The only two people in the town I thought could give me a challenge were Barry Vance or Merf. Barry had assured me he wanted nothing to do with Dawson politics anymore. Merf planned to retire before the election, so I figured he might be considering it. With Merf's ability to make the public believe he's a good guy, and me potentially raising rates twice in four years, I'd be vulnerable. I encouraged Ron to have Max Woodrum do a free water rate analysis. This would at least buy me some time, and if we weren't keeping up with future maintenance costs, I'd at least have justification for raising the rates.

We also discussed the issues we'd been having with Nick Constant, a 30-something guy who lived near my parents. Chickens were not allowed in the town but he had them anyway. This is now the second time I would have to force someone to get rid of chickens! Colonel Sanders must hate me! I personally had no problem with chickens. However, I was doing my best to improve the image of the town. With Nick's chickens running all over and not in cages, cars regularly had to stop in the road and honk to scare off the chickens. This was definitely not the image of a town on the rise. With a diminishing population, and a barely afloat school system, we needed to improve our image to save both. Ed Quentin chimed in and said we needed to do something, because those chickens are a health risk to everyone in our community, and, "They'll make you feel worse than the morning after a Mardis Gras parade!"

I told the board all I had done. I sent Nick letters, to which he never responded. I stopped by his house, to which he said he had received the letters, but he was keeping the chickens. I told him they're illegal, and he said he was keeping the chickens. I then told him I'm sorry for what I'll have to do next, because they have to go.

At the board meeting that evening, the board approved a forceful removal of the chickens. This almost sounds like the Mafia or some casino pit boss thugs would ransack the house, but that wasn't the case. I don't recall the exact verbiage, but the gist of it is that due to a citizen's actions causing a health risk to the community, the Village must step in. Free-range chickens are considered a health risk because of their feces. Before police and animal control could get involved, Nick took the chickens to a relative's house. I win again!

I asked if this scenario could be applied to the Green family's asphalt dumping, and our attorney Reggie Phillips said that he had already checked. The answer was no. Kara Gregory brought up that Ryan Green's wife had left yet another expletive-filled voicemail. I guess they were tired of getting warning letters from the town. Frustrated, I said to the board, "Well, we're tired of them being in the town!" Everyone in the room rose out of their chairs and gave a standing ovation! Meeting adjourned.

***

I was mowing the grass a few days later when I noticed Roman Green buzzing around on his dune buggy. Again, this wasn't street legal. I was certain that he was doing it just to annoy me and maybe incite me to engage him. I continued riding my mower as if he wasn't there. Then, I noticed he was driving the dune buggy along the edge of the road where it met my property. I continued mowing, choosing this as the perfect time to trim the edge of my grass. I turned my mower and quickly rode along the edge of the grass, right alongside the road. This caused a broadcast of small rocks and gravel to spray in Roman's direction. He fishtailed and the buggy crashed into a stop sign. The buggy rolled over and he fell out onto the ground. I continued mowing as if nothing had happened, keeping a close eye on him while I held in my laugh.

He yelled over, "What are you doing?!"

"What?" I said.

"I'm gonna call the cops on you!"

"You call the cops and explain why you're driving an illegal vehicle and trespassing with it on my property."

He angrily stormed into his house. The police never showed up, probably because they were never called. I got a phone call from Agnes Cobb a few minutes later, who had watched the entire scene play out from her picture window. "That was absolutely hilarious!" she said. "Thanks for giving this old lady a good laugh!"

***

I remember the weather that September being quite warm. I got a call from college student Fallon O'Neill who had a problem with the heat.

"Something reeks over by the Village Hall. I think it's the dumpster," she said.

"They'll empty it tomorrow, so it's probably okay," I responded.

"I can't jog past there anymore. It's terrible! It smells like hot garbage!"

"That's what it is, so...*I'll see what I can do.*"

***

I called Merf to check on him since he was still resting at home. I thought it might be a goodwill gesture, but it didn't take long for me to regret it.

"Merf, how are you feeling?" I asked.

"Oh, as good as I can be. Just disappointed," he said.

"Don't worry. You'll get better in no time."

"I'm not disappointed in my health! I'm disappointed with you!"

"What'd I do?"

"It's what you didn't do! A couple months ago I was driving the truck into the workshop and backed into my file cabinet. Now the truck and cabinet both have big dents!"

"What's that have to do with me?"

"If you appreciate me, you'll buy a new one."

"I don't think it'll be too hard to buy you a new file cabinet."

"No, I want a new work truck!"

***

When we met in October of 2015, Ed Quentin and Kyle Langley were absent. Sharon Yount kicked off the meeting by saying that the school bus stop had been moved to the fire station and it was very unsafe for the children in our neighborhood. She added that we need to get it moved right away before a kid got hit by a fire truck. Before I could answer, Johnny Lynch, being the father of two elementary school students, correctly told her that the school would need to handle that and it had nothing to do with us.

She said, "So you're telling me that the school and this town are separate units of government?"

Johnny looked like a deer in headlights, stunned that Sharon didn't know this. He was speechless.

I said, "That's correct. That's why they have a School Board and we have a Town Board. If people have an issue with the school, they need to contact the school, not us."

"But it's happening in our town," she argued.

"So do my walking farts, but no one cares!" said Margie Baggio.

Our attorney Reggie Phillips changed the subject to the continuing issues with the Green family. He had begun taking steps to apply fines due to their ordinance violations, which would be $300 a day. He said that to move forward, we needed to get photos of the house, showing both the address of the house and the equipment in the same picture. This would not be an easy task, because the address is on the front of the house, and most of the equipment was in the backyard. And since no one else was going to do it, it would be my job to somehow take this photo like some small-town paparazzi. Can't wait.

In addition to upsetting the Green family, I knew I was about to upset the entire town. We had run the numbers and it was clear that we needed to raise the water rates. I had talked to Max Woodrum with Ron Butcher present and he declared we needed to raise rates around 15%. Now, that's only $2 a month. But, my future political opponent could make me look really bad when he reminds voters that I raised rates 15% when I had already increased rates once. According to Max, most towns raise their rates around 25 cents every two years just to keep up with inflation. Under the two-plus decades of

Carl Donaldson as mayor, the rates were never raised, period. My recent rate increase was to cover those previously lost costs, of which I really had no choice. It needed to be done. Now, we needed to raise rates again, knowing that several big-ticket items were going to need replacing. But before we voted, I would need Max or Ron to argue for the increase as well, so I delayed the matter until all three of us could be at the meeting. With the three of us pushing for it, and widely agreed to be the three most knowledgeable figures on Dawson water rates, the board would almost have to agree.

Our annual debate over what night the town bonfire would take place then ensued. Margie said we had to do it October 31, which was the last Saturday in October, and "Dumb Buffalo is doing their event on our date again." I reminded her that when Buffalo does their event wouldn't matter, and that we probably shouldn't do it Halloween night anyway. If we have the event Halloween night, it would really limit the people's ability to treat kids to candy from their own houses. I suggested we hold the event on Friday night, October 30.

Rhonda, adjusting her short gray hair, said, "We can't do that because I've already told people it was going to be on Halloween night, and we'd have no way to inform the public of anything different, so that's what it's going to have to be."

At this point, I'd had enough of Rhonda trying to put her foot down, since she's not someone elected to make decisions.

I said, "I've already told people it would be on the 30th. I can post the date on our website, our Facebook page, on the sign board at the town entrance, in the town newsletter, and on the water bills, so that's what it's going to have to be!"

I pounded the gavel. Meeting adjourned.

***

A few days later, I got started on my CIA spy-like mission to take photos of the Green's property. I slowly drove toward their house and rolled down my window. I figured I could get a good angle from a diagonal perspective, capturing both the front of the house's address numbers and the equipment parked at the side and back of the house. I wanted to be quick, but I had to readjust a couple times, because from my angle a large tree blocked the address numbers. I snapped a couple photos when I heard the screen door pop open. It was Ryan Green, who stormed out past his porch with a shotgun! He fired it into the air as I began to speed off and head home. He yelled, "Next time it'll be at your face!"

***

It wasn't much longer when I got a call from Phyllis Ellison, an older widow, who seemed to be in a tizzy about something.

"Did we get attacked by Iran?!" she frantically asked.

"Umm, excuse me?" I asked while I laughed.

"A pothole just swallowed my Cadillac! The only thing big enough to do that is an Iranian missile strike!"

"We've budgeted to fix potholes this month, so don't worry, it's not a war zone."

"Better see what you can do!"

"Yes. *I'll see what I can do.*"

***

The town bonfire went off without a hitch. When we were there, I happened to notice the steel door that led into the park pavilion's kitchen seemed to have some marks on it near the dead bolt. I asked Merf if he'd noticed them before and he said no. The lock on that door had always been a little tricky, so we wondered if maybe someone who had reserved the park had some trouble getting into the kitchen. Besides, if the marks were from someone trying to break in, we couldn't figure why anyone would want to do that. It was a full commercial kitchen, with not much to steal besides hand-me-down pans, containers, and utensils. Plus, anyone who wanted to use the kitchen for a party was welcome to do so for free. We filed a police report so that it was documented, but still had no idea what to think or who to suspect.

Of course it wouldn't be the bonfire without one of our older ladies being upset at Buffalo for holding their event the same night. A trustee from Buffalo happened to visit our event and was cornered by Agnes Cobb. Cornered between an angry old woman and a stack of hot dogs, Trustee Dan Fleming had no reaction when Agnes Cobb poked him in the chest and called him "Dirtbag Danny."

***

I called Merf at home to try to be a good boss and check on him again. If I called, I knew he'd be mad, but if I didn't call, he'd also be mad.

"Merf, are you doing better?" I asked with a positive tone.

"Yep, feeling good about everything but my stapler," he responded.

"What's wrong with it?"

"The one at the workshop is a cheap plastic one. I'm not sure why you don't think I'm good enough to have a nice steel Swingline."

"If that'll make you happy, we'll get you one."

"Good, then I'll take the plastic one home. The one I have here is broke."

"I can't buy you office supplies just so can take them home."

"That's not what I said and you know it. I'm gonna start calling you 'Blender' cause you keep mixing my words!"

CHAPTER 12

COME WALL OR
HIGH WATER

I couldn't believe it. We met on November 2 with all six board members present. They had a reason to be there since the water rates were going to be voted on. Ron Butcher was seated next to Max Woodrum in the banquet chairs. Ron and I had met again with Max about a week prior to the meeting. We devised a strategy as to how it would go. Yes, even in a town of 500, the political powers held secret meetings to get things done!

Max would explain the doom and despair scenario, essentially saying the town had no choice but to raise rates. Ron would chime in here and there to agree. Max was a water industry expert, and Ron had run the town water system for decades. Between the two, they were very believable. I would play "good cop," pitching ideas as to how we could get around the rate increase. Ron and Max already knew what my pitches would be, so they had answers planned as to why my ideas wouldn't work. This way, the town would be aware that although I would ask the board to increase rates, it appeared I did all I could to avoid it, and clearly I didn't want to do it at all. Reelection here I come!

Max spoke, with some input from Ron, for two hours that night. That's how long it took to field all of the board's questions! I asked the pre-planned questions which were shot down by each of them. It seemed that between me and the board, there were no other ideas as to how we could avoid this. With Max's booming voice and "friendly farmer" look and sound, he was very likable and convincing. To my surprise, the board was then unanimous in approval of the rate increase. Per Reggie Phillips's odd procedures, this only approved the writing of the ordinance for rate increases. They'd have to vote next month to approve the ordinance.

Reggie then explained that he had sent the letter to the Green family, informing them of the upcoming fines, and that he included the pictures of their house that I took. It worked, because they moved all of their trucks and equipment to a commercial lot on Route 36, the highway that runs along the south side of town. It seemed we had finally won, but it also seemed odd that the Greens would just give up their fight after all they'd been doing. I was certain there was more to come.

I brought up the upcoming senior dinner and asked if the group wanted to cut back on food, which we seemed to discuss every year while cleaning up after the senior dinner. The idea of preparing a lighter and easier meal, such as soup and sandwiches, was suggested as it was every year. As you might guess, Margie Baggio fought back against it, insisting that we don't change the meal on our friends. Since Margie and Agnes Cobb almost always argue the same side, Agnes agreed not to change anything. The remaining four trustees gave resistance, as did I, but Agnes and Margie kept pushing back hard. I could have put my foot down, but Agnes and Margie voluntarily organize the event and do almost all the cooking. If I made them too angry, they'd refuse. I think Ed Quentin, who headed a household with two boys and one girl, was right on the money when he said, "This will work just like my house. The women are outvoted, but they're still going to get their way."

I laughed at Ed's joke, then moved on to pitch yet another improvement to the vacation policy. Without the funds to pay our staff big salaries, it was all the more important to me to take extra steps to keep the staff happy. I didn't think it was right that the staff's vacation days expired at the end of the year. I felt that allowing the days to build would be another way to keep the crew happy without breaking the bank. It seemed everyone was on board except Sharon Yount.

She said, "I don't think we should be helping these guys out. Ron and Merf are going to retire soon, so it only applies to the younger guys, and they don't do nothin'! My husband could work circles around them!"

Ed Quentin responded, "The only circles he can work around is donuts!"

Sharon and Ed sat next to each other, but they began yelling like they were three blocks apart. I got things settled down, then Agnes Cobb said that Sharon may have a point. Now that Agnes was agreeing, Margie was too. I quickly compromised by saying that we could cap the amount of vacation days allowed to be accumulated at 20. With that, everyone settled in, and unanimously approved an ordinance to be written. Again per Reggie's rules, this would also require a vote next month.

I then proposed that we hire Dan Jones full-time. He was already working around 30 hours a week, and with Merf planning to retire this summer, it was time to get him ready to take over completely. The board agreed, and Dan was now officially full-time. Meeting adjourned.

***

I had family over around Thanksgiving and noticed my cell phone kept ringing. I suspected it was mayor-related, but didn't want to be rude and take those types of calls with family around. A couple of the calls were from Agnes Cobb, and a couple more were from a number I didn't recognize, though I could tell it was local. Soon, there was knocking at my door. I excused myself from the dinner table and opened the door to Agnes Cobb and Lee Finley. Lee was the old man that suggested I shoot up the family of skunks in the abandoned house, and Agnes was his longtime friend since high school. As I opened the door, I noticed a ton of smoke coming from behind the Green's house.

"Do you see that?!" Lee said.

"When you're the mayor you have to take these calls, even on holidays. We've been trying to call you all night!" said Agnes.

"What exactly do you want me to do, Lee?" I asked.

"They're burning all their old equipment and chemicals! You need to stop them!"

"You think I should go argue with these guys, who have already threatened my life, right next to a giant fire?"

"You're the mayor! It's your job!" Lee shouted.

"Agnes, you know I can't do anything. We need to call the fire department to put out the fire," I appealed.

"Nope," Agnes said, "You need to go get 'em!"

I closed the door. My eyes burned from the smoke. I called the fire department and dispatch said they would be there soon; they had just left another call. I told my family what was going on and debated whether I should walk over. Against my wife's wishes, I started walking over. The stench of burning chemicals was overwhelming. I got about halfway there when the Greens noticed me.

Ryan, the father, turned around and shouted, "Took you long enough! I figured you'd be here sooner! Ready to fine me or what?!"

"I'd rather you just put out the fire and be done with this," I said as I continued walking closer.

"Look, here comes that tall pasty white chump! We've been ready for you, ya' ghost lookin' dork!" added the teenage Roman.

I continued walking closer to have a normal conversation, wondering what he meant by saying they were ready for me. Roman started reaching into the back of his waistband. I tried to look at what he was reaching for when the roar of the fire trucks got louder. The trucks zoomed up the road and parked right next to us in the back alley. I looked back at Roman, who just put a gun back into his waistband! They planned to kill me right there and I was saved by the fire trucks.

The fire chief, Lance Butcher, said, "We have to put this out right now!"

"Do what you have to do," said Roman, as he and Ryan walked back inside.

I told Lance what happened, and he said I should call the police. I called, and the same old thing happened.

The officer knocked at my door and said, "I talked to the Greens and they say that didn't happen."

"It did," I said with frustration.

I reminded him of all the other issues and times the officers had to come out.

"There's really nothing we can do at this time," he said. "Call us back out if you need us."

***

One day in late November, I stopped in the Village Hall to work. I noticed someone was in the men's room but didn't think much of it. As I worked away, I noticed that no one had left the bathroom the entire morning. That was until Merf stepped out.

"Are you okay?" I asked.

"Why wouldn't I be okay?" he replied.

"You just started working again and spent like five hours in the bathroom. I thought something might've happened."

"No. Just read *Huckleberry Finn* for a few hours. Not bad!"

"You can't spend your whole morning reading a book on the toilet!"

"How long until I call the Department of Labor?! How long?!"

***

We met on December 7 without Margie Baggio. Our first point of discussion was the findings of the annual audit, which was the same as every year. The board agreed that although

it was recommended for us to have more cross-checking between employees, we simply didn't have enough employees to
do so. Rhonda Brown and Kara Gregory would continue to
cross-check each other, I would look at specific payments, and
the board looked at the overall reports. As Ed Quentin put it,
"I think it's fine. If you steal money from my little town, you're
dumber than a fire alarm in a meat smoker."

With that, I took a deep breath as I proposed the vote for
the water rate increase. I gave a brief pitch, reminding the
group of the previous discussions from Ron Butcher and
Max Woodrum. Planning for a three-hour debate, I asked the
board for any comments. With that, Johnny Lynch motioned
to approve, Agnes Cobb made a second, and the vote passed
unanimously. Now the only thing I had to worry about was
whether the town was so upset by the increase that they'd vote
against me in 16 months.

For now, I knew I could at least make the staff a little hap-
pier if I could get the vacation ordinance passed and allow
vacation days to carry over. Everyone must've been in the
Christmas spirit, because with no debate, it passed unanimously as well!

On this night, I was basically taking my victory lap. The
property owner of the fourth abandoned house finally paid
us what they owed. We'd been mowing and cleaning up debris
for several months and our labor had been reimbursed. Not
long after, the house was cleaned up and remodeled, making
the area look much better. Now, all four abandoned houses
had been addressed and resolved after years of being ignored.
This was the house with the skunk family, so at least it smelled
better over there too!

As we wrapped up the meeting, I reminded the group that we'd eat our annual Christmas dinner at Boston Steakhouse. I stated it, rather than asking, because I wasn't about to have another hour-long debate over where we'd eat! I also reminded the group that we are leaders of the town, and we should lead by example. I shouldn't receive complaints about a trustee's yard or a trustee's dog being loose. This was absolutely in reference to Sharon Yount. I made it a point to have it listed in the meeting minutes so that the town voters knew I felt the same way they did. Sharon adjusted her glasses and fanned her t-shirt nervously, feeling she had been targeted. I feared that some of the trustees may have interpreted that statement as being directed at them. I wisely waited to the end of the meeting to make this statement, rather than right before they would vote for my initiatives. By this time I knew how to play the game! Meeting adjourned.

***

Throughout December, Sandra and I started hearing these faint noises late at night. It was almost a light popping sound. I happened to see Agnes Cobb outside one evening, we got to chatting, and she was hearing the same thing but couldn't quite figure it out either. A few days later, I ran into Hank White, the retired Marine that lived a couple houses down.

"Are you doing anything about the Greens?" he said.

I began explaining the entire situation, then he cut me off.

"The guns," he said.

I was puzzled still, and again tried to explain what was happening, before he cut me off again.

"They've got a basement no bigger than 300 square feet – I know because I used to visit there when the previous owner lived there. They set up a gun range in the basement! They're shooting guns throughout the night in that tiny basement!"

Ahhh, so that explained what we were all hearing.

"Maybe my problem with the Greens is going to work itself out naturally," I said. "Survival of the fittest!"

We both had a laugh, and I told him if he thought it was necessary, he could call the county police.

He responded, "Why would I call the police? I'm rooting for a stray bullet to end all our problems! I asked if you were doing anything about it because I was going to talk you out of it!"

We both had another big laugh and agreed. If the Greens were doing something that could end our troubles, we weren't about to stop them.

***

We got through our staff Christmas party and senior dinner with no problems except the rain. It's funny how fate works. By coincidence, my wife Sandra and I happened to sit next Johnny Lynch and his wife Renee at the Christmas party. We really connected, learning we had numerous things in common, including our love of pro wrestling. Likewise, at the senior dinner, it seemed like the chores and duties needing done that day often resulted in Renee working alongside Sandra, while simultaneously Johnny and I worked closely together. We soon invited them over for dinner and games, a friendship truly developed, and dinner and games became a recurring activity to this day.

Merf called me immediately after the party.

"If our budget is so tight, why did you have the party?" he asked.

"I just wanted to keep everyone happy, but you're right, it's pricey," I countered.

"If the budget is that tight, I think you should lay off Kara Gregory!" he blurted.

"There's no need to lay anyone off."

"I'd recommend you start with Kara. If you want to know who else to lay off, just let me know!"

"Thanks, Merf, I'll get on that."

Oh, but the rain. It seemed it rained almost every day that December. The weather was in the low 30s, so it never turned to snow or ice, just lots of cold water. The people of Dawson didn't really have to worry about their houses flooding, because the town wasn't near any bodies of water. In the back of the minds of the town leaders, though, we always had to worry about the water plant flooding. It sat a mere 25 feet from the banks of the Sangamon River. And although it was uphill, a heavy flood could put our water distribution in a world of hurt. Ron Butcher had been monitoring the rising waters, hoping the rain would stop. On December 26, he gave me the call I never wanted.

He said, "Mayor, it's Ron. The water is too high, and projected to go higher. It's time. We're going to have to start a sandbagging effort."

We organized the plan, our roles, and next steps. Ron really guided me, because he'd been through it all before. The plant seemed to be in danger of flooding about every 20 years or so. Twice before, a sandbagging effort was necessary, and each time, they saved the water plant. This time, we'd have to save it again. Ron would lead the staff and volunteers at the plant, in addition to maintaining the current water operations. Our full-time and part-time crews would help sandbag. Kara Gregory would stay at the office and handle the phone calls and emails from volunteers. Any media requests would be directed to me, and I knew there would be several. The last thing I needed was another awkward interview showing Rhonda's Bluetooth dangling from her 80-year-old ear! Kara and I would volunteer to sandbag when we had time. Rhonda would handle the day-to-day operations of the office.

Volunteers came and went, throughout the day, for the next few days. Just when we thought the sandbag wall was high enough, the waters went higher, and the volunteer crews came back. All in all, 80+ individuals volunteered in the effort. Lance Butcher brought many of the local Dawson firefighters and even acquired some insulated diving gear from another fire department. That allowed a couple guys to actually get on the other side of the sandbags, in the chilly river waters, and help seal the wall. Lance was instrumental in leading the effort alongside his father Ron. Lance also coordinated with the high school to get a school bus near the plant, so volunteers could take a break in a heated area.

The high school basketball team even came by and helped, and of course they made the freshmen do the hard stuff! Local businesses donated everything from food and water to spotlights and sump pumps. Some water would still seep through, so we had pumps to send it back over the wall into the river. The spotlights allowed crews to work overnight.

The river water was incredibly high. Traffic passed by on the county highway bridge over the river. The water was touching that bridge. Our sandbag walls were almost six feet high, on a hill, and the water was at the top. If water got to the plant, we would have to disconnect power and shut down water distribution. Then, we'd enact a boil order whenever the water finally cleared out of the plant and we had time to replace what was damaged. Luckily, through all the efforts, the plant was saved.

Houses and buildings in nearby Riverton and Spaulding weren't so lucky. The damage was so significant that Illinois Governor Bruce Rauner came to see it firsthand. Alongside him were Congressman Darin LaHood and State Representative Tim Butler. They visited Dawson, then the damage at Riverton, and then Spaulding. We looked at each site, with media present, along with Riverton Mayor Red Tomko and Spaulding Mayor Clint Daniels.

When the media circus ended, I had a good talk with Darin LaHood about how to get an actual wall built around the plant. I had tried to look into funding previously, but the Army Corps of Engineers blocked us from building anything on a flood plain. Darin gave me a plan, guided me on how to get a grant, and said he could work things out directly with the Corps of Engineers. I thought this was great. If we could get a wall built around the plant, the sandbag efforts would never be needed again.

Not long after, I got a call from an older resident, Danny Reynolds, with his own idea on how to prevent the floods from happening.

"You know, if you just dug out the river and rerouted it, you'd never have to worry about the plant flooding," he said.

I replied, "The river is almost 30 feet deep and just as wide. There's really no way we could do that."

"Yes you can! You just need the town backhoe. Heck, I'll do it! After you reroute it, the river isn't your problem anymore. The people in that subdivision would have to worry about it."

"I'll see what I can do."

Obviously, rerouting a large river isn't really doable. Even if it was, I wouldn't have attempted it. If I could, I'm sure my long-term political career would really get a boost by flooding out an entire subdivision!

The stresses of dealing with emergencies like this one, in addition to small-town complaints, the Green family, Merf, and a Town Board that may or may not share my vision, all added up to one thing. I was starting to wonder if I should pursue reelection. I would have to file my paperwork in December 2016 to get on the ballot, so I had about a year to make up my mind. As I pondered, Rob Dellomo called me to chat about final details in the comprehensive plan he'd been writing. He asked me, point-blank, if I'd run for reelection. I told him I couldn't say for sure, but it was 90% likely I would run.

He told me that if I didn't plan to run, he was going to recommend that the Village government be disbanded, the town become unincorporated, and the written plan would essentially be the steps to do so. This would mean that the town would be treated like a subdivision in the rural area of a county, with any taxpayer funded services coming from county government. He went on to say that after his numerous meetings and discussions with the town officials, as well as his public hearings and meetings with town citizens, he felt that there was no one else reasonably equipped to be mayor. I mentioned that I thought Ed Quentin or Barry Vance would do a good job, but neither had any interest at the time. Rob said that he felt the same, chatted with each directly, and neither was "dumb enough to do it." I then brought up Merf, who had worked and lived in the town for so long that he had to have some knowledge. Even though we butted heads at times, he was the only other person I could think of.

"Jeremy," Rob said, "he knows the maintenance and infrastructure, no doubt. But in my talks with him, it is abundantly clear that he has no idea how to balance finances ... or his emotions for that matter!"

I had always noticed Merf's emotional imbalance and his inability to budget. It was common for Merf to get mad because I couldn't make 12 mega-purchases within the same calendar year, totaling tens of thousands of dollars more than our entire operating budget.

Rob continued, "If you can't balance money, you can't lead a government. Your town needs you. You're all they've got. I can't get behind Merf as mayor when he pouts during a crisis like a millennial intern having to shovel manure at the State Fair."

I acknowledged and agreed that I'd run for reelection, thinking the stress of the flood had simply affected me temporarily.

***

It was January 2016 when we gathered without Agnes Cobb. I started the meeting by thanking Ron and the entire crew for their leadership and efforts to save the plant from the floodwaters. I also mentioned to the group that I had been speaking with Congressman LaHood on how we could go about getting approval to build a wall around the plant from the Corps of Engineers, as well as appropriate grant funding. Sharon Yount asked if we could instead simply tear down the old plant and build a new one on the other side of the county highway.

Ron said, "Our Village doesn't own the property on the other side of the highway, it belongs to the county."

"I recently heard about this 'eminent domain,' in which a government can seize property for their own use. We could do that," she said.

"We can't just seize county property, it doesn't work like that," I added. "They'd have to agree to sell it to us. And even if they did, you're looking at millions of dollars to build a new water plant."

"Could we seize someone else's property and simply move the entire water plant building there?" she asked.

"No," I said. "Let's move on."

I'm curious just what Sharon's intentions were, but I suspect if she ever became mayor, "eminent domain" would be a regular discussion in every meeting. In the meantime, I mentioned that we may want to consider a Neighborhood Watch. This was largely due to all the issues that the Green family had caused us. Of course, my intentions were selfish. The goal was to have the people of the town on board for a Neighborhood Watch. Once they were on board, they'd be given basic training from the County Sheriff's Office as to how to be a good witness and report a crime to police. This way, the calls would be going to the police, as they should be, rather than to me at all hours. And after a little discussion, the Town Board agreed that I should pursue it further.

I also pitched the idea of buying some new Christmas decorations that small towns tend to have attached to their light poles downtown on Main Street. We didn't have a downtown, but we did have a main highway that ran through town.

My idea was to get these new decorations on the main drag through the town, in order to present the town nicely to those driving through. The board didn't know, but I had already spent the better part of the last year getting approval from the utility company to put the decorations up there. We had bought decorations a couple years earlier to do that, but the electrical hookup on the highway utility poles didn't match those in the general part of town. I decided that those decorations would be used to replace the significantly damaged ones throughout town. We had previously been displaying damaged Christmas decorations that became known as "Rudolph the two-legged reindeer" and "Dislocated shoulder Santa."

We may have improved the mismatched decor that was already spread around town, but we still had nothing on the main drag. That night, Ed Quentin looked his usual self, unshaven and wearing a college sweatshirt. He summed it up perfectly when he said, "If we're trying to decorate the town to look nice for people passing through, we're really just polishing up a turd. But I agree, we need to shine it up." And with that, the vote passed unanimously. Meeting adjourned.

***

The next week, an old friend of mine called and said that his teenage daughter told him a story about hanging out with her friend, Cassie Green. Cassie was the younger sister of Roman Green and was about 13 years old. My friend said that his daughter was concerned that Cassie had been trying to break into the commercial kitchen at the park. Cassie thought it would be funny if she could get into the kitchen and cook roadkill animals that they'd get from the highway. This explained the marks we had previously seen on the doorway.

I called the police about this but was told the same thing as before.

The officer said, "You didn't see anything; you're just hearing secondhand. There's nothing we can do."

The officer suggested I get security cameras installed at the park. I agreed, but this was just one more expense we'd have to deal with because of the Greens. We had to have Cassie Green on camera to do anything about it, but this was urgent, and I was afraid of a significant gas explosion. If you don't know what you're doing in a commercial kitchen, you can release a ton of natural gas. We needed to stop this before it got really bad, and without cameras, we'd have no proof of who blew up the park!

I called Merf and tried to explain the situation. He cut me off pretty quickly.

"That explains the loud clicking sound I kept hearing from that kitchen," he said.

"A clicking sound? Like the sound when you're trying to get a grill to light?" I asked.

"Not that. My ink pens! They click too loud! Haha, I got ya' that time!"

I laughed, confused as to why Merf was suddenly joking with me.

"I need new pens! These click too loud!" he added. "If I click it repeatedly people think a horse is trotting down the road!"

"Seriously though, could you check to see if you can make that more secure?"

"I'll see what I can do," Merf added, using my own catch-phrase against me.

✲✲✲

In mid-January, an older lady named Sonya Chapman called me.

"You've been doing a good job of keeping the roadkill off the road, but not good enough!" she said.

"We really don't have a 'roadkill removal' program. What do you mean?" I countered.

"Those teenage girls have been scooping up roadkill all over, but there's a dead squirrel over here that they haven't touched!"

"You've seen them pick up roadkill?"

"Yes sir, except this one. I've been forced to stare at it for weeks! It's like some sort of military torture to get me to talk! Come pick it up and I'll tell you anything you want to know!"

"I'll see what I can do."

CHAPTER 13

SITTIN' ON THE DOCK
OF THE PAY

It was February 1 when we met again, this time with every board member present! This night was one of the most memorable nights of my tenure. Merf had come to speak about staff salaries. Each November we reviewed staff salaries. In each of my first two years, the board agreed to give some kind of raise. This past November, we agreed to put raises on hold until spring, because the Illinois Government was withholding funds to municipalities, and it was unclear how much, if any, state funding we'd receive. Similarly, the water fund was in question, and we weren't sure how much of an impact the rate increase would have. We needed a clearer picture. As Merf adjusted his flannel shirt and ball cap and prepared to speak, I knew I could trust him as much as a car salesman desperately trying to meet his month-end quota.

Merf said, "Two years ago we got a 1% raise, and last year got a .5% raise. This year, the town didn't give raises, but somehow had money to buy some dumb Christmas decorations. That shows where we are on the totem pole, down at the bottom. I talked to the other employees and they're really disappointed with this leadership!"

My first thought was his information was wrong, and I'll get to that in a second. My next thought was Merf was doing his usual task of stirring the pot to turn the staff against me. Between the town and the staff, Merf seemed to always be trying to get people to turn on me. I still suspected it was because he planned to run against me for the mayor's seat. I listened to his words closely, knowing I was about to turn everything against him like I was in a Presidential debate!

Merf continued, "I'm retiring this summer, so I don't need a raise, I'm good. Don't worry about giving me a raise. But, it's important you take care of the new guys. I'm here to speak for Dan and Will, not for me."

I paused to think it was odd that Dan, who recently got a nice raise for becoming full-time, already wanted more money. Similarly, Will was still fairly new to full-time work and we had given him an even higher salary than he requested when we hired him.

I responded, "I'm confused as to why the staff doesn't understand. I spoke with you all directly and told you that we would revisit raises in the spring since we weren't sure how the State's withheld funds would shake out, and we weren't sure how the water budget would look after the rate increases. I told you all this directly, so the confusion makes no sense to me. The past raises you received were 2% and 1% respectively, so your figures are also wrong. Do you have any other misconstrued information to present?"

Ed Quentin added, "Merf, are you in the media? This all sounds like fake news!"

This is what I believe to be the first use of the phrase "fake news." Now, I noticed Merf look at Kara Gregory when I stated the amounts of the raises, so my question as to who was leaking him confidential information was answered. I added that the Christmas decorations were purchased from a completely different line item on the budget, from a completely different fund, in a completely different account, so that purchase had no impact on raises whatsoever. If he was going to try to make me look bad, I was going to make sure everyone knew he had no idea how budgets worked. I didn't think he could write a budget for his own household, let alone the town!

So, from my soapbox, I asked, "Do you understand how the budget works?"

"I think so," he replied.

Knowing his statements would be a factor later, I asked him for clarification, saying, "So to be clear, you have no interest in a raise, you are just here lobbying for Dan Jones and Will Baggio?"

"That's right," he said. "I don't want a raise. Give the money to them. Those guys have to work really hard, for a lot of hours, and their wage just doesn't meet what they're required to do. We all feel unappreciated, especially after the flood."

I responded, telling him I'd been very vocal about the great work that the staff did, saying so in every media interview or statement I issued. I also made numerous trips to the water plant in the midst of the flood to thank them directly. I continued, reminding him that the staff was on overtime, so they got time and a half for all the extra hours, and even double time at points. I allowed it to be paid out as cash, rather than requiring comp time.

Merf responded, "Yes, I'm aware of all that."

I added, "Each of them has automatic raises built into their contracts for each of the three levels of water license they receive, and another raise if they get licensed to spray for mosquitoes. Though I agree that they deserve a raise, and I'm sure we'll give them one, they can get a raise any time they want if they'd just pursue these licenses. The town even pays for the training and courses, and they'd have a $12 an hour raise if they got all four licenses, so I'm not sure what's not to like about that. They were each hired full-time in order to replace you and Ron, who are each licensed workers for either water works or mosquito spraying. If they are truly to replace you, they need to be licensed, and are contracted to be paid very well once they get licensed. When that happens, they'll be paid like supervisors and not subordinates."

"I know, that's correct," he said.

"He is right," said Margie Baggio. "Everyone in town knows these guys need to get off their lazy butts and do something!"

I wasn't sure if she realized she was talking about her own grandson. If Margie was on my side, I knew the whole board was, because she was the hardest sell with her grandson immediately impacted. Sorry, Merf, you lose this round.

We then moved on to talk about funding for that new flood wall to build around the water plant. The idea was that it would be similar to the concrete dividers you see on the interstate that separate the road from construction crews. I'm not sure the science behind it, but they would be a little thicker, about double the height, and waterproof. We had all the figures we needed. It would be up to me to work with Congressman

LaHood to apply for the grant and hopefully get it. Of course, it's politics, so who knows how long that process could take!

The conversation then turned to a lengthy discussion on whether we would legalize golf carts. They weren't street legal in Illinois, but plenty of people were driving them around the town anyway. Does that surprise you? I figured we might as well make it legal; that way it kept our people out of any trouble with police. We agreed to a registration form and a $15 one-time fee to cover printing costs for the form and the fancy registration sticker. Everyone voted to approve the legalization, with the exception of Johnny Lynch. He told me after that he liked the idea, he just voted that way to distance himself from my opinion this time. He felt he knew it would pass, so it was a safe topic to alter his vote on and allow the public to recognize he didn't always vote with the mayor. People were recognizing that we had become friends, and he wanted to be perceived as he was, which was his own man, not the mayor's crony. For some reason Reggie Phillips felt that an additional vote for the ordinance wasn't necessary this time around, so the golf cart legalization was a done deal.

The local public library was holding a fundraiser trivia night and once again requested a small donation from the Village to help pay for door prizes. Before I even brought it up, I knew the older ladies were somehow going to have a problem with it!

Rhonda Brown jumped in, "I'd suggest you donate the same amount to them that you gave the Town Team for their trivia night!"

"How much was that?" I asked.

"Zero!"

Rhonda and Agnes agreed that we should give nothing.

I followed up, saying, "I was not aware of the Town Team asking for a donation."

"We didn't get anything!" she said.

Ed Quentin jumped in, "You've gotta ask the right people for the money, or you're not getting your money. Just ask Will and Dan!"

I laughed at his hilarious observation.

Ed added, "Those two never asked Jeremy for anything either. They just counted on Merf's dog and pony show."

With the donation talk going nowhere, we switched the topic to security cameras for the park. We needed to do what we could to catch Cassie Green and her friends breaking into the park kitchen. The Greens alone were incredibly frustrating, as was the cost of dealing with them, which continued to skyrocket. In typical Dawson fashion, the board chose to wait a month before voting.

I notified the board that I had spoken with Sheriff Wes Barr, who was willing to help develop the Neighborhood Watch program. Ed suggested that instead of a Neighborhood Watch, we call it "Green Watch," which made complete sense.

The next subject was my suggestion to make Martin Luther King, Jr. Day a paid holiday for our staff. Honestly, I was surprised that it wasn't already a paid holiday. I realized it when I happened to see our crew out working on Martin Luther King, Jr. Day that January. I wanted to get that fixed right away. Our entire board was in support, although Sharon Yount was hesitant.

"Who is Martin King anyways?" she asked.

After we filled her in, she asked if it was appropriate that a staff of all white employees should be granted such a day off. When everyone else in the room suggested her argument was irrelevant, she joined in agreement, and this motion passed unanimously.

We closed off public admission so we could discuss raises, as Merf requested. As I suspected, the board was on my side. We were all in agreement that although we wanted to give raises, it wouldn't be prudent to do so without knowing our financial situation. Meeting adjourned.

After the meeting, Ron Butcher pulled me to the side and said that like Merf, he didn't want a raise either. Ron said he felt it was better to tell me privately, rather than through "Merf's dog and pony show," echoing Ed. He agreed that the newer guys worked hard, but felt we were right to wait for raises until we had a full understanding of the finances.

***

A couple days later, Sandra and I were awakened in the middle of the night. Thump ... thump ... thump! I looked out and saw two shadowy figures run back toward the Green's house. I was certain that one was Roman Green and the other was either Ryan or a large friend. I knew they were up to something but decided I'd take a look in the morning. When I woke up and looked outside, sure enough, they had egged the house. We called the police, yet again, and filed a report. And yet again, the police said that just because we say we saw the Greens do this, didn't mean they could do anything about it. We had to prove it, or all the police could do was talk to them. Yet again, I was reminded that somehow we had to get them out of this town.

***

As the weather began to turn from winter to spring, we had a close call with a tornado. Luckily, the town was spared when the tornado made its way through a nearby field instead. That didn't stop Brandi Thompson, a middle-aged mother, from calling me with a complaint.

"I want to know why they sounded those storm sirens!" she exclaimed.

"A tornado was in the area," I replied.

"It was way too soon! If they would have waited, they would have seen the tornado went around us, and would've never had to sound them in the first place."

"But if they waited that long and the tornado hit our town, they would have given the people no advance warning."

"So what! They need to wait! That siren about made me crap my pants!"

"I'll see what I can do."

***

As I sat at my desk preparing for the March meeting, Merf approached me.

"Do you think we'd have the money to get a new microwave?" he asked.

"If it's broken we probably should get one," I answered.

"It's not broken. It's disgusting! There's chili all over it!"

"Can't you ask whoever did that to clean it up?"

"No."

"Why? You don't know who did it?"

"I did it!"

"Can't you clean it?"

"Are you asking me to do work on my lunch hour? I just want clarity before I submit a report!"

"No. I'm asking you to clean up after yourself."

"Unbelievable!"

***

The next meeting was March 7, with everyone present except Agnes Cobb. We were again kicking the tires on extending our water system to the rural subdivisions. With Merf back on the job, and Dan Jones and Will Baggio full-timers, we were in good shape to begin the labor. Although Merf could no longer do significant labor, he was comfortable operating a tractor or backhoe. We had George O'Reilly still doing some part-time work for us, and Ron's grandson Austin Butcher had expressed a willingness to do some part-time work. We had the staff to make it happen, but it would also require the finances of the residents in those subdivisions to make it happen. We decided to put out a mailer and see what kind of response we got. If the residents were willing to pay, we were going to do it.

Ed suggested we hurry before Merf retired that summer, because, as he said, "You know if Merf doesn't want to do it, he'll take his ball and go home."

We then voted on the official ordinance approval of Martin Luther King, Jr. Day as a paid holiday.

"Well, if we have to, I guess we should," said Sharon.

"We don't have to but it's the right thing to do," I responded.

Sharon rolled her eyes and voted yes, passing the vote unanimously.

The board then also unanimously approved the purchase of security cameras for the park.

As Ed put it, "The Greens have to go. They're more annoying than a tick in your crack!"

The best part of this comment is knowing that Ed was an avid hunter, so I was certain he had experienced that exact phrase! It seemed to be a recurring problem since it wasn't even the first time he mentioned ticks inside his pants.

A local elderly man had passed away and donated $10,000 to the town. Agnes Cobb had previously suggested to me that we plant a Red Oak tree, with a plaque in his honor, at the park. The board agreed to do so. That still left roughly $9,500 to spend. I told the board I would consider options and would revisit. I secretly knew exactly what I wanted to do with that money: eliminate the flashing arrow sign at the town entrance and replace it with a legitimate LED sign. If you recall, I had planned to do so before, but the funds were shifted to purchase the 20-year comprehensive plan. But like a good marriage, I knew I had to keep some things a secret!

Ron nearly revealed my plan, without his knowledge, when I brought up storm sirens. Ron was still looking older by the day, but on this night, I could tell he really had something on his mind. I informed the board that the storm siren that Spaulding had given us was fully functional. The local sewer commission gave me verbal approval to put the siren on the post at their substation, so we were in business. I wouldn't have to spend any of that extra money on another storm siren. This would keep the people on the east side of town happy. I discussed that, then brought up that the siren at the park no longer worked because it was struck by lightning. We were simply waiting for the insurance money to come in.

"Let's use the extra money to buy a nice sign for our town entrance!" Ron blurted out.

I responded, "We still have to get the insurance money for the siren at the park. If for some reason they don't send it, we'd need to purchase an additional siren. In the meantime, we've got to wait for attorneys and boards to create and sign off on a contract to put the other siren at the sewer station. Until those things happen, we should hold the money, because the town's safety is number one."

To prevent Margie from planning a reason to vote against it, I had successfully diverted the thought of the new sign. On top of that, I thought I'd look smart in the papers and score some points by saying safety comes first.

Ed must've agreed, saying, "I'm gonna start calling you poker star, because you've gotta be stacking a lot of chips after that big play."

Maybe I'd be running for reelection after all. Meeting adjourned.

***

This month was oddly quiet regarding the Greens until I began mowing that March. Roman was zooming around on his dune buggy again as soon as he heard my blades turn on. Every lap I'd make in the yard, he'd make it a point to zoom back in front of me along the road. Once again, I timed my lap to spray him with roadside gravel. This time, he drove off, middle finger raised high in the air. I was content to have the middle finger directed at me, so long as his guns weren't involved again.

***

I later talked to Merf and made sure he still planned to get his mosquito license this year. He agreed that he would do the spraying until he retired this summer. I wanted Dan Jones to do it, but he'd been unable to pass the licensing exam. Merf even agreed to work part-time and spray after he retired, in the event that Dan was still unable to pass the exam. In the same conversation, Merf suggested I reach out to Benny Fowler, who had made so much money doing subdivision developments in the area that most of the community called him Donald Trump.

Benny had already established some subdivisions in nearby Mechanicsburg and also in nearby Rochester. The folks at the local Tri-City School weren't really happy with him though, because he made his money by convincing the town to establish Tax Increment Financing (TIF) districts in these areas, which of course limits the total tax revenue that the school receives. The Tri-City School was already struggling, so I certainly didn't want to be the person responsible for putting it out of its misery like it's the last Blockbuster Video in America! However, I was also aware that Dawson was dwindling in population and the majority of those still around were getting older. If we could get a nice 40-50 house subdivision, that would help with our revenues, help maintain the town's population, and even add enrollment to the Tri-City School. As long as Benny was reasonable in his needs, I thought we could be like Monty Hall and make a deal.

I sat down with Benny Fowler late that March. He was around 45, about 5'6", with a buzzed head that was nearly bald. When we met, he was wearing a t-shirt and gym shorts, carrying a catalog of common subdivision home designs. He was certainly open to developing, and even had an idea as to where, although I didn't know quite yet. He also reminded me that this moved quite slowly, so I needed to be patient. He said the first step was to have his TIF attorney come to a board meeting and explain how these things worked. He told me not to mention to anyone, even the board, why it was happening. To the community, the thought of having Benny make more money off of a TIF district was an automatic negative response. We needed to get the Town Board, and the community, in agreement with the idea before revealing that Benny was behind the subdivision development.

***

Fire Chief Lance Butcher had been telling me that a lot of cars had recently been parking in the Village Hall lot, which was causing delays in fire response. There were only eight spaces, lined up directly off of the street and alley. When the firemen rushed to the firehouse to respond to a call, they'd often have to circle around and park in the street when the spaces were full. After some talk, we suspected that they were patrons of the nearby Mr. Ribeye Lounge. With an emergency call, time is of the essence, so we had to make sure those spaces were clear. I had signs put up in front of every space that said, "Parking for Village Hall only. All others will be towed." As you read this paragraph you already have to know that soon this is going to make someone mad!

***

My parents joined me for dinner for my mom's birthday that month. As we ate, I got a knock on the door from Vivian

Aguilera, a young millennial who lived with her parents (surprise).

"I just got back from the store in Riverton and they're outta bread!" she yelled.

"Did you ask them if they had more?" I replied.

"No, I want you to! Now I have to make French toast with hamburger buns!"

"I grew up poor, and that's how we did it!" I joked.

"That's not how I do it. Fix it," she said as she glared back at me.

"I'll see what I can do."

***

I stopped in the Village Hall to prepare for the April board meeting. Merf was in the office, making copies, and looked like a kid that just got caught stealing baseball cards. I didn't think much of it.

"How's it going?" I asked.

"It's going," he replied, which was his typical response.

"I'm just prepping for the board meeting. Is everything okay?"

"I'm just making copies of my grandson's birthday party invites."

"You're doing that on our copier?"

"I work here, don't I?!"

"You can't do that, Merf."

"You're saying I can't use the copy machine?"

"How many copies are you making?"

"Three hundred. It's gonna be huge!"

"No."

***

On April 4, the entire group was in attendance. Benny Fowler's TIF attorney stopped in to take some questions and answers. I introduced him to the group, saying that there are a lot of TIF districts around us, and this gentleman has been kind enough to help explain how they work. Simple enough! This poor guy, he got peppered with questions for the next hour! Eventually though, it felt like the negative stigma that accompanied TIF districts had been lifted. My next step would be to get the school on board. At this point, no one but Benny, his attorney, and I knew the plan.

We had a little discussion with Ron Butcher about the future of the water plant. I had recently asked him to gather some information and paperwork for the flood wall grant. He continued to drag his feet on that, just like he had been dragging his feet about the generator. He felt that rather than a flood wall, we should tear down and rebuild the water plant on higher ground. This of course would cost millions, and I knew from my previous research that a grant would only pay 25%. Plus, the plant was nearly at the top of the incline anyway, so moving it would only add about five more feet of elevation. It seemed much more logical to simply build a wall around the plant. But, with Ron delaying the paperwork, I had no idea what would come of this.

Ed Quentin jokingly said, "I think we should seize that farmer's property to the east!"

Sharon didn't know it was a joke, replying, "Yeah, let's eminent domain that guy! Problem solved!"

I simply replied, "No."

The plan to get water to that rural subdivision wasn't looking good. The responses to the mailed letters were minimal. A handful of residents had been calling me and begging me to make it happen. But if only a handful of houses were interested, there was just no way. We would continue to try, but this plan was now on life support.

I was able to celebrate though. Agnes and Margie had finally completed the sorting and destruction of all the old documents that had been in the Village Hall attic. For decades, totes and totes of old files and documents were thrown up there without a concern for organization or the structural integrity of the building. Finally, this was no longer an issue. I instructed Rhonda and Kara that any documents that now went up there needed to be thoroughly organized and labeled. I would make sure this would never be allowed to happen again.

My victory lap continued as Johnny Lynch and Ed Quentin had each completed their big tasks as well. Ever since Johnny had finished comparing the employee handbook with the ordinance book, he was working with Ed to get the electronic ordinances online. If you remember, Reggie Phillips wouldn't give up the electronic version of these documents, keeping them to himself like they were Heaven's Gate cult handbooks. Ed scanned the entire ordinance book, one page at a time, to create our own electronic version. He then adjusted those PDF files into Word documents. In the meantime, he had sent the PDF versions to Johnny, who would get them uploaded onto the town website. After all of their hard work, we now had an entire ordinance book in Word version, and the entire ordinance book on the website. As time went on, someone representing the town would simply need to change out a page here and there to keep it updated. The Word versions would assist our town's future boards for decades to come. Likewise, the online PDFs would serve as an easy reference point for the people of the town for decades.

I told the group that the Green family had started their drama again. They were once again parking the commercial equipment and dumping chemicals in their yard. Reggie suggested I reach out to him at his law office to talk privately about what could be done. He said he had an idea, but that it was important that nothing got back to the Greens. I was curious, and couldn't wait to see what he had come up with. If anything, I love a good scheme, especially from an old attorney!

The debate of the night then began. Our fire department had asked if we would donate toward the purchase of insulated diving suits, so that they would have them available in the event that they ever had to get into the cold Sangamon River waters again. They asked for $2,200 to pay for the suits and a gigantic chain saw, which would be used to help cut up large pieces of trees after a disaster. Now, the fire department also received a $10,000 donation from that elderly man that passed, which they put toward the down payment of a new fire truck. They were asking us to give up part of our donation to help them even more. Some of the board felt that our money was ours, and the fire department was responsible for their own money. On the other hand, they were asking for money for items that would help them help us, which they didn't really have to do in the first place. The fire department didn't have to help stop river waters, and likewise they didn't have to help clean up debris from a tornado. The debate rolled on for an hour! Finally, Agnes Cobb made the motion to donate $2,200, with Margie Baggio giving the second. Ed Quentin voted in favor of the donation. The remaining three trustees,

Johnny Lynch, Sharon Yount, and Kyle Langley, voted no. It was interesting that the older trustees wanted to help the fire department, while the younger trustees didn't. With a 3-3 tie, it was up to me to cast the vote.

"As the shrink says, 'Help me help you,'" joked Ed.

Johnny Lynch countered, saying, "When do they stop asking our Village for money? Will they come back later like Oliver Twist" – (doing a child's voice) – "'Please sir, I want some more'?"

To this day I still don't know if I made the right vote. But I considered that the department is made up of volunteers, who risk their lives and don't have to. They were asking us to fund gear that would be used for tasks that had nothing to do with fire or medical emergency, it was simply to go above and beyond. The department was motivated, cleaning up their section of the building, willingly painting and improving the look of the building. I felt there was no reason to turn away from all of these efforts, so I agreed to make the donation.

Sharon Yount brushed back her hair and adjusted her smudged glasses. She then asked what the plans were for the remaining donated money, because she thought it would be great to put an electronic sign at the town entrance. With the cat now out of the bag, I was in agreement.

The usually silent Kyle Langley joked, "Does the dollar store sell LED signs? Asking for a friend."

I had previously secretly increased the budget line for the sign to $15,000, and adding the remaining $7,300 of donation funds, we had enough money to buy a sign big enough to make Times Square jealous. I agreed to come back to a future meeting with some samples and pricing. I couldn't get a read on who might be interested, but with Sharon Yount behind it,

I had my work cut out for me. I was going to have to hope for Ron Butcher to get vocal when it was time to vote. Meeting adjourned.

***

In mid-April, I stopped by the Hall early one afternoon on my way back from a comedy tour. Will Baggio had recently been deployed as part of his role with the National Guard. I wanted to see how the guys were doing without him. The utility truck was locked in the garage and all the lights were out. No sign of Merf or Dan Jones anywhere. It was obvious what happened – they snuck out early. I didn't tell anyone that I had discovered this, because I didn't want anything to leak back to Merf and Dan. I stopped by the Hall the next morning while they were still sitting around sipping coffee.

"What time did you guys leave yesterday?" I asked.

"Four o'clock. Same as every day," Merf said, as he tugged on his trademark ball cap.

"That's funny. I stopped by City Hall at 1:30 and everything was shut down. Why would that be?"

"DO YOU KNOW WHAT TIME WE STARTED?!"

"No. That's why I asked."

"It was earlier than usual!"

I had to at least hear him out, because I had given the crew permission to start early if they wanted to leave early, so long as they were still putting in a full eight-hour day. However, I suspected it was a lie because I had previously recognized Merf's penchant for sneaking out early. Plus, I considered that he said he worked until 4:00, then when I questioned him, he implied that they left early because they started early. If that was truly the case, why would he have said he worked until 4:00? On top of that, I looked at family friend Dan Jones, who sat with his head down, both hands rubbing his shaved head, looking quite disappointed and uncomfortable. I was about to earn my detective badge.

I responded, "If you left at 1:30, that's two and a half hours early. You normally start at 7:00, so you're telling me you started yesterday morning at 4:30 a.m.?"

"No. Not that early," he said.

"Then you stole time."

"That's not stealing."

"Yes. That's stealing time."

"No, stealing is what I did with that gas can last week!"

I ignored the comment and told them that they would have to use vacation time for the time that they skipped out at the end of the day, and that the next time it happened I would dock their pay. I told them if their weekly timesheet wasn't accurate, that was cause for discipline, including termination. I left, leaving Dan with his head down, and Merf with a blank, angry stare, mouth agape. I had enough and hoped the message was received.

As I walked away, I heard Merf yell from down the hall, "Stalin!"

I returned back, "What did you say?"

"Oh, um, I said, uh, 'We're not stalling, we're on it.'"

The next week, the timesheets were turned in, accurately claiming vacation time for the time skipped out. After looking those over, I stopped by the school and chatted with the board president and the superintendent about the TIF district possibility. They were understandably concerned about losing tax money but were willing to listen. I told them that as Benny

Fowler suggested, I wanted to at least give them a heads up, and not let something so significant come as a surprise to them.

By this time, I was aware that Sharon Yount's father, Greg Emerson, was planning to sell his large property to Benny Fowler. Benny asked me not to share that information, again, because if any of this leaked, the angry pitchfork-carrying mob would come out! So as the two school representatives pressured me to know what area, I just told them it would be developed into around a 40-50 house subdivision. Benny had already shared the blueprints of the development with me and I was excited. After learning that many people could be coming to Dawson, and that I didn't plan to create a very large TIF district, they gave their nod of approval. Next up was the long, drawn-out paperwork and negotiations. With two small units of government involved, a snail would be moving faster.

***

I got an interesting email message from someone who complained that I refused to repair the potholes in the alley behind her house.

"The weather is nice, the potholes are terrible, so there's no reason for you to be refusing to do this," she wrote.

I called her and said that I had already planned for the potholes to be repaired in the coming weeks, and wasn't sure where she was getting her information.

"That's what Merf told me," she replied.

"I'll see what I can do."

I had upset Merf enough that he was now significantly lying about me to the townspeople. But, I had bigger problems at the moment.

The Greens seemed to start back up with their taunting efforts. Any time one of them drove by, they waved a middle finger at me. The teenage daughter, Cassie, wasn't yet old enough to drive. But even when she walked by, she waived a middle finger my way. Whoever it was, I would just smile and wave back. I called our attorney Reggie Phillips as he requested, and he said he had finally completed his research and thought he might know how to end the problem. He suggested I go to the county building and file a request on behalf of the town, which essentially worked like a restraining order. It would ban the Greens from any of the town's properties and also restrict them from being near any town officials.

I wasted no time and went to the county building right away. You wouldn't be surprised to know that at a government building, no one wanted to help me! One by one, each office I entered said that I needed to talk to another office. After going to five different offices, I was about to give up. I decided as I approached the last window, if I was passed along again, I would just leave. After explaining the situation, the lady at the counter again passed me on.

She caught my attention when she said, "Roman Green is causing all this trouble? We know him very well around here. I'd suggest you go talk to his probation officer; he sits right down the hall."

It wasn't my original intention, but I was certainly willing to give this a shot. The probation officer listened to everything I had to say. I told him about the middle fingers, the waved guns, the attempted fights, the dune buggy, vandalism, the day they lured me to the house with their guns ready, everything. This guy looked stunned. He told me that Roman had a probation hearing next week, and that he would present this information to the judge. He'd keep me filled in as to what happened.

I called Reggie Phillips to tell him what happened. "You talked to his probation officer?! It's over! It's done, Jeremy! It is done!" He then yelled a bunch of celebratory swear words that would make a sailor uncomfortable! I'd never heard Reggie so much as say something minutely offensive, so this series of swears really proved just how frustrated the elderly attorney had become also. Did I really win? I had no idea, but I couldn't wait to find out.

My joy was deflated when I received a phone call from Alvin Wilson, an old man who had lived in the town for decades.

"Why are the cars driving so fast?" he asked.

"What do you mean?" I said.

"The cars are so fast in our town, I'm concerned. My hand-me-down Model T never went nearly this fast."

"Are you complaining about a certain driver?"

"No. Cars these days are fast! My Model T never went that fast!"

"That's because you couldn't," I joked, realizing this man hadn't been outside in 80 years. *"I'll see what I can do."*

CHAPTER 14

PUT THE 'IRE" IN "RETIREMENT"

It was May 2016 when we met again. This time, we only had three trustees in the room. Ed Quentin, Sharon Yount, and Kyle Langley were nowhere to be found. I was excited because we had finally completed everything requested by Congressman LaHood's office to get moving on a grant for the flood wall. I was thrilled that Ron Butcher finally helped out. My only concern was that it could take a full year before we got any type of grant approval. If it was a full year, that put things at May 2017, when a new mayor would potentially take over the town, and could potentially take the credit for the work. I was still undecided on reelection, but after all the small-town complaints, dealing with the Greens, and dealing with Merf, I was now feeling like I was ready to be done. Someone else could deal with it. I felt I was doing a lot of good, but the past couple months really flipped my thinking. I still had time to decide, but at this point, I was about 90% sure I was done. But, as Ed Quentin often said, "It ain't over until my mother-in-law sings."

Ron Butcher, Merf, and Dan Jones had recently taken a little more aggressive approach to gauging interest of those rural subdivision residents wanting water. We had done mailers but didn't get much response. This month, Ron asked me to create a brief flyer to be distributed door to door. The three guys dropped off the flyers, door to door, to all 45 or so houses that would be impacted. The flyer required a phone call to the Village office to state whether or not the homeowner was interested. At the board meeting this night, Ron announced that only six people had responded and only one was interested. I officially declared this plan dead. I called Ed Quentin and told him the news, to which he responded, "I guess my mother-in-law is singing."

I could see the disappointment on Ron's face. He really thought this would be great and I did too. I told Ron that maybe in time we can revisit it. Ron responded, "I don't have that much time." I moved on to the next topic, acting like he was joking, but I knew he was right. His health had gotten noticeably worse. He had just been diagnosed with lung cancer and the chemotherapy was wiping him out. He started traveling with oxygen hooked to his nose wherever he went. As much as I was worried about Ron, I was worried about how we'd operate the water plant without him. Ron was the only licensed operator. Merf had worked alongside him for years, but had never been able to get the license. With Merf retiring soon, I knew he'd help out if we needed him, but that didn't solve the problem of being required to have a licensed operator running things.

I changed the subject, celebrating the fact that the water tower painting was finally completed amid the string of nice weather we'd been having. Johnny Lynch quickly cut me off, saying, "Speaking of nice things, I think we should really reconsider not making a donation to the Tri-City Library Trivia Night Fundraiser." He rubbed his buzz-cut head as he continued, "We're the only of the three towns that didn't give anything." I had brought up making a donation a few months ago but the board wasn't interested. I agreed with Johnny, though, saying that the board would need to vote to approve it. With only Agnes Cobb and Margie Baggio in attendance, I had a feeling I knew where this would go.

"They operate on their own tax money. We operate on ours," Agnes said, staring right at Margie.

"That's right," Margie said, staring straight back at Agnes. They still regularly voted the same, being part of the same elder generation. Johnny shook his head, knowing it wasn't going to happen.

Under his breath, Johnny said, "I guess there's no convincing the Golden Girls."

The storm siren at the park had been repaired with the insurance money, so things were looking up. We would be able to add the Spaulding storm siren to the east side of town after all. The sewer commission was still on board and the siren was finally installed shortly thereafter.

I had finally completed a deal with Sheriff Wes Barr to help us launch the Neighborhood Watch program. Honestly, it was still largely to put more eyes on the Green family, especially Roman. The amount of break-ins to cars, sheds, and garages seemed to be increasing, and someone fitting Roman's description seemed to always be noticed fleeing the scene. With the help of the sheriff, I thought we could slow things down a bit. And knowing that the media wouldn't miss the opportunity to film the popular sheriff helping out this lowly little town, we were going to get more free press. Of course, Agnes Cobb didn't see it that way.

"You think it's a good idea to make it known to the public that my town doesn't have cops?" she said.

"I think it's a good idea to make it known to the public that the people of this town are watching," I responded.

"Those late-night gangsters watch the news and look for places to rob!"

"You really think gangsters are watching the news to figure out where they can rob that night?"

"Oh yeah! That's how they roll!"

I laughed out loud after a woman in her eighties used the phrase "That's how they roll."

Margie Baggio soon jumped in to help her friend, saying, "It's no laughing matter. Those highway robbers will getcha! I don't need John Dillinger in this town!"

I replied, "The watch is going to happen, whether you like it or not. Plus, there are enough guns hidden in houses around here to fight off a small army. The ghost of John Dillinger would have no chance."

Kara Gregory chimed in, saying that the new security cameras at the park weren't helping much with violent crime.

"Violent crime?!" I said concernedly to my old high school peer.

Kara said, "Some young girls were at the park, Cassie Green was one of them, and they were smoking the marijuana."

Margie jumped in, "They're smoking that mary jane at the park?!"

Rhonda yelled, "The devil's lettuce!"

"The wacky tobaccy?!" said Agnes.

Margie said, "Well it's happening! The gangs are taking us over!"

I calmed everyone by saying that smoking marijuana isn't a violent crime, though I understood the concern that teenage girls were doing it at the park. Kara said that a mother and young boy happened to be at the park and noticed the teens, and the mother called the Village Hall to complain.

"I had no idea what to do or what to tell her," said Kara.

"Did you call the police?" I asked.

"No. All I knew was that people were breaking the law! Who would you call when that happens? I told the lady to call you!"

I laughed and said, "Next time you're aware of a crime, it's best to call the police. This is an example of basic guidance that Neighborhood Watch training will give."

I couldn't believe someone in her mid-30s didn't think to just call the police, and instead resorted to the same tactic as the older folks in the town: "Call the mayor. He's supposed to fix it." That lady did call me and leave a voicemail, but it was the day after the "violent" marijuana smoking took place.

I moved the discussion along, saying, "Speaking of the park, I think it's time to fix up the baseball field a little bit." The backstop, which is the fencing behind home plate, had gotten bad. It was quite rusty and curling up at the bottom. The fence along each baseline was doing the same. Coaches and parents were regularly telling us that it was a safety issue, with kids tripping and falling on the fence about every game.

"We better do something! They'll get the tetanus!" Margie said.

Her lifelong friend Agnes added, "If a kid gets that lockjaw, they'll be shutting down our field!"

And with that, the three in attendance agreed to spend a little less than $3,000 to replace the fencing. I then pitched the idea of putting yellow tubing across the top of the outfield fence.

"That way, we aren't just fixing our problems, we are improving and beautifying the field," I said.

Agnes and Margie voted to approve, but Johnny voted against it. I was surprised that someone who was still young enough that his kids played on that field wouldn't want to spend the measly $500 to upgrade it. But nonetheless, with my vote, the bright yellow tubing was on the way. Johnny would later tell me he liked the idea, but voted against me again just because he still worried that it looked like he voted along with everything I wanted.

We talked a little more about getting that brand new sign at the town entrance.

Ron Butcher removed his oxygen hose briefly and shouted, "We need a sign so big they can see it from space!"

Everyone else laughed, but it was clear Ron was serious. The three board members weren't quite sure if they wanted to spend the extra money for a big fancy LED sign or be conservative and have a basic, amber lit sign. We had time to sort it out.

Either way, I had recently talked to the local grain elevator operator about allowing us to put a new sign on their property at the main corridor. The operator told me that the town just put the flashing arrow there one day, without so much as asking.

He then said, "And a few days later, those jerks at Mr. Ribeye followed suit and dumped their junky arrow right next to it!"

I told him I wanted to clean up the entrance and I needed his approval to make it happen. He agreed, saying the only condition was to fix "that," as he pointed up. I looked, and an orange extension cord had been attached to the top of the street light, dangling down all the way to the arrow sign, as the duct taped wire dangled in the wind.

I laughed and said, "Yes, we're going to fix that."

I relayed this story to the board and mentioned the need to create an ordinance restricting flashing arrows to the property of that business. I was met with three nodding heads, but no real acknowledgment. I looked at the clock and it was already 10 p.m. We had been at it for three hours, so it was time to go. Meeting adjourned.

***

Just a few days later I got a call from the lady that lives on the south side of the Green family. She had noticed, like me, that it seemed like they had removed and packed up a few things here and there.

"Are they moving?" she asked.

I didn't know, but I was keeping an eye on it. She went on to tell me that a large tree in front of her house, in the Village right-of-way, was leaning badly and might fall over soon. Several other people had started mentioning this, so it was already on my to-do list, which is what I told her.

She added, "I told Merf, and he told me you said you weren't going to do anything because you didn't like me."

"I never said that. We're working on it," I responded.

"Thank you. Please come over and join me for a butter-scotch anytime."

"I'll see what I can do."

I called Merf later because I wanted to have him start spraying the mosquito repellent.

"DID YOU GO OVER MY HEAD?!" he yelled through the phone.

"No. What are you talking about?" I asked.

"You told that lady you'd cut that tree down!"

"I said that because we need to cut it down. Why'd you tell her I said otherwise?"

"Because we don't need to! Just like those potholes in the alley! You never should have fixed those!"

"First, I make the decisions, not you. And I don't need you speaking on my behalf."

"I do the work!"

"I think you use the word 'work' pretty loosely. Speaking of, when are you going to do the first spray for mosquitoes?"

"I didn't get licensed."

"I asked you to get licensed and you said you would."

"Nope. Not doing it. There's too much bull going on around here and I'm just not doing it."

"Do we need to sit and talk?"

"There's nothing to talk about. I'm not getting a license."

"So just to be clear, I'm your boss, and I'm telling you to do this, and you're saying no."

"That's right."

"I guess that's all I need to know too. I'll have to figure out how we're spraying for mosquitoes."

"You're supposed to be the smart one. Figure it out, Wonder-Boy."

"I'm not going to let you talk to me like that, and I still don't know why you're mad."

"You never gave me a raise!"

"We're talking about raises in the near future, but you said very clearly that you didn't want a raise."

"I never said that. Here goes the blender mixing my words again!"

"You told me that directly and you told the entire Town Board at a meeting a few months ago."

"I've said all I need to say to you, Castro."

We ended the call and my next call was to Reggie Phillips. I wanted to gather his thoughts on terminating Merf or at least suspending him until his retirement date. Merf was retiring very soon so I needed to tread lightly. Likewise, I wanted to keep him away from the staff. With two fairly new full-timers, I didn't want them to pick up Merf's bad habits.

Reggie said, "Jeremy, he retires in less than two months. If you do anything significant, he'll sue us for discrimination, based on his age or heart condition. I trust him as far as I can throw him, and that's not very far! I'd suggest you ride it out."

"But he's endangering the public's health, he's being quite disrespectful, and he's insubordinate," I argued.

"You can ride out these two months, or deal with him and a lawsuit for another year. I really think you should let it be."

Reggie was right. I had to swallow my pride and let Merf run rampant for the final two months.

My next call was to Riverton Mayor Red Tomko. On that call, we worked out an intergovernmental agreement to have their crew do the mosquito spraying for Dawson. All it took was our board's approval next month, and Riverton's board approval the following week, which was approved unanimously. Two days after Riverton's board approved, Merf called.

"I heard you're having Riverton do the spraying," he said.

"That's right. I worked out an agreement since you didn't get licensed," I responded.

"They can't do that."

"Why not?"

"If I'm not doing it, no one can do it. I AM this town!"

"It's going to be Riverton's crew doing the work now."

"What if I get licensed?"

"Then I'd be happy to have you spray."

"Good. I heard about this and got my license this afternoon."

"So you didn't want to get licensed because you hoped to make me look bad?"

"Oh no, not at all. I'm not like that."

Clearly, that was the plan. And once again, this Wonder-Boy wins.

***

Later in the month, I got word from Roman Green's probation officer that the judge hearing Roman's case was not happy with him at all and came down hard. Roman's probation was extended. Not only that, but none of the four members of his family was allowed on any Village-owned property ever again: the park, the Village Hall, the water plant, you name it. The judge referred to the Green family as a disgrace to Illinois. That's saying something! On top of that, the judge ordered the family to move out of the town immediately! I thanked the probation officer for his time, then celebrated with my wife in the living room like we had just won the Super Bowl.

***

I came back from a comedy tour a few days later and there were cars parked at the Village Hall, right in front of the no parking signs I had recently put up. I typed up a warning note on the town letterhead, stating that they would be towed if they did it again. Not long after, I got a call from the owner of Mr. Ribeye.

"Why are you running off my customers?! Are you trying to put me out of business?!" she said.

"I'm not trying to put anyone out of business. You bring the town revenue. That would make no sense."

"Then why did you put warning letters on their vehicles?"

"I had a right to tow them but I gave them warnings instead. We have to have those spaces open for the firemen."

"That's bogus. I know you play favorites because that gray van has been parked there for weeks!"

"That van belongs to the fire department."

"You're saying that they can park there but my patrons can't?"

"That's right."

"Your sign says the parking is for the Village Hall!"

"Correct. The firehouse is in the Village Hall."

"Uh–Well–I just–"

"I think we're done here, buh-bye."

As I hung up, she screamed, "Evil dictator!"

It felt great to not try to play the nice guy and smooth things over. To just let things out and speak the truth was quite a freeing experience. I knew then that I for sure wouldn't run for reelection. Someone else could handle all of this and I was going to enjoy the ride to May 2017. The next time Merf or the

Mr. Ribeye owner called me a Communist, I knew I could tell them they were wrong. A Communist wouldn't willfully give up their power!

***

It was June 6 when we met again, this time with every board member present. My first order of business was to get approval to cut down that tree that had been leaning. Merf had insisted it didn't need to be cut down, but the board unanimously agreed that it did. With their approval, it was taken down the next week. Sorry, Merf!

Next up was the discussion on purchasing a new sign for the town entrance. I was stunned when the board, without hesitation, approved the purchase of a four-foot by seven-foot, full-color, LED sign board. It took me more than three years, but my goal was finally met. We were going to beautify and upgrade this old town and it didn't matter who agreed. I knew I could lose the old folks' vote come reelection, but I didn't care because I knew I wouldn't run again. The old folks' vote mattered to me as much as any vote in Cuba matters ... not at all.

The only slight pushback was from Agnes Cobb, who aggressively said, "Are you trying to modernize our town?! I'm not sure about this!"

I successfully derailed her argument and got it approved.

Johnny Lynch, as he did last month, pitched the need to donate to the library fundraiser. Like last time, he uncomfortably rubbed his dark buzzed hair, saying, "It looks bad that the other two towns donated $100 and we didn't give anything."

I agreed, again saying that I couldn't just send the money without board approval. Then, something odd happened. Without any further discussion, the board unanimously approved a $100 donation to the library.

Next up, we needed to discuss that most of the zoning board's members had either moved away or died. I needed to fill the entire board, with the exception of Ron Butcher. Ron was a member of the board, but his term had expired. It was my duty to appoint the members of the zoning board with the approval of the Town Board. It is important to note that before the final comprehensive plan's adoption is approved by the Town Board, it is first reviewed and approved by the zoning board. I had just received the finalized version of the plan, so stacking the zoning board in my favor was next on my to-do list. I also knew that if we had the entire zoning board, which is made up of volunteers, unanimously approve the comprehensive plan, it would be very difficult for the Village trustees to vote against it. Knowing that Ron Butcher was in strong support of the plan, I reappointed him. I also added a local tree-trimming business owner, Zach Bloomfield, who had just done some work for me and was about my age. We had chatted previously and he was in agreement with my plans for the town.

My lifelong friend, Matt Butler, had left the town years ago. But his mother, who watched me grow up, was still there. She'd be the third appointee. I still had four more people to appoint, but I didn't want to make it obvious that I was stacking the deck like a Vegas card shark, so I postponed the next four until July's meeting.

Although Merf had acquired his mosquito license, I wasn't about to trust him to be willing to spray throughout the entire summer. I told the full story to the board and made sure it was in the meeting minutes so the people of our town would know. I wanted the Riverton agreement in place to cover our bases.

Ed Quentin added, "Merf seems to be about as reliable as a $50 Ford Tempo."

The board members nodded in approval, and the intergovernmental agreement was passed unanimously. We'd only call Riverton if we needed them, but I at least had this as a backup plan in case Merf threw another tantrum.

I then pitched the idea of a town improvement contest. We would award prizes of $150, $100, and $50 to the homes that made the best improvements, whether landscaping, displays, exterior home repairs, you name it. I thought at the very least, we'd essentially be bribing a handful of homeowners to clean things up. With my goal to improve the town's appearance, I thought this was a simple way to do it. I also realized that if people wouldn't clean up their property even if we were paying them, it just wasn't going to happen.

Agnes Cobb said, "If they want to clean up their property they will! You don't need to bribe people. It's their right to do what they want with their property! That's how it works in our town 'cause that's how it works in the good ol' U.S. of A!"

I agreed with her, but also discussed my views and goals of the town beautification. I knew why Agnes was vocal, and so did everyone else. Johnny Lynch and Ed Quentin both smirked and looked at me out of the corner of their eyes. Sharon Yount's property was the worst looking in town. Agnes Cobb's was probably the second worst. When I had to go after someone for not keeping up their property, the first thing they would do is point out Sharon Yount's yard, saying that if a board member's house looks the way it does, I have no right to address anyone else's house. If they weren't pointing out Sharon's house, they were sure to point out Agnes Cobb's. No more discussion was needed, and the proposition passed 5-1, with Agnes being the lone holdout.

We finally had a clear picture of our financial future. Since things had finally become clear, I proposed we get the staff the raises that I felt were overdue. Agnes asked if we should consider a raise for Merf, even though he would be retiring at the end of the month. I reminded her that he said we should not give him a raise. I suggested that the funds that we could have given to him should go to the rest of the staff. The board agreed, remembering Merf's words, and unanimously approved raises for all staff, effective July 1. Merf would be retiring June 30, so he'd be left out. It was 10 p.m. and I had once again had enough. Meeting adjourned.

***

The coming days and weeks were extremely busy. The next week, Sheriff Wes Barr came to the town to host the Neighborhood Watch launch meeting. We had about 50 people in attendance, which I think would be considered a success in a town of 500. The sheriff explained how the program would work and then went on to take questions. With grace, he handled questions such as, "How fast should a four-wheeler be going before we call you?," "Can we report someone that slows down at a stop sign but doesn't completely stop?," and "If my neighbor's dog comes on to my property, am I allowed to shoot it?" I was so impressed with the sheriff and so was the local media. With a clever press release, I drew quite a lot of media attention, including a live interview for both myself and the sheriff on the local TV news station. I found it odd that several people at the event were asking me why Merf didn't get a raise. I responded to each of them saying that I couldn't discuss these things, but in short, Merf requested that we divert the raise funds for him and give them to the other staff. "That's not what he said" was a common response.

I was also stopped by someone at the event who said she was disappointed that I didn't do more to make people aware that the town had recently been under a boil order.

"I didn't even know about the boil order until I saw that it was lifted! I could've got AIDS!" she said.

"That wouldn't give you AIDS. And we did announce it on both TV and the radio," I replied.

"I don't watch TV and I don't listen to the radio."

"It was in the newspaper."

"I don't read the paper."

"It was in the town newsletter."

"I don't read that."

"It was on the town website and Facebook page."

"I don't read those either."

"It was on the sign at the town entrance."

"I don't drive that road."

"I can't help you if you live under a rock. Have a nice day!"

Once again, it was so freeing to just speak the truth. She looked at me like I was crazy. The only thing that made me crazy was running for mayor in the first place!

Shortly after, I called Merf to discuss plans for his upcoming retirement and clear up any financial confusion.

"Why didn't I get a raise?" he asked.

"You made it clear that you didn't want one and told us to give the money to the new staff," I responded.

"Whatever, Jeremy. You know I changed my mind last week," he said.

"You change your mind so often, I don't know what to think."

"That's what I tell my wife!" Merf joked.

I went on to discuss plans for a retirement party for him. I would be out of town for a couple of weeks on a comedy tour, so I wouldn't be around until his final day on the job. I suggested that we have a party in the office with our entire staff, including the part-timers, as well as Merf's wife. I told him to order any food they wanted and for the group to take their time during lunch. Merf was very thankful, adding that his family would be hosting a party at his house that would be open to the public as well. I offered to hold a public party for him and invite all the people of the town to the park for a big gathering.

"No. I think two parties is plenty. Having a third seems a bit much," he said.

I knew Dan Jones was nearby, because I heard Merf ask him, "What do you think, Dan? Isn't a third party a bit much for me?"

"Have you ever been shy about receiving accolades?" Dan responded.

Merf laughed, then told me he was thankful that I offered, but felt two parties was plenty.

***

The following Saturday, I was mowing grass as I noticed a large U-Haul in the Green family's drive. They were moving! I couldn't believe it. They were finishing packing up as I finished mowing. The U-Haul drove by, followed by a truck driven by Ryan Green, and another one driven by Roman. As they drove past, Ryan sternly waved his middle finger at me one last time. I smiled and waved goodbye as I rode my mower. As Roman drove by, he waved his gun at me. It wasn't pointed; he just waived it in the air, and kept driving. Since I didn't anticipate him trying to shoot me, and knowing that even if he did I had nowhere to run, I blew him a kiss as I rode on my mower. It seemed this nightmare was finally over.

***

With the town improvement contest going on, I was able to get some free press out of it. With the recent media coverage, I was thinking that my goal of making people in the surrounding area aware of Dawson was nearly met. The local newspaper interviewed me about the idea, came to the town and took photos, and even interviewed some locals. The story was printed on the first page of the local news section ... above the fold!

I got back into town late on June 29, and made it a point to be at the office early the next morning to greet Merf on his final day. I felt it was my duty as a good boss to be there, and at least try to wish him well and smooth things over on his final day. I had a really nice plaque made for him that read something like, "ON BEHALF OF A GRATEFUL COMMUNITY, THIS PLAQUE IS PRESENTED TO BILL MURPHY IN APPRECIATION OF 38 YEARS OF SERVICE." I wanted to do more for him, but now I understood why the same gift was given to Mayor Carl Donaldson. With our budget, there wasn't much more that could be done, aside from throwing the staff party, and hosting a public party, which he had declined. On that morning I said the same to him. I also told him that I wished to bury the hatchet. I added that he and I both cared about the town deeply and we seemed to butt heads simply because we were passionate about our views.

Merf's response was quite odd, saying, "Thanks. This plaque means a lot. And I agree, we can forget the past and move forward. But you and I both know that this should have been presented to me at the board meeting. You didn't do that; you gave it to me here on my last day. And at the very least, you could have given me a small parade, which wouldn't have cost much. This was one final jab as you push me out the door and let it hit me in the backside!"

"Is that really how you feel?" I said.

"Yes! I think you threw me out like an unwanted piece of meat, but we can move on if you want."

"I'm a bit perplexed, but yes, let's move on. Why don't you spend the morning packing up your things and take it easy. Once you've got things gathered up, go ahead and take the rest of the day off with pay."

"Wow, that's awful nice, thanks."

"We appreciate you. Are you sure you don't want me to throw you a public party at the park?"

"No, no, you've done plenty."

"By the way, I heard you're thinking about running for mayor."

"It's nothing personal. It's just something I've always thought about and wanted to do. I just have to weigh out whether I can handle all the stress with my age and heart condition."

"I'm not running for reelection. I haven't told many people, but I'm done. And just so you know, it's the most stressful thing I've ever encountered. You can't comprehend it until you experience it."

"How do I know you're not trying to talk me out of it so you can run unopposed?"

"I'm telling you the truth. That's all I can say."

We ended our conversation as he talked about looking forward to having lunches with his grandkids at the local Subway. I felt good that maybe things were finally cleared up with Merf. Dealing with Merf was finally behind me, as was dealing with the Greens. Once the upcoming fireworks extravaganza concluded, I could breathe easy for my final 10 months, and maybe be lucky enough to finish up my projects and goals.

***

In the previous three years, I never had to make a decision whether to cancel the fireworks. In a way, it wasn't really my call because the Town Team was running the event, not the Village. As we approached July 3, it rained and rained for days in a row. The sun came out early on July 3, but storms were in the forecast for that night. Rhonda Brown, being the leader of the group, even though she insists they have no leader, called me and asked my thoughts. I told her it was all a Town Team event, and the Town Team's money that was spent on the fireworks. It was entirely up to that group. I suggested delaying the event for about 30 minutes to get a better idea of what direction the approaching storm would go, since it was looking like it may go around us. About two hours before the event was to start, Rhonda canceled and rescheduled for July 6. You're not going to believe this, but the pitchforks came out!

Several locals complained on Facebook, saying the mayor made a terrible decision. I was stunned that they didn't realize I had nothing to do with it. To help clarify, and also give some backup to Rhonda and the Town Team, I responded to the group complaints.

I wrote, "The fireworks event is run by the Town Team and is in no way affiliated with the Village. I was not a part of the decision to cancel the event, though I understand why it was done."

I thought that would clear things up, but instead I saw a post from Rhonda saying, "I was also disappointed that the mayor canceled the event, but he has the power to do it."

I immediately called Rhonda and she said, "I've been telling every person that calls that you were the one that canceled. I'm not willing to take the heat for this! But really, we had to cancel. Even if the rain held off, we've got three days' worth of water on that park grass, it's just a swamp down there. But yes, I'm not letting the people get after me for this! It's your job to take it!"

***

As we approached the July meeting, I was getting all sorts of calls and emails from people complaining that there was no public retirement party held for Merf.

"He insisted that the staff party and his family party were plenty, and he didn't want a third," I would reply.

"That's not what he told me," was the common response.

It all felt a little odd, but I pushed forward at the July meeting. Kyle Langley was the only trustee missing this time. Ron Butcher's health was really declining and forced him to stay home that night. I was proud of myself for sprucing up the room. I had swung by the local party store and picked up some discounted patriotic bunting to display, right in front of the head of the U-shaped tables. It really did help brighten up the drab room, which could have easily doubled as an abandoned haunted house.

As I sat down, Rhonda leaned in and whispered, "You know Merf isn't very happy that you bought the bunting with our Village funds. He says it's a tacky waste of money."

I was curious how Merf even knew, since he was retired and would only be coming to the office once a month to prepare for mosquito spraying. But nonetheless, it was time to start the meeting.

It was my time to appoint the remaining four members of the zoning board. If the Town Board approved them, I really knew I had stacked the deck in my favor to get the comprehensive plan approved. I first started with Candy Lipton. Candy had been a trustee at one point and was regularly active in town volunteer opportunities. She was part of the old guard, but from my talks with her, she was in favor of planning a future with needed changes for improvement. Similar was Sharon Yount's father, Greg Emerson. Greg was already a member of the zoning board; his term had simply expired. If you recall, Greg was the mayor at one time many years ago and was still part of the old guard. However, from my talks with Sharon, Greg had the same feelings that Candy did. Without making it too obvious that I was stacking the board,

I thought these were two good picks. My final two picks were Johnny Lynch's wife, Renee, and my wife, Sandra. I had talked to Renee and Sandra about the idea at one of our recurring game nights, and both were willing. Obviously the two of them were in favor of making changes for the future, which Johnny and I both agreed to as well. To my surprise, there was no pushback or debate at all, and the board approved the appointments unanimously. Maybe I could be a Vegas card shark after all.

As we moved on, for the official record I thanked Merf for his years of service to the town. Ed Quentin asked if we would be throwing a retirement party for him. I spoke clearly, knowing my statement would be in the public meeting minutes, saying that we gave Merf a staff party which was open to the public, and Merf's family was also giving him a party. I went on to say that Merf said he felt a third party would be a bit much.

"Merf told me that he was disappointed that we didn't give him a third retirement party," said Agnes Cobb, looking toward her peer Margie Baggio for approval.

"He's telling me something different, so I'll call him and check," I replied.

Johnny Lynch, not knowing the full story, joked, "What else can we do? Throw this guy a parade?"

I ignored the question and moved on. The last item of business was that Ron Butcher had asked me to bring up hiring a licensed water operator to work under him. Our new employees just didn't seem to be willing to try to get licensed, even with those nice salary incentives to do so. Ron had told me that he'd work as long as he could, but he just didn't know how much longer he could do it. I had previously talked to

Max Woodrum, the water works consultant, who was licensed and willing to run the plant until we could make a long-term hire. The only problem was that Max just informed us he was moving to Ohio.

"I guess we need a plan C," said Ed, "but you've found your way to a plan Z before." He directed his eyes and nodded his head toward Sharon, reminding me just how many people declined before I was stuck appointing her.

If we could hire someone who was already licensed, we'd be able to get by if something abruptly happened to Ron. The other option involved the nearby town of Illiopolis; it had been working with a water coop wanting to create a large partnership among several nearby towns. In that scenario, we'd essentially be giving up control of our water system, and the 80% of our income that came with it. If we went that route, we'd also probably only have room for one full-time employee if we were lucky. I had privately told Will Baggio and Dan Jones that as long as I was mayor, I wouldn't let it happen. We could contract with a company to run the plant for us, but the labor involved with the plant would largely fall on Will and Dan, who were still very new to the water system. We'd have to start the candidate search, but I had no idea if we'd be able to lure someone away by offering less money and benefits. And with this stingy board, I doubted they'd be willing to change that.

Ed leaned in and said, "This is your mission, should you choose to accept it."

Meeting adjourned.

***

I called Merf and asked about all these rumors I was hearing that he was disappointed he didn't get a third retirement party.

"That would have been awful nice of you to do," he said.

"Why didn't you just say that then?" I asked.

"You should have known what I wanted."

"It's not too late. I can make it happen this weekend."

"It's too late now. What's done is done."

"It's not too late. I can get this done for you."

"I don't want a third party. You can swing by the party at my house in a couple weeks. It'll be my only party."

"It's not your only party. You had the staff party that was open to the public also."

"I know, Jeremy, but this is what you wanted."

"Merf, I just want to send you off happy."

"I AM HAPPY!" he yelled into the phone.

It was yet another odd call with Merf, but at least my interactions with him would soon be over. When the day came for the party at his house, I took my dad along. I did it for two reasons. One, Dad had known Merf for decades and respected him, though the respect had dwindled because of how Merf had treated me. The other reason was that I thought Merf would be a little friendlier with Dad around. With Merf living right across the street from the Village Hall, I made some quick signs to cover up those no parking signs at the Village Hall lot. It read "PARKING FOR MERF'S RETIREMENT PARTY PERMITTED – PER AUTHORITY OF THE MAYOR." With all the visitors I expected Merf to have, it would certainly help. Plus, I didn't need Merf or anyone else complaining that I was somehow restricting his party by not allowing parking nearby.

Not that Merf would take the opportunity to try to make me look bad or anything ...

When we arrived, there were about 20 people present at the garage party, most of whom were Merf's family. Merf walked up and greeted us, as happy as could be. He sat and talked with Dad and me for a good 30 minutes, sharing stories and laughs. In that moment, I really understood just how good Merf was at balancing two different personalities, and why so few people believed my stories about his negative traits. A few more guests arrived, so he excused himself and went to chat with them. I shook a couple hands of other guests, making sure that the residents of the town that happened to be there saw me.

"You ready to go?" Dad whispered. "I think enough people have seen you that he can't say you never showed up. 'Cause you know he would."

I nodded. I dropped into the gift basket a congratulatory card with a $50 Subway gift card enclosed, with a note that read, "Have your next couple lunches with the grandkids on me. Congratulations, Jeremy Nunes."

As Dad and I stepped out of the garage, I waved to Merf. Once we were back in the car, I asked Dad, "How did you know I thought Merf might lie and say I didn't come?"

He replied, "Because I've known him for decades. He can be a great guy and very friendly, but a few people have seen how negative he is with no one around. He'd be a great President!"

A little later I got a phone call from Dan Jones, who was soon to be handling most of Merf's workload.

"A lot of people at Merf's party were saying what a shame it was that you didn't throw him a party from the Village," he said. "Mayor, I heard him tell you, several times, that he didn't want that party. Then he would tell me and Will that he was going to make you look bad and complain that he didn't get the party. He's saying he's gotta do it so you can't beat him in the election. It's terrible that Boa's doing that," he finished, sounding as if he was about to cry.

"Why don't you correct people when they bring it up to you? And who is Boa?" I replied.

"I don't want to get in the middle of it. And if you aren't really running for reelection, he's probably going to be my boss. And we call Merf 'Boa' because he's a snake!" he said laughing.

I couldn't blame him for not getting involved, and I understood. Finally, my suspicions of what was going on with the retirement party fiasco were confirmed.

***

Before we would meet in August, I was doing some yard work and noticed an unfamiliar vehicle parked at the Green's house. I saw a woman going in and out but didn't recognize her. Knowing that the Greens had left, I kept a close eye, but went about my business. I stood in my garage as the vehicle pulled into my driveway. Not knowing what would happen next and sensing that the Greens had finally figured out how to finish me off, I grabbed a pistol I'd been keeping for protection. I kept this gun in my garage in case the Greens approached me outside. I had it locked and loaded, obscuring it from the driver of the vehicle.

A woman, about 45, got out of the car. "You Jeremy Nunes?" she asked.

"Yes," I replied, still ready to pull the trigger.

"I'm the landlord of that house over there," she said, gesturing toward the Green's old place.

"What can I do for you?" I countered.

"I'm just here to apologize. I had no idea how terrible that family had been to you and the town."

"Thanks. We tried to track you down but couldn't figure out who actually owned the property."

"My dad's cousin's estate left it to my brother's niece's uncle's neighbor's son, so I ended up with it."

"I don't understand."

"It's that way to dodge the Feds. Anyways, I just wanted to tell you that now I know the Greens were terrible. They left without paying their last two months' rent. The yard can't even grow grass because there's so much chemical waste there. I just went into the house; they tore out a load-bearing wall! And they plugged the drain in the shower and left the water running! Now the floor is rotted and the basement is flooded! And it looks like they created some sort of gun shooting range in the basement. How they didn't shoot themselves in that tiny basement I'll never know."

"It's unfortunate they didn't get hurt," I joked.

We ended our discussion and she pulled out of the drive. Relieved, I put the pistol away. I couldn't believe just how terrible the Greens were, but the good news is they were now in the past. I'd spend the next month or two looking over my shoulder, but eventually I stopped being concerned. I finally put the guns away and never looked back.

***

The zoning board met to discuss the comprehensive plan on the last Tuesday of July at 7:00 p.m. I didn't attend so that they could talk freely without being concerned with my presence. I'm told the meeting went like this:

Ron Butcher thanked everyone for coming. Then he said, "Did everyone get a chance to read the plan?"

The group all confirmed they had. Though in reality, I'm certain that neither my wife nor Johnny Lynch's wife had actually read it; they just went to vote yes.

"I think this is great for the town. We need to have a plan for sustained growth for both the town and the school," Ron said, adding, "Does everyone agree?"

The group silently nodded in approval.

"Let's vote. Raise your hand if you want to send our approval to the Village Board," he said. All seven hands were raised.

Ron continued, "It's unanimous, so I think we're done here. Candy Lipton made pie. Let's eat!"

And with that, their meeting was closed at 7:03 p.m.

***

Sandra, sitting at our kitchen table, was filling me in on the meeting details at about 7:15 when I got a call from Chad Matthews. Chad was a former college frat boy who was now around 40.

"I just got a ticket on Route 36 for going five over the speed limit!" he yelled.

"Sorry to hear that," I replied.

"Whatever happened to a hometown discount?"

"That would've been a county officer. We don't have police."

"I told him and I'm telling you. My taxes pay your salary, pal!"

"And I appreciate it. Good luck, lead foot," I said as I hung up.

CHAPTER 15

GOOD BUY FOR GOODBYE

When we met on August 1, every trustee was present. It wasn't a surprise that we had full attendance, since we'd be voting on the 20-year comprehensive plan. Rob Dellomo, representing the planning commission, started off the meeting by discussing the generalities of what was in the 20-year plan. After workshopping and studying options, he gave our town the motto of "You're with Friends Here." He went on to remind the board that a comprehensive plan is almost always a requirement to receive a grant, and even if it's not a requirement, your town is given bonus points for having a plan.

"Planning schmanning!" said Agnes Cobb.

"How long is this spanning?" asked Sharon Yount, wearing her Marlboro t-shirt.

Rob Dellomo, serious as can be, replied, "A twenty-year plan is twenty years spanning."

Ed Quentin jumped in, "Peyton Manning tomato canning with Dakota Fanning!" He paused, looked at the stares, and said, "What – I thought we were rhyming!"

I moved things along, saying, "Let's vote before this transcript needs banning."

"Good one," added Ed.

Agnes Cobb voted no, Margie Baggio voted present, and the remaining four voted in approval. I got it done!

Gary Whitcomb, our engineer, had privately told me about his concerns that Ron Butcher's health was getting worse. The only existing maps of our water system were of the original plans. Once additions or revisions were made to the actual water routes, they were never added to any maps. It was simply all kept in Ron's head. Gary urged me to fund new water route maps, because if something happened to Ron, we were in big trouble. We knew Ron wouldn't be high on the idea, and we certainly didn't want to tell him we were concerned that he might die. Our plan was that at this board meeting, I would casually bring it up.

"Gary," I said, "weren't you wanting to draw up some maps of the water system?"

"I forgot to mention," he replied, doing his best academy award level acting job, "I was wondering if we should have those drawn up so we can go for grants soon. It's a new requirement for almost every water grant now."

"Never used to be," said Ron.

"It is now. So we better draw up where the water lines are," Gary replied.

"What's that going to cost? Whatever it is, it's too much!" added Ron.

Gary said, "I'll give you the maps, you draw on there any revisions or changes, and I can get the maps digitized for very minimal cost."

"Okay, that's a fair deal for our town," Ron replied, as he fell into a scary coughing fit.

Speaking of the water system, I was excited that Congressman Lahood's office had reviewed documentation for the flood wall barrier and submitted it to the Army Corps of Engineers. I had some back and forth with them, so the good news is that this was continuing to move forward.

The baseball field had begun to look so good that the board was excited to make more improvements. I knew that if we could just get the ball rolling on improvements, people would recognize it, and join in my viewpoint. After recently approving the backstop fencing, the board now approved replacing the fencing along the dugouts of the ballpark. They even approved having a large American flag display, including landscaping, a spotlight, and an industrial pole to hang it from. We could be accused of many things, but we couldn't be labeled unpatriotic!

The first step in the 20-year plan was improving the sidewalks that were in such bad shape. The main drag that bordered the west end of town was Constant Street. While traffic was largely slow in most of the town, and most people just walked in the road instead of using the sidewalks, that was not the case for Constant Street. It was a county highway that was quite busy, and not safe at all to be walking on. It was necessary to use the sidewalks, which were largely broken or overgrown, and so difficult to navigate that they'd compare to an Army obstacle course! I had planned to divide Constant into two sections and replace the entire northern half. The funding would be set up so that whoever was mayor next year could replace the entire southern half. However, it was incredibly expensive. We only had the funding to replace about a third, rather than half. I made it a point to draw out a map of the worse sidewalks, specifically noting the area right in front of Ed Quentin's house as the worst. If Ed recognized that it would improve his property, that gave me one vote. I just needed two more, because I'd break a 3-3 tie. To my surprise, the board voted unanimously to make the improvement.

As we wrapped up, Ron Butcher made a plea for additional help. He really wanted a licensed operator to learn under him. We had already been discussing this, it was still just so difficult to recruit someone, considering the circumstances. With Merf's retirement, Ron currently only had two workers: Dan Jones and Will Baggio. Historically the crew was limited to only Merf and Ron, with George O'Reilly working part-time, which is a large reason why very few improvements were ever made; only sustaining work was done. With Merf and George both now working part-time, and Dan, Will, and Ron working full-time, we had more laborers than ever. However, our full-timers Dan and Will were still very new, and not experienced enough to get licensed to oversee the health and wellness of an entire community. I told the board I would reach out to other mayors and water coops to gather their input and advice. I'd reach out to the water works training groups as well to see if they had any ideas. But one thing was for sure: we needed to do something and do it fast. Meeting adjourned.

***

To my surprise, Merf continued to happily work part-time. He sprayed for mosquitoes two more times and continued to help the crew read the water meters each month. His attitude seemed to have improved significantly. He was joyful and courteous now that he had retired. Getting away from the Village Hall will relax even the grouchiest of people!

***

Late in the month I got a knock on my door. A very unkempt middle-aged man named Newt Daulton, who I recognized from numerous police run-ins of the past, stood on my porch.

"Them new guys can't put straight lines on the baseball field! They's all crooked!" he said.

"I'm having dinner with my family, but I'll remind the guys to slow down and keep those lines straight," I replied.

"You need to do more than that! You need to fix 'em yourself right now!"

"I can't, and my guys are capable. I'll let them know, thank you," I said as I began to shut the door.

"My tax dollars pay for better!"

"I hardly think you pay your taxes," I said as I closed the door. I thought of that line after the recent complainer said that his taxes pay my salary. I thought, "If I ever get the chance, I'm gonna say that to someone."

***

The leaves were changing as we met in September. Only Kyle Langley was absent. I was excited that the Corps of Engineers, with some urging from Congressman LaHood, approved our plans to build the flood wall. The next step was to secure funding. The next round of grant applications wasn't being accepted until spring, so we would have to wait for now.

I was excited that a big part of fixing our water system would finally be completed. Another big concern was completing those electronic maps of the water system. Ron adjusted his oxygen hose and Cubs baseball cap as he described the work he was doing with Gary Whitcomb. Ron added that as our engineer, Gary would be able to get the maps perfected in electronic form. Luckily, Ron had taken a liking to the idea. My only concern was whether the maps would get done before Ron's health took a turn for the worst. Ron seemed to know it as well, because he again pushed for the hire of a licensed operator to work as his understudy. We had posted vacancies in a couple of the water operator magazines and had drawn very little interest. In fact, one of the comments under the online posting read, "I don't think I want to work for minimum wage in Podunk!" Another read, "This town looks like a real life *Hee Haw.* No thanks." Ron agreed to review any applications we'd receive and assist with interviews, but time was precious.

With the new electronic signage now installed and looking great at the town entrance, some of the older folks in town were a little concerned as to how much money we spent on it. Margie Baggio got a little angry and voiced displeasure as a representative of the greatest generation.

"There's a lot of people in our town, including me, wondering where we got the funds for this fancy new sign. I think you're spending money just willie nillie!" she said.

I reminded her that an elderly man's estate donated a lot of the funding, and we got donations from the local church, the fire department, and the Town Team.

"Plus," I said, "Our entire board voted for the purchase, including you."

"That's right. My bad!" she said, as she laughed and leaned into Ed Quentin for approval. It was fairly common for Margie, whether in the board room or by phone, to disagree with something that she had already approved. And I found it hilarious to hear an elderly woman say, "My bad."

Agnes Cobb chimed in, "I'm concerned that the sign is going to cause an accident. I stopped the car to read all the messages on the sign, and some guy came up behind me and almost rear-ended me!"

"You stopped on the county highway?" I asked.

"Yes! How else would I read it?!" she responded, adding, "You need to do something!"

I told her that we would just limit the sign to two messages and that way no one would be tempted to stop.

Ed said, "I think you should just do nothing and let the chips fall where they may!"

We all had a laugh except Agnes, who stared daggers at Ed across the table. I told the group that I had a meeting with the volunteer block captains for the Neighborhood Watch. The volunteers were excited and thrilled to help. At Sheriff Barr's suggestion, the block captains would meet about every six months, unless things really got out of control. With the board's urging, I agreed that the mayor would serve as the overseer of the program and run the meetings. I didn't really want to, but I also didn't want to look bad if the board felt I should do it, and after all, it was my idea in the first place.

I did find a way to dodge it though, saying, "Since this will be the mayor's project, we might as well extend the next meeting eight months into May. There's no reason for me to guide the program in March, then just a few weeks later a new mayor comes in with new ideas for the program. I'll know by

March if I'm running unopposed, and if so, we can just keep the meeting in March."

The board agreed except Johnny Lynch, who said, "I thought you weren't running for reelection?"

He was right. I had told him privately. His family was still regularly hanging out with my family and we'd become close friends.

"I'm still thinking it over," I replied, staring back and raising my eyebrows to indicate that my decision was still largely a secret.

"Oh, then I agree completely," he said.

I was thrilled to announce that we had finally received yet another grant. We would finally be funded to replace all the old light bulbs throughout all of our facilities and replace them with energy efficient ones. The grant that we had already been awarded was finally going to be financed. Even more of our bulbs and ballasts had become obsolete, so this was going to have to be done eventually anyway. To be paid to replace bulbs that would cut utility costs was a big win. Getting yet another grant in a town as small as Dawson was quite an accomplishment, and I hoped the town saw it that way. Meeting adjourned.

***

Throughout the month, Ron was in and out of the hospital about four times. Between the lung cancer and the treatments, things weren't looking good. Luckily, we were still collecting applications and would be able to hire another water operator before long. When Ron had the strength, he was still working with our engineering firm to complete the water system maps.

He was such a warrior, even finding ways to come into the water plant and teach Dan Jones and Will Baggio anything he could. I hoped Ron would be around forever, but I was realizing it wouldn't happen.

One day Ron was showing me the top candidates for the job that he wanted to consider. He was really favoring candidates that were into new techniques and technology. We looked at one application that he originally liked.

I asked, "Did you see his email address here?"

"No," he replied.

"His email address is convictedkiller247@aol.com!"

"That's scary."

"I know! I cannot hire someone who still uses AOL!"

***

Benny Fowler knocked on my door in mid-September.

"Are you still sticking with your decision that you're not running for reelection?" he asked.

"I'm done with it," I said.

"Would you reconsider?"

"I'm sorry, Benny. I'm done."

I could see the disappointment in his face. He went on to tell me that he verbally agreed on a price to purchase Greg Emerson's property right next to the town park. He was certain he would have enough room for 46 houses. He showed me the blueprints of the subdivision, complete with the road layout, water lines, and sewer lines.

"Jeremy, you've even got the school on board for the TIF district, but it'll take the mayor to make it happen next summer. Who's running?" he asked.

"I'm not sure, but I heard rumblings that Merf might," I said in response.

"He won't do anything productive. Who else?"

I told him I halfway suspected Sharon Yount might run, but otherwise everyone I could possibly think of running wasn't interested.

"Sharon Yount? Why don't I just throw my life savings in a burn barrel!" he said.

I knew no one else was interested because I had lobbied them all, wanting someone with brains and experience to take over my precious work. Ed Quentin and Barry Vance were the two best fits, being experienced, smart, and willing to adapt to the new era, and both declined interest. I pushed Johnny Lynch, and he said no also. Kyle Langley was very new to the board, and was really smart, but he wasn't sure if he even wanted to continue being a trustee. The remaining trustees were Agnes Cobb and Margie Baggio, both with lots of experience, but both absolutely represented the old guard. Rhonda Brown had been on the board before spending years as clerk, but she was also old guard. Between Agnes, Margie, and Rhonda, I don't think any of them had the slightest desire to do it anyway. Merf was a fit for the experience, but someone with thin skin, burned out on the town, and no ability to budget wasn't the best fit. The bottom line was that I was the best person for the job, and I just didn't want to continue. Benny ended the conversation saying that he was just going to have to put things on hold until he knew who would take over and how that person felt about the development.

***

A fifty-something-year-old woman named Emily O'Brien called me, clearly furious about something.

"I've got a trespasser and I need you to fix it!" she shouted.

"You should call the police," I replied, hoping to end the call right then.

"It's not a problem at the moment. It's my neighbor Gus! When he mows his yard, the wheels of his mower touch my property!"

"And your empty beer cans touch his property. Don't care."

***

We met on October 3, 2016, with all trustees present except Agnes Cobb. Even Ron Butcher made it, although he was looking a little frail, a little pale, and was having coughing fits throughout the night. Ron said that he had completed marking up the old maps with any new routes and revisions. Although Gary wasn't in attendance that night, Ron added that Gary had since completely finalized the electronic water system map. With Ron's health getting worse by the day, this was a big relief.

The annual argument over what night to hold the bonfire and wiener roast then commenced.

Rhonda chimed in, saying, "I am sick and tired of Buffalo doing their event the same night as ours. We did it first in our community, so there's no reason to change it!"

The older ladies like Rhonda, Margie, and Agnes always seemed to be the most upset by Buffalo. Without Agnes around, Margie spoke up too, saying with her Italian venom, "I'll plan the party for you, but only if we do it the last Saturday, like we always have. Those no good morons in Buffalo will have to worry about their own thing. I'm not changing!"

I looked to the younger guys in the group, Kyle and Johnny, who both were holding back their laughter. Since I really didn't care, and certainly didn't want anything to do with planning a party, I agreed with keeping our traditional date.

Sharon Yount, wearing a faded AC/DC shirt, added, "I'll help set up. You know our useless new employees won't get it done."

Rhonda replied, "What a terrible thing to say."

Sharon said, "It's true! I still say my husband Harry could work circles around Will 'n Dan! They should be fired 'n Harry hired to replace 'em! If I'm ever mayor, that's what I'll do!"

"Your husband couldn't work circles around a dead guy!" replied Margie.

"Do we have a problem?" Sharon asked.

"We've got a problem. You're the problem," said Margie.

"I'll be happy to finish your problem!" yelled Sharon.

I banged my gavel, trying to get them to settle down. Everyone else in the room sat stunned, with large eyes, except for Ed Quentin. With Sharon on his left and Margie on his right, he said, "Ladies, calm down. I haven't had two women fight with me between them in 30 years!"

The tension slowly left as everyone cautiously laughed. I said, "So it's settled. Margie and Sharon will be planning the bonfire event."

Before anyone could question me, I immediately asked Ron for an update on the applications for the new water operator.

He said, "But are you done talking about –"

"Yes, that's done, we're on to you," I interrupted.

He smirked, had a coughing fit, and unbuttoned his dusty flannel shirt as if he was uncomfortable. He went on to say that we only had two applicants that met the criteria. One was from Peoria, a little over an hour's drive away. The other was from Chicago, a little over three hours away. Ron agreed to interview each, show them around the facilities, and gauge which would be the best fit. Meeting adjourned.

***

Two weeks later, Ron Butcher called me. I was nervous to answer, because any time he called, it was often to tell me some machinery broke and it would cost thousands to repair it. This time, it was different.

"Mayor," he said, "I'm in the hospital again and it's bad. Grab a notepad and a pen and write down everything I say."

"What are you talking about?" I asked.

"They're telling me things are worse, much worse."

"You've always pushed through. I'm sure you'll be fine in no time."

"Not this time, Jeremy. They tell me I'm not leaving the hospital."

I didn't know what to say. For about 30 minutes, Ron told me every detail of everything I might need to know. He individually called Merf, Dan Jones, and Will Baggio as well. I don't know about them, but I wrote and wrote until my fingers were hurting and Ron was done talking.

"I talked to both guys that applied," he said, "And the guy from Peoria is definitely the best. You should hire him. If he says no, I wouldn't hire the guy from Chicago. He's just not right."

The next day, Ron's son Lance, still working as fire chief, called and told me that Ron had passed away. I was stunned that one of Ron's incredible final acts was to call so many people to make sure the town would be okay. What a selfless hero. Looking back, it's disappointing to know that Ron, a lifelong Cubs fan, passed away just a couple weeks before the Cubs finally won their coveted World Series Championship. I recall Ron's death being so heartbreaking, but I didn't have time to mourn. Without Ron, there wasn't a licensed operator for the plant. With water being distributed to the town and outlying rural areas, totaling around 800 households, a safe water supply was in the balance, so I had to get to work.

Legally, we could operate two weeks without a licensed operator. The local water works association could run the water plant for one month, at no cost, since we were members of the association. After that, they would charge us to run the plant, but would do nothing more. They wouldn't assist with water line breaks, machinery repairs, or anything else. I called the water coop that wanted us to join with Illiopolis, who offered to run the plant for a fee, but also wouldn't do anything more. I called the water coop that was operating south of town, the one Ron was so concerned about invading our territory, who also offered the same plan. I wasn't sure those would work, because Will and Dan were just too new to handle all of the other work on their own. I called the applicant from Peoria, who was no longer interested when he found out he was going to have to be the superintendent, not an assistant.

"I don't want to be the lightning rod for small-town complaints!" he said.

I certainly understood! Being desperate, I even called that candidate from Chicago to at least have a conversation with him and see if I agreed with Ron's assessment. A big part of the job is understanding the ever-changing rules and regulations.

I asked him, "Can you tell me the difference between a regulation and a statute?"

"Sure," he said. "A regulation is a rule or a code you have to follow. A statute is a sculpture like the Statute of Liberty."

And with that, I knew I had nowhere to go but to ask Mayor Red Tomko if Riverton was willing to assist in the interim until I could sort things out. After three days of frantic phone calls, gathering information between doing comedy shows, and issuing statements to the town regarding the status of the water system, I sat down with Red Tomko at the Riverton Village Hall. Joining us that morning was the township supervisor, Andy Lewison. Andy was in his mid-40s, about 5'10", with a slight husky "working man" type build. Andy and Red were both incredibly helpful. They were willing to have the Riverton operator oversee our plant in the short term until we could find a full-time replacement; we just had to pay his hourly wage for the work he did. They also said that having the Riverton operator oversee the plant long-term was another option, but that was completely at the discretion of the operator himself.

Red said, "We can't make him take a second job. As much as the employees think so, we aren't slave drivers!"

Red and I had previously signed off on an intergovernmental agreement, allowing either town to use the other town's employees in a short-term crisis. This of course was a crisis. But long-term assistance was a different story. In our discussion, I learned that Andy's son, Cody, was the lone water operator for Riverton. Cody also happened to be longtime friends with Will Baggio. Now, on one hand I knew that Cody would be accepted by the crew; however, I was concerned that Cody and Will might take over the work and push aside Dan Jones. Or worse, do a lot of goofing off and leave Dan to do the work. With them both being millennials, I envisioned them yelling, "Scrub that water basin, old man!"

I didn't think something like that would happen, but I really had no idea what to expect. With the options sorted out, I left our meeting and drove to Des Moines for a comedy show. I'd have to juggle shows, mourning, and decision-making in the coming days and weeks.

I got back from Iowa just in time for Johnny Lynch to join me at Ron's visitation. Ron's wife sat on a couch greeting guests, flanked by her two daughters and two sons (I haven't mentioned the second son because he wasn't really involved with our town like the others). Johnny and I shook hands and offered condolences. As I walked out, I noticed Merf, seated alone with his head down. The two had worked with each other, as the lone full-time labor employees, for almost four decades. I didn't know what to say or do, so I patted him on the shoulder and kept walking. Rhonda Brown, Agnes Cobb, and Margie Baggio were seated with some guests, and each stood up and hugged me. I later heard that the remaining three trustees, Ed Quentin, Sharon Yount, and Kyle Langley, didn't attend.

Johnny couldn't make the funeral the next day, so I went by myself. I told Dan Jones, Will Baggio, and Kara Gregory that as long as the essential work was done, they could take off the time they needed to attend without using vacation time. Both of Ron's sons spoke, giving great stories that were funny, riveting, and emotional. The funeral home was packed, including Rhonda, Agnes, and Margie. I was still a little disappointed that our Town Board wasn't better represented, but I didn't show it, in an attempt to keep things focused on where they should be. The speeches ran so long that I wasn't able to accompany the caravan to the cemetery because I had to catch a flight to Las Vegas for a comedy show.

While I sat at my gate at the St. Louis airport, I got a call from Dan Jones, who was speaking as if he was trying to not be overheard.

"Merf just talked to Will at the reception after the funeral. He told Will that the mayor is in a vulnerable spot and Will should take advantage," he said.

I replied, "What did he mean by that?"

"Merf said it's time to stick it to the mayor like a key in a stolen car! He said now is the time to demand a massive raise from the gangly mayor! He told Will to tell you he would quit on the spot if you didn't give it to him."

"What did Will do?"

"He sort of stood there quietly, just thinking it over."

"Thanks for letting me know, but it doesn't work that way. If he tries it, I guess I'll send him on his way."

I left that last statement a little vague because I wasn't sure if Dan would relay the message back to Will. If he did, the statement could be interpreted as I would fire him, or that I would just let him quit. Either way, I wasn't going to be bullied. And sadly, this problem was created by Merf, who I thought had finally changed for the better.

I got home from Vegas and was unloading my car when my cell rang. I looked at the screen, which read, "WILL BAGGIO."

"Here we go," I thought. "This could get ugly."

"I've been thinking about the workload at the water plant," he said.

"Yep," I said as I rolled my eyes.

"I really think you should hire Cody Lewison. He's right down the road, so you don't have to worry about talking someone into moving here. He's got the experience, he's a good guy, a hard worker, all those things."

"I've heard good things about him. I'm still weighing all the options," I said, not wanting to reveal my hand, but knowing hiring Cody seemed to be the correct and logical choice.

"I just want you to know he's a great fit. You really should bring him in."

With Will lobbying for his friend to be hired, it made me a little more leery to do it. I was envisioning more bullying, like Will saying, "Dan, is that what you call digging a trench? Dig deeper, Grandpa!"

But alternatively, we didn't have much choice. The next day I sat with Cody and talked out terms of a contract. Cody was in his early 30s, with a thick muscular build, dark hair and dark eyes. Ed Quentin and Kyle Langley joined me that day. I had Ed be part of the discussions because of all of the trustees, he was most familiar with the water operations. Kyle had been part of the hiring process at his company since he graduated high school about 20 years earlier. We wrapped up our meeting with an agreement in principle that needed to be approved by the Town Board at a special meeting.

Ed joked to Cody, "I'd tell you to take all this extra money you're going to make and bet it in Vegas, but Jeremy was just there and it clearly didn't work out for him!"

"How do you know?" I asked.

"Because your shirt still has a big hole in the armpit."

I looked down. He was right. And the fact that he said "still" means he had noticed it before. Whoops!

***

On October 20, 2016, we held the first and only special meeting of my tenure. All six trustees were present as Cody Lewison sat in the beat-up banquet chairs. I laid out all of the options I had researched as to how we could continue a legal and licensed operation of the plant. In our discussions, Cody had agreed to make a salary about 20% less than what Ron had been making. I thought that was fair, because Cody didn't have the experience that Ron did. But I agreed that he should be making near what Ron made, because Ron was vastly underpaid. After years of Ron refusing raises and bonuses, his salary wasn't near what it should have been. My concern was that at least some of the trustees wouldn't see it that way. One statement I expected was something like, "If Ron was making this much, someone with half the experience should make half that." We'd still be saving money if we paid Cody the salary that he wanted. Not only would we pay him less than Ron's salary, but we didn't have to pay for any of his benefits, since he was already getting them from Riverton.

Surprisingly, the trustees all agreed except for one. Sharon Yount complained that this was just way too much money to pay someone, and the best thing to do was have Dan and Will operate the plant without a license.

"We can't just run the plant illegally without a license," I said.

"It'll save us money! And who's gonna know? It's not illegal until you get caught!" she replied.

"Every report we turn in to the EPA is signed off on by the licensed operator, which is tracked in their database."

"Forge the papers then!"

Ed Quentin chimed in, saying, "Some tools are sharper than others!"

"Ed is right," Sharon said. "We need to save money to buy better tools!"

I could see Ed's smirk through his unshaven face as he looked at me out of the corner of his eyes. I called for a vote, which passed 5-1 to hire Cody, with only Sharon voting against it.

Secretly, upon their retirement, I had previously planned to name the water plant after Ron Butcher and the town park after Merf. Of course, by now I had figured out that I wouldn't be naming anything after Merf. Well, that's not entirely true. Whenever my friends or I are pleasant to someone, then complain about them when the person leaves, we call it "Pulling a Merf."

In the previous days, I had been in touch with the Butcher family about my intentions to hold a ceremony and dedicate the water plant in his honor. I pitched the idea to the board, who agreed to spend money on a nice sign to honor Ron's legacy. Sharon almost didn't vote for the sign though.

"I'm only voting for it if there's still going to be enough money to replace them tools!" she said.

"Don't forget some bulbs are brighter than others!" added Ed Quentin.

"I thought we just replaced all those bulbs with them energy efficient ones," Sharon replied.

"Everything is fine and there's plenty of money to fix what we need to," I said.

I looked around and everyone was smirking as they held in their laughs, with the exception of Sharon, who seemed concerned and angry, but also not sure why she felt that way.

After reviewing the pricing for a sign to honor Ron at the water plant, Johnny Lynch said, "That's a good buy for a goodbye!"

I was so proud that I had found Ron's replacement and a way to honor his legacy, only one week after his passing. Meeting adjourned.

***

Not long after, we were gathered at the park to set up for the annual bonfire and wiener roast. I stood in the commercial kitchen with Sharon Yount, Agnes Cobb, Margie Baggio, and Rhonda Brown. We were each doing our own duties, some mixing hot chocolate, others dicing onions, and others running paper plates and napkins back and forth to the tables. The conversation went as it did every year, with the ladies complaining that Buffalo had hijacked our night once again.

"Maybe we need to send our men over to have a chat with their men," said Margie, seeming more Italian than ever.

"Jeremy, you need to make appropriate changes next year," added Sharon.

"He won't be the mayor next year," said Rhonda.

Confused, Sharon asked, "Why not?"

"I haven't really made it public yet, but I'm not running for reelection," I told her.

Sharon paused and stared into blank space, clearly thinking something over, then saying, "Now is my chance."

"What do you mean?" I asked.

She was clearly startled, and must've been thinking it was her chance, and not intending to say it.

"Well, um, I've been thinkin' about runnin' for years now, and maybe it's the time. I can get in there and fire Will 'n Dan, hire my husband, and get this town fixed up!" she said.

Her statement was met with silence. No one agreed with her stance to fire our two newest employees, but no one dared argue with her either. I think everyone just thought that the town was in trouble if someone didn't step up. I certainly felt that way, but after all I'd been through, it wasn't going to be me.

The only noise was from Rhonda, who murmured, "Fixed up to her must mean turning the town into the New York City landfill."

As the night went on, people from the town came and went. I noticed Merf and his wife, and waved hello, but didn't initially chat with him. As the night wound down, I pulled Merf to the side.

"I really hope you'll run for mayor. Like I told you, I'm not," I said.

"I'm not sure my heart can handle it, but I'm concerned that everyone is saying Sharon is running," he replied.

"That's a fact. She just told me."

"I won't let that happen. I tried to work with her on the park budget a while ago, and I learned right then that I couldn't use her to undermine you! She's not all there. If she's serious, I'll run."

Like I said before, I didn't think Merf was the best choice, largely because of his inability to budget and understand finances. His thin skin wouldn't help either. I didn't appreciate the confirmation that he wanted to undermine me, but with a choice between Merf and Sharon, it was like choosing between a bruised apple or a pile of mud for dinner.

As we packed up for the night, Johnny Lynch's boys agreed to put out the fire ... by peeing on it. When they didn't quite get it extinguished, Kyle Langley put it out ... also by peeing on it.

The very next day was the water plant dedication in Ron Butcher's honor. There was a crowd of about 40 people there. I saw many of Ron's family members, as well as many people from the town gathered in anticipation. Ron's son Lance, still the fire chief, had worked with the fire department to have the sign covered. I would say a few words, then the firemen, who were positioned on top of the building, would release the covering and reveal the new sign, now attached to the east side of the water plant.

I spoke to the crowd, giving all the respect I could to Ron. His widow stood front and center, again flanked by their two daughters and two sons. As the covering was dropped, I heard Mrs. Butcher gasp and say, "It's beautiful." I was touched that she loved it so much. The sign simply read, "BUTCHER WATER PLANT, DAWSON, IL."

Lance Butcher then said a few words, bringing some joy and laughter, and then he dismissed the crowd.

As they began to depart, Merf shouted over to me, "Where are the trustees?!"

It was loud enough that about 10 or 15 heard his unnecessary remark. I had noticed that I was the only elected official there, but didn't want to point it out. This was a day about Ron and his family, not being petty about who showed up or didn't.

"I don't know where they are, but I'm disappointed," I replied, hoping to show that I had nothing to do with their absence.

"It is disappointing," he said, then turned to the crowd around him for approval. "Am I right?" No one replied, most just looked at him with blank stares. He seemed to be trying to fire up the crowd against me, but none seemed interested.

I just thought, "You're trying to grow a raucous campaign against a person who isn't running, in a town with 140 voters, in which maybe 100 actually vote. Pull it back a little there, Mayor Daley."

***

The following day, Paula Fallon called me. Paula was possibly the oldest of all the ladies in the Blue Hair Club.

"I noticed you didn't have whole wheat buns at the bonfire. You only had white buns, which is so inconsiderate," she said.

"I'll be sure that we have wheat buns next year," I replied.

"Mayor, I don't even know if you'll be around next year."

"Well, Paula, I don't know if you'll be around next year."

CHAPTER 16

I GOT A JOB IN HER VIEW

It was November 9 when we held our first regular meeting since Ron's passing. All six trustees were present, though our engineer Gary Whitcomb and attorney Reggie Phillips were not. The annual audit had just been completed, echoing the same concerns as every year. There were no issues with the accounts, but the auditors again raised concerns at the limited checks and balances in place. We discussed it as a board, but again there wasn't really much we could do. The clerk and the treasurer, Rhonda and Kara, cross-check each other. The mayor reviews any payments going out. There really aren't any other personnel that could be involved, as all three people with access to the money are a part of the process. The board agreed that we shouldn't give new access to the funds to anyone else. I was just happy this was the last time I'd deal with it. If a sound was made when I read that report, by now it was sounding like Charlie Brown's teacher!

We had previously agreed to hire a third full-time labor employee to join Will and Dan. I had agreed to have Johnny

Lynch and Kyle Langley review the applications, since I personally knew some of the applicants. Since Johnny and Kyle did hiring as part of their full-time jobs, I felt they were the best options to help. Once they selected the best candidates, they would be a part of the interview process with me.

"How old are the applicants?" asked Sharon, as she looked over her glasses at me.

"It's against the law to consider age when hiring," I replied.

"I'm going to fight this if you hire someone old," she said.

"Again, we can't consider age."

"They better get a full water operator's license their first week!"

"Again, you have to have three years' experience to get the license. We will provide guidance and support to get them their licensing, including substantial raises once they get it."

"I'd fire them if they don't get it the first year!"

I then used the crisis at hand to make a point and get change done. I alerted the board to the fact that the water operator from Peoria was really concerned that he wouldn't get vacation time until he had worked an entire year. Our crew can get called in at three in the morning for a water emergency, then still have to work a full day the next day because they don't have time to take off. In that scenario, I had always let the guys apply the time they worked overnight to their regularly scheduled day, but I wasn't telling the board that!

"This is a very challenging and tiring job, and the health and safety of our town depends on them," I said. The board then unanimously approved granting vacation days as soon as the 90-day probation period was complete.

I pitched the flashing arrow ordinance again, restricting the sign to the site of the business, in an effort to clean up our town entrance. With no debate, the group passed this unanimously as well.

Ed Quentin joked, "You're red hot, what else do you want to pitch? Just don't crap out, no sevens buddy!"

Ed was right. For some reason the board was in a good mood, so now was my chance. I had originally only planned to plant the seed for another small raise for our now three full-timers, Will, Dan, and Kara. I had run the numbers, and we had room in the budget to take care of them. I knew they were really going to be working hard with Ron gone. In addition, his replacement Cody Lewison was only working part-time.

Sharon Yount gave pushback, saying, "Will and Dan don't do nothin'! They should be fired, not given raisins!"

"Did you say raisins?" said Kyle.

"I don't like raisins in my oatmeal cookies," said Margie, as she looked at Agnes.

"Yuck," said Agnes.

"Okay, let's take a vote on the raises, not raisins," I said.

"Calm down now, raisin bran helps you stay regular," said Rhonda, wearing a Christmas sweatshirt a month early.

"I vote fire 'em all!" said Sharon.

With everyone else voting for the raise, it passed 5-1, and I finally felt the crew would be compensated fairly. At this point, three-and-a-half years into my tenure, I felt I had finally accomplished my major goals. No more complaints from the crew about low pay, Merf wasn't around to complain anymore, the Greens were gone, the comprehensive plan was complete, and with the exception of Kara Gregory, I had hired every active employee. With the small-town complainers starting to back away, I had six months left to focus on getting anything else done. Meeting adjourned.

***

Kyle Langley and Johnny Lynch helped me prepare for the interviews. We had three great candidates but one withdrew because, as he said, "I'd make more money selling water to sailors!" The final two candidates were Ron Butcher's grandson, Austin Butcher, and Ed Quentin's son, Corey Quentin. It was a Tuesday at noon when I called each and set up an interview. I called Austin first, who was excited and couldn't wait to chat with us. I called Corey next, still around noon, who answered the phone like I just woke him up. I found it a bit odd, but didn't think much of it, because he was a young guy, to my knowledge unemployed, so if he was choosing to sleep that late, so be it.

We met with Austin that Thursday evening at about 7:00. Austin Butcher was about 21, with short buzzed blond hair, a medium build, and looked almost exactly like what you'd think Ron looked like in his youth. He was professionally dressed, wearing a blue button-down shirt with a tie and khakis. He gave reasonable answers throughout the discussion, and wasn't necessarily impressive, but wasn't unimpressive either. Johnny, Kyle, and I were discussing how we felt the interview went, and agreed that Corey could easily impress us and get the job. As we were talking, the door opened back up. It was Austin.

He said, "I just wanted to say that it would mean a lot to me to work for this town. I would love to honor my grandpa's legacy. I've been in and out of that water plant with him more times that I can count, and I love it here."

It was quite a way to end, as we had been questioning his passion, and now he could've swayed us. We'd have to see where the interview with Corey would lead.

Corey Quentin had agreed to meet us that Saturday at 10:00 a.m. Kyle, Johnny, and I were surprised as 10:00 rolled around and Corey hadn't yet arrived. Soon it was 10:05, then 10:10. I tried to call him but no answer.

About 10:15, Ed called me, saying, "I saw you called Corey. What's up?"

"I was checking to see if he was coming to the interview," I replied.

"I'll see if I can wake him up. He seemed to think it was 10:00 tonight."

"Why would we do an interview at 10:00 on a Saturday night?"

"That's what I told him, but he insisted. You know how these millennial kids are these days! I'll wake him up and have him there in a few minutes."

I told Johnny and Kyle what happened, and they had a good laugh. It was only a few minutes later when a large pickup truck came barreling down the road. Corey hustled in, wearing a t-shirt, ball cap, and sweatpants. He was clearly unshowered and unshaven, and maybe a little hungover. He gave really brief answers to everything, and only seemed to be there because his dad was pushing for his 22-year-old son to get a job and move out. I specifically remember asking him what his plans were in the next five years.

He replied, "I haven't planned past today, brother."

"Why do you want to work for our little town?" I asked.

He replied, "Why not, man."

As we dismissed him, it was an easy decision. We'd be hiring Austin Butcher.

***

I soon got a knock on my door from an angry middle-aged mother named Gina Rizzo. Gina had lived in the town for years and was notorious for complaining. That November evening was no different.

"You know that 'Deer Crossing' sign out on the county highway?" she asked.

"Umm, yes," I said, wondering where this was leading.

"It's in the wrong spot!"

"Uh-oh, are you going to tell me the deer don't know where to cross so we need to move it?" I joked.

"No, I'm not stupid, Mr. Mayor! I'm telling you that because the deer cross about a half mile south of that sign, and it needs moved to the appropriate location. So move it!"

"I don't have the ability to move a sign on a county highway. The county office would have to handle that."

"The mayor of a municipality doesn't have the ability to move a county sign? You are a joke! I thought you said you would help!"

"And I thought you said you weren't stupid," I said as I shut the door.

***

We met in early December for our final meeting of 2016. All trustees, plus engineer Gary Whitcomb and attorney Reggie Phillips, were in attendance. We planned to have some snacks after the meeting, so it seemed no one wanted to miss it. Either that, or they needed to be present for the small talk when we decided what restaurant we'd visit for the Christmas party!

Reggie Phillips, dressed in his usual navy business suit, then pitched the written vacation ordinance that the board allowed for last month. Margie Baggio's complaint was that it wasn't fair to the current employees to give new hires vacation time right away, when the current employees all had to work a year first. She was clearly fighting for her grandson Will, but she had a point. I suggested we give each current employee three vacation days to make up for the change. No one on the board agreed to do so, so that idea died. However, the new vacation ordinance passed unanimously anyway.

Reggie then pitched the flashing arrow ordinance, which didn't seem to match what we had discussed. Since no one liked what he wrote, the idea was tabled. Reggie would rewrite the ordinance and have it ready next month.

Ed Quentin joked to Reggie, "You'd think everyone in here was female, with so many people telling you that you're doing it wrong!"

Just before the meeting started, I had pulled Ed aside and told him about our hiring decision, and even explained why. He was disappointed but understood. I was a little surprised when in the meeting he fought to have a second round of interviews.

Sharon Yount agreed, but for a different reason, saying, "All we need in here is another young guy, especially a Butcher. I'd keep that family out of it! Will and Dan already need fired so that we can hire my husband!"

Reggie Phillips told Ed that he should recuse himself from the discussion and vote since his own son was being discussed. Ed ignored Reggie, voting against hiring Austin, as he joined forces with Sharon, who also voted against it. The vote passed 4-2. Meeting adjourned.

***

After the meeting we had our annual December potluck. As we packed up, I found myself alone with Ed.

I jokingly asked, "So have you gone so politically extreme that you're partnering up with Sharon to get things done for your town?"

He replied, "Let's not get carried away. I think I had a little too much to drink before the meeting, and my beer goggles had me thinking those ideas were looking good."

For our Christmas party dinner, we once again went to Boston Steakhouse. To keep things friendly, I even invited Merf and his wife. Merf was still working part-time, once a month, to help read water meters. The evening was fine until the end of the night. Everyone had left our private room, except for my wife and I, who were waiting for the copy of the check to sign. The receipt arrived and I began to fill out the tip and sign the paper. At that moment, I heard a thud-bang-thump-thud-thud sound.

Someone had fallen down the stairs from the second floor party room!

I heard someone groan out the word, "Owwwww."

Soon, a few staff members of the restaurant rushed over.

The victim said, "My back hurts, my arm hurts, and I can't feel my legs."

Then a waitress added, "Let's pick him up and put him on this chair!"

I told Sandra, "That's our cue to go! No reason to be subpoenaed as a witness to this!"

***

December was the time to file for reelection. The trustees who were up for reelection had a decision to make, as did I. Johnny Lynch, Agnes Cobb, and Ed Quentin, whose terms were up, had all privately told me they wouldn't run for reelection. Kyle Langley had the choice to run for the remaining two years on his partial term, since it was an appointed position. He could also run for a full term for Johnny, Agnes, or Ed's seat. He had originally told me that he was done, but Merf had stopped by his house and talked him into finishing out the final two years. Merf told Kyle not to tell anyone, but that he was running for mayor, and he respected Kyle as someone valuable to have on the board. I took the moment as an opportunity to get the media's attention once again. I sent press releases to every media source I could think of, and highlighted the story as a small-town mayor not running for reelection in order to become a standup comedian. At this point I'd been a comedian for 15 years, but "to become" sounded way more interesting than "to focus on." With that press release, I generated a magazine article, was interviewed on the local TV news station, was on three different radio stations, and in two different newspapers. The publicity helped me gain more of a following on social media and on my email list, and even helped me book a few private shows. If I got nothing else out of being mayor, at least I got some comedy work!

Rhonda Brown, who as clerk would be receiving the applications for those wanting to get on the ballot, filled me in on who was running. Even Rhonda's term was up, and she'd chosen to be finished. Merf would run unopposed for mayor. Agnes Cobb's daughter Julie, a returning Mike Madison, and a guy I'd never heard of, would be running unopposed for the three empty trustee seats. The only position that would have a race would be for Rhonda's clerk position, which would be a lady who served on the fire department running against Will Baggio's mother, who is also Margie's daughter-in-law. There seemed to be some concern in the town that the Baggio family would be taking over our small-town government. That would be for the voters to decide in April. And since the Baggio family seemed to make up 20% of the town, when I say "for the voters to decide," I mean "for the Baggio family to decide!"

I received a nice email from Reggie Phillips right before our meeting in January. He said he had seen the articles about me not running for reelection. He told me I had been doing a wonderful job, and was getting far more done than any previous mayor that he or his father worked for. He went on to say that he was concerned that Merf wouldn't be able to continue with the forward progress, and was sad that I wasn't going to be around much longer. It made my day and I was surprised to know that even Reggie recognized what was happening around him. He later frantically called me and said it was unprofessional of him to say something like that about the future mayor, and asked me to delete the email without showing anyone. To this day, that email is printed and framed, displayed on my office desk.

***

When Johnny and Renee Lynch were visiting Sandra and me that December, Johnny joked that we should start a podcast about all the things we deal with. We joked that we could even make fun of what people complained about in all the surrounding towns, not just Dawson. Soon after, *The Back Table Podcast* was born. The guy who I originally considered to be my biggest threat was now doing a podcast with me. We anticipated some pushback, but at this point, we didn't care anymore!

***

I soon received a phone call from Saul Hackenberg. Saul was an older man who himself had served on the Town Board. His complaint was one I figured many people in the town were in agreement with.

"Jeremy, it's not right when one family secretly runs a town," he said.

"I know. It's pretty common in small towns, though. Not much we can do," I countered.

"You've got the Butchers running things, and the Baggios running things; it's like they're the small-town Gambino crime family!"

"And you seem like the snitch they're gonna whack!"

***

I was feeling good when we met on January 3, 2017, with only Agnes Cobb missing. The first Monday of May would be my last day as mayor, so with just a handful of months to go, I could see the light at the end of the tunnel. These last few meetings were going to be shorter and getting less done, because my major goals were complete, it was just time for finishing touches.

I was also feeling good because aside from the crazy fall down the stairs, the Christmas party went just fine. Likewise, there was an ice storm on the day I hosted my final senior dinner, but fortunately no one took a spill. It was also the first time in the history of the dinner that all six trustees and the mayor participated.

I was impressed that Merf sat in on this meeting from the public seats. It was wise of him to be aware of what was being discussed and voted on, because including this night, there would only be four discussions before he took over.

The meeting started as Reggie Phillips presented the revised ordinance to restrict flashing arrow signs. Kyle Langley adjusted his fashionable glasses and asked if this would impact temporary banner signs, which it wouldn't. I reminded the group that Springfield had outright banned the flashing arrows and we were merely restricting them.

Ed Quentin contributed, saying, "I'm for it. Otherwise, our town fits the subject of a Jeff Foxworthy joke."

And with that, the ordinance passed 5-0.

Cody Lewison talked about the numerous quick fixes at the water plant that he had discovered that were actually illegal and quite unsafe. He had already identified nearly $40,000 in urgent repairs that were needed. Merf also added to the discussion to help clarify what needed to be fixed.

Sharon Yount was not happy at all, saying, "You mean Ron just did band-aids on all these things? That is absolutely disgusting and disappointing for our community!"

"The Village has been asking Ron to do quick fixes instead of full repairs for forty years! How can you be mad at him?" said engineer Gary Whitcomb.

"I don't care. He should have overruled all the mayors and done did it right!" she replied.

Ed Quentin added, "I think you know all about ignoring the mayor's request. Have you started leashing up your dog yet?"

Sharon stared daggers back at Ed as we all held in our laughs. I had completely forgotten about the issues with Sharon's dog running around and her husband wanting to fight me for bringing it up.

"Speaking of trustees not getting things done," I said, hoping to change the subject, "I was just notified by the county that our hazard mitigation qualification process was not completed by our trustee."

What I didn't think of was that Sharon was the one who dropped the ball. Sharon was supposed to have been attending the meetings to make us eligible for natural disaster relief in the event of a large-scale emergency. This is the same set of meetings in which she pushed to be the representative of the town and I reluctantly allowed it. I had also started to wonder if things weren't getting done because of her hesitancy to answer my questions about it over the past few months.

"Wasn't someone from here supposed to be doing that?" asked Johnny Lynch.

"I thought a trustee volunteered to address that," said Kyle.

"Don't look at me. I don't volunteer for anything, not even charity work!" added Ed.

"Me and Agnes spent a lot of time sorting all those papers in the attic, so it wasn't us," said Margie Baggio.

All heads turned toward Sharon.

"Umm, I'm not sure who it was neither," she said, as uncomfortable as she could be.

"I'd have to look at the notes to see who was supposed to be doing this. I'll cancel my vacation to get this done. I guess I'll miss those time-SHARONS after all," I said. Meeting adjourned.

***

Aside from working on the hazard mitigation project, the rest of the month went fairly slow. I only got one unusual complaint, which was a call from Jenna Tyson. Jenna was in her late 30s, married with a few kids.

"I was walking around the park with my kids and noticed that last house over there. They've got a huge marijuana field in their backyard!"

"Did you call the police?" I asked.

"No, I think you need to go burn it down!"

"That's not a good idea; they did that once before. Though I think the whole town was relaxed for a week," I joked.

"Why do you think I'm telling you to do it?" she said seriously.

"That's a half-baked idea."

CHAPTER 17

YOUR WISH HAS BEEN GRANTED

We met on February 6, again with everyone present except Agnes Cobb. Merf didn't attend, so I figured he already felt he knew what he needed to know.

The first item up for discussion was another $6,000 in repairs for the water plant. I wasn't that concerned because we had recently raised the rates, knowing that several infrastructure items were old and needing repair. Kyle Langley asked when these repairs would stop because it was getting too pricey. I agreed it was pricey but told the board that I had instructed Cody Lewison to prioritize the repair of the things that risked the water safety.

Sharon Yount chimed in, saying, "I still think it's unacceptable that Ron didn't fully fix these things. He should've been fired!"

Our engineer Gary Whitcomb stood up in his usual perfectly erect manner, saying, "He did what your board always asked him to do. Why would you be mad?"

Ed Quentin added, "At least he tried to do what he was told, unlike some people around here!"

"What's that supposed to mean?!" said Sharon.

"Okay, let's get back to business," I said.

I informed the group that I spent the better part of the month completing the forms and paperwork to get us eligible for hazard mitigation funding. Rhonda Brown and Kara Gregory had helped me gather the information, so I gave them a well-deserved thanks.

If there was ever a time for my proposal to get shot down, I figured this would be it. With Ron Butcher's passing, the zoning board now had a vacancy. I wasn't going to need the zoning board to approve anything for me before I moved on, so I didn't have that much of a concern. But I had thought it would be nice to have someone on the inside who I knew would relay back to me anything shady that Merf would try to do as mayor. I had my own wife and Johnny Lynch's wife on there, but I didn't think either would stick with it for long since their respective spouses were no longer going to be involved. I then nominated my dad to fill the vacant seat. With no push-back whatsoever, he was approved unanimously!

I told the board I was impressed with the work getting done by our labor crew of Will, Dan, and Austin. All three were working part-time elsewhere and still on call 24/7 with us. It was a tough job to balance, so maybe we needed to give them raises large enough to allow them to give up their part-time jobs. I wanted to help them, but we also had to be able to honor the large raises we promised them if they were to get the various levels of water licensing. The discussion seemed to agree with just that, except for one person.

"Those guys don't do nothin' they's asked. They need fired," said Sharon.

Ed Quentin replied, "If you got fired for not doing what you're asked, you'd have been impeached a long time ago!"

"Let's regroup and see where things lead next month," I said. Meeting adjourned.

***

As the weather began to change, we got some significant storms, which at one point caused the power to go out. I was on the phone with Will Baggio to check on how things were going.

"We're a little delayed on reading the meters since the power went out," he said.

"You're driving around reading meters. That doesn't require electricity," I responded.

"Right, but we're short a guy. Merf is refusing to work. He says we can't be forced to work without electricity."

"Okay, let me talk to him."

"He already left. He said if you refused to pay him, he'd just pay himself when he became mayor."

***

As I came to the realization that there wasn't much I could do regarding Merf, I got a phone call. This time, it was from Wendy Kendall. Wendy was new to town, single, and right on the age cutoff between millennial and Gen-Z.

"Did you know they're remodeling that McDonald's in Riverton, so it's drive through only?" she asked.

"I guess so," I said, not yet sure what to expect.

"I work in the medical field, and drive through only is a great way to prevent the spread of disease. So maybe they should make that permanent. It would help a lot with people staying healthy with the gross Yount family running around here."

"You'd need to talk to the restaurant about that."

"You need to try. Who knows what kind of diseases that family is walking around with!"

"If the rumor mill is true, probably the same diseases you're walking around with."

***

We met on March 6 with every trustee present. With her recent absences, I thought for sure Agnes Cobb had simply quit, but she proved me wrong. I had also thought Merf had given up on attending the meetings, but there he sat, proving me wrong also.

Cody Lewison wore his signature ball cap, with a tight t-shirt, explaining the need for $4,000 to repair something else at the plant. After ogling his muscles, Sharon Yount had more frustration to let out.

"You're telling me you found something else Ron didn't do right?" she said.

"It's not that he didn't do it right, it's that he had a quick fix on it, and it's not going to last much longer," Cody replied.

"I'm tired of people not doing what they're supposed to around here!"

"Pot, meet kettle," joked Ed Quentin.

I quickly moved the discussion on to the good news that Congressman LaHood's office had worked to finally get us the grant for that flood wall. They were confirming the details, but it was looking like we were finally going to have a chance to get the funding. My only concern was that it may take a couple months before we could sign off on it, and my time as mayor was limited. I was concerned that when Merf became mayor, he may oppose it, simply because it was my project. In reality, Merf had probably moved more sandbags around that water plant than anybody, so he'd certainly seem to be in favor of a flood barrier. On the other hand, anything that made me look good was something Merf would oppose.

There was one more bit of unfinished business. Remember that generator setup for the water plant that Ron Butcher kept pushing off? Without Ron to argue against it or delay it, and with Cody Lewison now pushing for it, the Board approved $15,000 to fund the electrical setup and the generator installation. We were spending all kinds of money to get the plant up to speed, but I kept reminding myself that we knew this would be coming, and that's a big reason why we raised the rates a second time. This generator was one more thing I had hoped would get done before Merf took over. It made absolute sense for the water plant to have some sort of electrical backup in the event that there was no power, but that wouldn't matter to Merf. Meeting adjourned.

***

The friendship that Sandra and I had developed with Johnny and Renee Lynch continued to grow. We had moved beyond game nights and dinners together. In late March, our families flew to Orlando, Florida to vacation together. We all stayed in an Airbnb together for a week. We were a little nervous what a week together in the same house would do to our friendship. The only thing that made it hard was learning that everyone farts. And some worse than others!

***

I was chatting with Kara Gregory as she was preparing to order office supplies. She regularly checked with me to see if I needed anything.

"Is it okay if I order a paper shredder that cuts a little finer than the one we have now? Merf wants it," she said.

"Why does Merf need a paper shredder?" I asked.

"He says the one you've been using doesn't cut small enough. He's been able to piece together some of the reports on him that you shredded."

"Did you know he was doing this?"

"No. I thought it was odd though that he always volunteered to empty your shredded paper. He would always just take it and say he would be back after he put some things back together."

"Don't order anything. I'm going to add paper shredders to the required board approval list. I'd love to hear him explain to his board why he wants approval for a new shredder!"

***

It wasn't long after when I got a knock on my door from Lita Yelich. Lita was a middle-aged, married mother of two. Both of her kids had recently moved out, so she had plenty of time on her hands.

"My neighbor just got Weed and Feed all over my yard!" she shouted.

308

"So much that it's killing your grass?" I asked.

"No! He treated his own yard and then treated mine!"

"Then what's the problem?"

"I like dandelions! Fine him for littering the Weed and Feed!"

"But honestly your yard needed it," I said as I hung up quickly.

***

When we met on April 5, it would be the final time I would run an entire meeting. Every trustee was present for our final meeting together. At the May meeting, we would start the meeting, then vote to approve meeting minutes and finances. At that time, the newly elected officials would be sworn in and take over. If I had any last-minute items to complete, it was now or never. My only concern was that Merf, who looked on from the public chairs, would interrupt and oppose something.

I started with good news, because I knew I'd be pushing for a big decision in my final action as mayor. I had been working hard to get us a grant for corridor improvement, which was a 100% funded grant that helped clean up and improve the town's entryway. Aside from our new LED sign board, there wasn't much to look at, and the nicer homes were all tucked away a few blocks into the town. To a passerby, the town looked worse than it really was. Through my work, we were awarded this grant, now the third in my tenure. In addition to the road sign grant and the light bulb replacement grant, I thought this was impressive. But I still had a fourth grant to announce!

Congressman Lahood's office confirmed with me that we were going to get a grant to build the flood wall! After years of dealing with the fears of the plant flooding out, it was finally over. It would take about a month for the paperwork to come in. The only concern was that since it was going to take a month, that meant the final board approval would fall into the hands of Merf and his new trustees. Knowing this, I made a point to confirm with Kyle Langley, Sharon Yount, and Margie Baggio that this was a significant win, since the three of them would be continuing their service as trustees.

Our engineer Gary Whitcomb, finally showing his personality, said, "Wow, you got this town four grants in four years? That's rarer than a celibate honeymoon!"

Attorney Reggie Phillips added, "Yep, we're losing a good guy."

I thanked the men for their kind words as Merf looked on in disgust. Knowing that he'd have a plan to eliminate my progress, I dumped a couple things on him right away, in hopes of slowing his efforts. I told the board that the comprehensive plan should be reviewed regularly and monitored for progress, and we were currently due to do so. But with a new administration coming in, we shouldn't put effort toward any new projects since the new administration would have their own goals and views. The board agreed, so I was ready for more.

I also told the board that the Neighborhood Watch program was due to be reviewed, with new goals and plans to be set. But again, with the new administration coming next month, there was no point in doing so because their objectives may differ. Again, the board agreed. Merf, wearing his faded flannel shirt, scratched his beard as he stared back at me with anger.

I informed the board that I had been recruiting a gas station chain to open up on Route 36. Our town had been without a gas station for about 25 years. But with my persistence, it looked like it was going to happen. The only concern, again, was that it would be at least mid-May before they'd agree to commercial development terms. That also meant that it was going to fall on Merf to make the final call. I didn't tell the board that, I just pumped them up knowing that we had a gas station in our future.

Ed Quentin said, "I've been married long enough to know that when you butter us up this much, you're about to ask for a nice favor!"

"Easy now, you're gonna give me dirty flashbacks," said Agnes Cobb.

"I hear you!" added Margie Baggio, as the rest of us uncomfortably laughed at the adult-humored undertones.

I told the board how impressed I was with the work of our new crew. They had been getting projects done and working harder than ever. Will Baggio had really taken the lead on things and Dan Jones was right there with him. The newest employee, Austin Butcher, was picking up rather quickly. I asked for a 5% raise for each of them, knowing that with a new administration, they may not see a raise for a while. The group agreed that it was a little too early to give Austin a raise. However, only Sharon disagreed with a raise for the other two.

"What employer gives someone a raise when they should be fired?" she asked.

"State government!" said Johnny Lynch.

As the group laughed, the board voted to approve. Although Sharon voted no, the raises for Will and Dan both passed 5-1. I pounded my gavel for the final time. Meeting adjourned.

***

I largely took the month off with nothing much left to accomplish. I was enjoying the calm of knowing I wouldn't be dealing with any more bizarre small-town complaints. That's when the phone rang. Amy Mussina, one of the few unmarried area millennials, was on the phone. If the PC Police had a chief, she was it.

"Did you know the school we played baseball against last week has an Indian for a mascot?! They should be banned from the conference for being so offensive! How is that acceptable?!"

"How is it acceptable that you bring home a different guy every night from Mr. Ribeye Lounge? Bye!" I said as I hung up.

The phone rang again, but this time it was Kara Gregory calling to once again talk about office supplies.

"Merf wants to know if you're okay with buying a new desk," she said.

"We have really nice desks. If he wants to do that, he's going to have to do it himself. What's wrong with our desks?" I asked her.

"He says that since the desks don't lock, it's easy for an employee to snoop around in it."

"Did he used to look around in my desk?"

"He didn't used to. He still does!"

Immediately, I got a third consecutive call, this time from Will Baggio.

"Are you able to make a rule that we can't play cards in the break room?" he inquired.

"I guess I could but I have no reason to," I said.

"Merf says when he's mayor we can't play euchre in the break room anymore."

"Why?"

"He hears us say 'Trump' and finds it offensive."

"Good luck with your next four years, buddy."

CHAPTER 18

THE FINAL CHAPTER

I drove myself to the Village Hall for the final time on May 1, 2017. Merf followed me into the office, happy as could be. I chatted with him about where he could find files on various items, where I kept the office supplies, and where the phone directories were. I began to chat with him about the status of current projects while the current and new officials made their way into the meeting room across the hall. Several of Merf's family and friends piled into the public seating area.

I opened the meeting and had the minutes and finances approved in mere seconds. With that, I thanked everyone for their willingness to serve, congratulated the new officials, and wished everyone the best. Agnes Cobb and Rhonda Brown each left their seat and joined the public gallery. Will Baggio's mother Jan had won the race for the clerk position. Jan Baggio, Merf, and the three new trustees each walked toward the front of the room to be sworn in. Ed Quentin, Johnny Lynch, and I each left the room and walked toward our cars.

I was concerned that Merf may be in over his head or would pull some crazy stunts with so many new people in there, since all five people whose full term expired chose to step away. Merf would be the new mayor, but he'd also be without long-time Clerk Rhonda Brown, who was replaced by Jan Baggio. Agnes Cobb and Ed Quentin had been trustees for ages and they would be replaced by brand new trustees. Johnny Lynch's four years of experience would be replaced by that of Mike Madison, who had previously been on the board, but quit coming to meetings and was nearly given a Bill Clinton-like impeachment before he resigned. The only returning trustees were Margie Baggio, who had been there a while but didn't always remember things correctly, Kyle Langley, who had only been there two years, and Sharon Yount, who had been there about three years, and well, you know Sharon.

I mentally told myself I would have to disconnect as I walked toward the parking lot with Ed Quentin and Johnny Lynch. The three of us reached the pavement and turned to chat before walking away from the Village Hall for the final time.

"I don't know why I want to cry. I hate this place!" said Ed as he laughed and wiped a tear.

"I'm not crying. I feel better than ever," said Johnny, as he rubbed his signature buzz-cut hair. "I feel like I just kicked a bad roommate out of my house! I win!" he said as he laughed.

Johnny was right. I felt like I had been carrying a heavy book bag on my back for four years. At that moment, I felt free. It was interesting to think that Johnny was the one who I walked out with. When it all started, I thought Johnny would be my biggest enemy, and Merf my strongest ally. It didn't take long for those roles to flip entirely.

I don't know why, but the three of us each hugged on the way out that night. It felt like a goodbye, and maybe it was for Ed, who I knew I'd still see now and then around the town. For Johnny, we regularly spent time at each other's houses with each other's families, so we'd still be seeing each other. Only this time, no Dawson drama would be weighing on us! After the embrace, it was all over.

Not long after I got home, Kyle Langley called me. I knew he would be updating me on something Merf had done as soon as I saw his name light up on my cell.

"You're not going to believe what Merf did!" he said.

"What?" I replied.

"He got the board to buy a new water truck, without a loan, that wasn't even budgeted!"

"That's like 20% of the budget in one day!" I shouted.

"I know! I guess you were right; he doesn't know the finances!"

"Hopefully that's the last crazy thing he does."

"He also mentioned that Benny Fowler had been working to develop a subdivision, but he was going to block it, because it wasn't necessary," Kyle added.

"Are you serious?"

"Serious as a Sharon Yount eminent domain attempt! Remember you had that sidewalk replacement process going for Constant Street?"

"I do."

"He said the section that got done was more than enough. He cut the rest of that funding from the budget entirely."

"Of course he did."

"You know that corridor grant to improve the town entrance?"

"Yes," I said, feeling very concerned.

"He declined the grant. And he also declined the flood wall grant. He said it would be better to spend millions to move the plant up the hill."

"He declined both grants? There's barely any room for the water plant to be moved to! Why did the board just allow him to do these things without any push-back?"

"I know what you mean, but it's just how he talks. He's so convincing that anything he says you want to go along with him. He's almost a perfect politician. It's like the board disagreed with everything, but by the time he was done talking, everyone joined his cause. Maybe he should run for President!" Kyle joked, agreeing with my dad's previous assessment.

In just one hour, Merf had undone nearly everything I had worked to accomplish over four years. When I ran for mayor, nearly the entire town was behind me. Throughout my four years, I gave all I had to make the town better. And we did make it better, accomplishing things that had never been done, completing projects that hadn't been addressed in decades, maintaining a balanced budget, and even getting those four grants. Had it not been for Merf, the Greens, so many within the town who complained about petty things, and so many who turned against me when Merf lied to them so many times about me, I would have run again. I could have made the town incredible. Instead, the only way I could honor my work and give some laughs to all those who support me, was this book.

***

You may be wondering what happened to the town and the major players since I left in May 2017. Some things changed, some stayed the same, and some were outright stunning.

Spaulding Mayor Clint Daniels chose, like me, not to run for reelection. Riverton Mayor Red Tomko ran for reelection and was unopposed. He is still the mayor to this day.

After the Green family left Dawson, no one heard from them again. No one has any idea where they are, which is why they are jokingly referred to as "Hoffa."

Barry Vance never sought office again after stepping away in the middle of my mayoral term. Sadly, he passed away in his sleep at the age of 66.

Attorney Reggie Phillips and engineer Gary Whitcomb still serve in their roles for the town.

Lance Butcher retired and no longer serves as fire chief.

After their final night in office, Agnes Cobb, Ed Quentin, and Rhonda Brown have not sought to serve in an elected capacity again, although Rhonda has assisted Merf from time to time. All three still live in Dawson.

The four employees that I directly hired, Will Baggio, Dan Jones, Austin Butcher, and Cody Lewison, all still work for the Village. I remember being nervous when I hired each of them, but looking back, it's clear that all were the right choice.

Kara Gregory was relieved of her duties as treasurer. About a year after I left, in the first audit of Merf's tenure, funds in the neighborhood of $125,000 were determined to be missing. It seemed that those audit warnings of limited checks and balances had finally caught up to the town. My suspicion is that with a new and inexperienced clerk and mayor, Kara's activities were able to slip by unnoticed until the audit happened. I also suspect that she was able to make up the financial procedures, since the new mayor and clerk wouldn't know any better. She was sentenced to four years' probation and ordered to pay full restitution.

The trustees that were new to the board on my final night still continue to serve in their roles.

The three trustees that were holdovers from my time as mayor were all reelected, unopposed, in April 2019. Kyle Langley received the most votes, with Margie Baggio second, and Sharon Yount a distant third. Sharon continues to push for the crew to be fired and be replaced by her husband.

The stress of being mayor has taken its toll on Merf, resulting in his being hospitalized on a few occasions, though he continues to serve as mayor. I take no joy in his health issues, and have the utmost respect for him for stepping into the role to save his town from Sharon Yount, despite knowing the health risks.

That being said, Merf's actions as mayor are just as frustrating as his first night in office.

He has allowed Nick Constant, who I battled to remove chickens from his property, to raise chickens once again.

Remember that gas station chain I recruited to come to town? Shortly into Merf's tenure they expressed interest in coming to Dawson. Merf declined to work with them on a deal.

The Neighborhood Watch program is not maintained and is essentially nonexistent. The 20-year comprehensive plan has been discarded.

As part of discarding the 20-year plan, he terminated the town's motto of "You're with Friends Here," including destroying all letterhead and logos bearing the phrase. Merf created his own motto, the more exclusive-sounding "The Town of 500 Friends."

The town website has not been updated in nearly three years and sits unmonitored.

The town Facebook page, which I created to routinely keep the public informed, is now only used a handful of times per year, largely to announce that someone's dog got loose.

The opportunity to move forward on the flood wall grant has passed. The water plant still sits in its original location.

When the time comes that Merf no longer wants to serve as mayor, Sharon Yount still seems to be the only person interested in the position. God help us!

Although Merf undid most of my significant accomplishments, the giant LED sign still sits at the town entrance. It is so large and bright that it is literally noticeable from five miles away!

Johnny Lynch and his family moved out of Dawson, but still remain in Central Illinois. We remain close friends to this day.

As for me, we sold our house and moved to Riverton just one month after I left office. We didn't necessarily want to leave Dawson, but we welcomed our second child, a baby girl, and needed more space. The housing options in Dawson were quite limited.

Red Tomko asked me to serve as treasurer for the Village of Riverton, but I declined. Though, I have fun by routinely tricking my wife into thinking I want to run for mayor of Riverton. Will I run for political office sometime in the future? Never say never, but probably never!

The Back Table Podcast lasted for four years. Johnny Lynch couldn't continue doing the show, as it was taking too much time away from his family. I now host a comedy podcast about professional wrestling called *Dynamite Drop In.*

My successful tenure as mayor parlayed into a side hustle of consulting government entities on anything from grant writing to hiring to growth planning.

I continue to tour nationwide doing stand-up comedy. I hope you enjoyed this book as much as my stand-up audiences enjoy the show.

And with that, I'll bang my gavel. Meeting adjourned.

DISCLAIMER

This book is a work of fiction. Although it is based on a true story, characters, businesses, dialogue, events and incidents are significantly exaggerated or concocted entirely for comedic effect.

This novel's story and characters are fictitious. Certain long-standing institutions, agencies, public offices, and notable public figures are mentioned, but in no way should the characters, businesses, dialogue, events, or incidents be interpreted as true or factual in any way.

This book is merely based upon the author's present recollections of experiences over time and is not an accurate representation of reality. Names and characteristics have been concocted, businesses have been concocted, dialogue has been concocted, and events and incidents have been concocted. As such, it is a work of fiction.

Again, this book should not be interpreted as factual. Additionally, there is no intention whatsoever for this book to defame anyone. There is no intention to damage anyone's reputation or to harm anyone in any way.

ACKNOWLEDGMENTS

I wanted to take a moment to thank all of the incredible people that made this book possible. First, I thank you, reader! If you've gotten this far you must have really enjoyed it! Thank you for spending your money on this form of entertainment. Likewise, thank you to all the people who have paid money to see me perform over the years. Without an audience, there is no medium. And without promotion, it is very hard to draw an audience. So, I want to thank all of the media folks out there who have willingly promoted me. A big thanks to Springfield, IL radio icon Jim Leach, who is always willing to help.

The entire team at Clovercroft Publishing worked incredibly hard, from start to edit to proofread to layout to finish. I am grateful for them. They took a chance on me, as have so many comedy club owners, talent scouts, agents, and executives. Comedians like David Scott, Chris Speyrer, and David Graham have helped and mentored me for decades. Thank you all for believing in me.

The comedy business is a long road of physical, mental, and emotional turmoil. My friends, family, and especially my wife, have helped me along the way, and I thank them. Similarly, so many old friends and associates were willing to stick their neck out for me to endorse this book, and I thank them as well.

Had the people of Dawson, Illinois not voted for me, this story never would have happened. So to my friends in my hometown, thank you!

Last but not least, I thank God, through whom all things are possible.

MORE INFORMATION

To learn more about Jeremy Nunes or to inquire about hiring him for your next event, visit www.jeremynunes.com.

You can follow Jeremy on social media at facebook.com/comedianjeremynunes, on Twitter @jeremynunes, on Instagram @frontporchcomedy, on TikTok @frontporchcomedy, and on Parler @jeremynunes.

The *Dynamite Drop In* podcast is available on all major podcast platforms.

Jeremy's comedy special *Who's With Me?!* is available on Amazon Prime, ChristianCinema.com, and ChristianBook.com.

Jeremy's comedy special *Neighborhood Sasq-watch* is available on the Dry Bar Comedy app.